# Group Work Experts Share Their Favorite Activities Volume 2

## A Guide to Choosing, Planning, Conducting, and Processing

Edited By:
Kerrie R. Fineran
Benjamin J. Houltberg
Amy G. Nitza
Jacqueline B. McCoy
Sarah M. Roberts

*ASSOCIATION FOR SPECIALISTS IN GROUP WORK*

# Other Books in the ASGW Group Activity Series

(Available at www.asgw.org)

Group Work Experts Share Their Favorite Activities: A Guide to Choosing, Planning, Conducting, and Processing  Vol. 1

School Counselors Share their Favorite Group Activities: A Guide to Choosing, Planning, Conducting, and Processing  Vol. 1

Group Work Experts Share their Favorite Multicultural Activities: A Guide to Choosing, Planning, Conducting, and Processing

Online Group Activities to Enhance Counselor Education

## New in 2014:

School Counselors Share their Favorite Group Activities: A Guide to Choosing, Planning, Conducting, and Processing Vol. 2

School counselors Share Their Favorite classroom guidance lessons: A Guide to Choosing, Planning, Conducting, and Processing

## DVDs also available from ASGW:

Group Work: Leading in the Here and Now (Carroll)

Developmental Aspects of Group Counseling (Stockton)

Leading Groups with Adolescents (DeLucia-Waack, Segrist, & Horne)

Group Counseling with Children: A Multicultural Approach (Bauman & Steen)

Group Counseling with Adolescents: A Multicultural Approach (Bauman & Steen)

Published by Association for Specialists in Group Work
5999 Stevenson Ave. Alexandria VA 22304
Copyright © 2014 by the Association for Specialists in Group Work
IBSN: 978-1-55620-345-9

# Table of Contents

# Adolescents

# Older Adolescents/ Adults

# Adults

# Adults (cont.)

# Older Adults

***\*See Index at back of book for a listing of activities by Topic and Type\****

# About the Editors

**Kerrie R. Fineran** is an Assistant Professor of Counselor Education at Indiana University-Purdue University, Fort Wayne. She serves as the Coordinator of School Counseling and is currently Acting Director of the Counselor Education Program. She is a long time member of the **Association for Specialists in Group Work** and participated in the very first Advanced Group Work Institute developed by the organization. Kerrie is an alumna of The College of William and Mary (B.S.), Shippensburg University (M.Ed.), and The University of Toledo (Ph.D., Counselor Education and Supervision). Her professional interests include counselor preparation; suicide assessment, prevention, and postvention; and working with individuals with substance and behavioral addictions both individually and in group formats.

**Benjamin J. Houltberg** is an Assistant Professor of Counselor Education at Indiana University-Purdue University, Fort Wayne. He serves as the Coordinator of the Couples and Family program. He has a master's degree with an emphasis of marriage and family therapy from Oral Roberts University and doctorate in human development and family science from Oklahoma State University. His research focus is on understanding socialization factors across interacting systems that impact emotion regulation and mental health outcomes. He is particularly interested in examining these processes within adverse circumstances in order to identify protective processes and apply research-informed approaches that promote resilience. He is a member of ASGW and enjoys working in group formats.

**Amy G. Nitza** is an Associate Professor of Counselor Education at Indiana University-Purdue University, Fort Wayne. She typically serves as the Director of the Counselor Education Programs. She has a master's degree in mental health counseling from Purdue University and a doctorate in counseling psychology from Indiana University. She has experience counseling children, adolescents, and families in school and community settings, as well as in the supervision of school and agency counselor trainees. Amy has extensive group work experience and is particularly interested in cross-cultural groups. She has traveled to numerous countries to lead and research groups, including Botswana and Bhutan. She is a long time member of the **Association for Specialists in Group Work** and has served the organization in numerous capacities, including as Secretary on the Executive Board.

**Jacqueline B. McCoy** is a Graduate Student in the Couples and Family Counseling Program at Indiana University- Purdue University, Fort Wayne. She graduated from The University of Evansville and has experience working with children, adolescents, and at-risk families. She intends to pursue doctoral level work upon graduation. She is a member of the **Association for Specialists in Group Work** and is interested in challenging stigma and discrimination on all levels, as well as working with women's and GLBTQQA issues in group settings.

**Sarah M. Roberts** is a graduate of Ball State University and is a graduate student in the School Counseling Program at Indiana University- Purdue University, Fort Wayne. She is currently a School Counseling Intern in the Warsaw Community School District, member of the **Association for Specialists in Group Work,** and is looking forward to pursuing a career in counseling with an emphasis on working with grief and school students through the modality of group work.

# Acknowledgements

This book contains many diverse activities with different goals, modalities, and rationales. In order to provide a comprehensive picture of what group leaders are using in the field, we included as many high quality submissions as possible. Please note that activities included in this book are constructed from the point of view of the author(s). We encourage group leaders to be conscientious and selective in choosing activities to utilize in practice. The author(s) were asked to ensure that appropriate credit was given when presenting any activities that were adapted from other sources, and retain the copyright to original material. Please contact the author(s) with questions or concerns about the use of the presented material.

The editors would like to thank Dr. Janice DeLucia-Waack, Executive Director of the **Association for Specialists in Group Work** for her guidance and support during the creation of this book. Additionally, we would like to thank Dr. James Burg and Dr. Jane Leatherman in the Department of Professional Studies at Indiana University- Purdue University, Fort Wayne, for their support of us personally and professionally during the development of this project. Thank you also to our colleagues, friends, and family who have kept us grounded throughout the years, and particularly during this time: Lidija, Dawn, Jeong-Il, Carol, Stella, Rama, Andrew, Laura, Ted, Eden, Hope, Trey, and Shane.

# Reflections of Beginning Group Workers

## *Karen M. Eckert and Leslie A. Malkemus*

We count on group members to have emotional reactions, but we often discount the group's ability to provoke reactions within ourselves as leaders. Those of us who are new to facilitating group experiences may struggle with performance anxiety, receiving criticism, perceiving resistance from group members, or conflict among participants. Rest assured every new group leader experiences discomfort, fear, and anxiety; it's common to feel intimidated or uncertain when learning new skills. As fledgling group leaders ourselves, we continue to make mistakes, encounter novel challenges, and learn about groups every day. Preparation, remembrance of basic interpersonal and counseling skills, and a positive attitude can go a long way in the learning process. Despite our initial apprehensions, group work has also been a fulfilling endeavor that gets richer with practice. The purpose of this chapter is to walk metaphorically alongside new group workers by sharing our recent experiences and providing suggestions to guide the reader through the use of this book as a resource.

### Choosing an Activity

In an age where resources are abundant, it is easy to become overwhelmed with selecting an ideal activity for a group. Structured activities can be utilized for any kind of group or even the counseling room, though the activities should be customized to best serve the goals and members of a group. This book presents activities in a format that assists group leaders with skillful implementation. Take note of all information the authors have provided for the activity: population, stage of group work, type of group work, rationale or theory behind the activity, specific goals, needed materials, time allotment, step-by-step instructions, suggested processing questions, special considerations or precautions, and possible adaptations to other populations or settings. Each of these sections not only provide guidance for how to prepare and lead the activity, but can also guide your own thoughts for how to further adapt the activity to your group. Each author provides references if you wish to read further on the theoretical context or inspiration for the activity. If you have any further questions or need for clarification, contact information is also provided for the first author of each activity.

Ideally, a resource will accommodate your search for an activity by providing some or all of the sections listed above. Once an activity looks as if it serves the purpose of the group, consider how the activity will work with the size of the group, the group makeup, and the setting within which the group is held. It's perfectly normal to alter an activity to fit the needs and abilities of members, the limitations of resources, or the stage of development the group is currently experiencing. As leaders we often expect our groups to fluidly follow the textbook developmental stages, but this is not always the case. For example, some groups may never reach the working stage, so it is important to reflect on where the group is at any given time and consider the suggested stage for each activity.

If possible, it can be beneficial to do a trial run of the activity on location to determine how to adapt it for the group's setting. Even prepping the activity beforehand or envisioning the location can assist with preparing sufficient supplies. Activities in this book provide a list of needed materials, though group leaders should consider how the room should be set up for the activity. For example, an activity that involves writing or art may require tables, but an activity with a lot of movement may necessitate open space.

Another useful resource to utilize when choosing an activity is the Association for Specialists in Group Work (ASGW) Best Practice Guidelines (Thomas & Pender, 2007). When deciding upon an activity to use from this book, reflect on the goals for each activity. The authors have carefully identified desired objectives that should be taken into consideration when choosing an appropriate activity for your group session. The importance of this is highlighted in the ASGW Best Practice Guidelines, which state, "Group Workers concisely state in writing the purpose and goals of the group" (Thomas & Pender, 2007, p. 113).

## Implementing the Activity

Along with determining guidelines for the group to follow, adequate preparation may also include deciding how to best introduce and explain the activity to the group. Instructions that you give to members likely will need to be as clear and concise as possible, and may need to be repeated or reworded. It may be useful to develop a habit of asking members if there are any questions after instructions are given. Be mindful of how the instructions impact the group's ability to appropriately complete the task. A more complex activity with multiple steps may require giving instructions for one step at a time, rather than describing the entire activity at the beginning. If the activity is more interpretive or open-ended, you may want to give intentionally less detailed instructions.

It is also helpful to think about what could go "wrong" with the activity and how these issues might be addressed. The special considerations section for each activity includes the possible roadblocks identified by the authors. Think about how the activity will impact each member of the group, and weigh the risk of how certain tasks could cause discomfort or harm. For instance, if members struggle with reading or comprehension, simplify difficult text or structure the group in a way that allows them to get help from another member. If the activity involves acting or standing in front of the group, having members perform or present in pairs can reduce anxiety. Often, it is important for members to be challenged by the activity, but being overwhelmed can overshadow the purpose of the activity and may lead to less desired outcomes.

Additionally, as a leader you may notice the tension between silence and action in the group. It can be beneficial to remain silent to let a group make connections, find their own solutions, and fully engage in the experience. Long silences may also be an opportunity to check in with the group and discuss the hesitation to speak or participate at that moment. In the earlier stages of a group, the leader may be speaking more to provide structure and solicit participation. It may be very appropriate and even necessary for a leader to intervene at times, especially to enforce the safety of group members, though the intervention may simply be asking the group to enforce or clarify guidelines. Allowing and encouraging members to "own" the group may increase trust and participation. In environments such as school or correctional settings, members may need to be reminded of their power when they are conditioned to defer to teachers or staff members.

Also, we notice that more often than not, time seems to pass quickly during sessions. Group leaders should always leave time for debriefing and processing as part of the session in which the activity takes place. This could mean having a contingency plan of which steps of an activity to exclude if time is running out, or additional steps to add if the group moves through the activity quickly. Additionally, evaluation is continuous throughout sessions. Carefully look at the activity and decide what the most important pieces are in order to arrive at the processing questions. Pay close attention to the time allotment suggested in the activities and consider that groups may need time to settle in, get comfortable and complete a check-in before beginning an activity. As a new group leader, it is easy to feel pressure to complete every piece of the suggested activity plan. Trust yourself as a leader and make decisions based on the needs of your groups. The ASGW Best Practice Guidelines (Thomas & Pender, 2007) emphasize that "Group Workers apply and modify knowledge, skills and techniques appropriate to group type and stage, and to the unique needs of various cultural and ethnic groups" (p. 115). Even if an adaptation is not planned prior to the session, it may be necessary to make some changes during the session to attend to the group's needs.

## Processing the Activity

Just as group members debrief and process through activities to reflect on the experience and summarize what they have learned, debriefing is also important for group leaders. The ASGW Best Practice Guidelines (Thomas & Pender, 2007) acknowledge both formal and informal evaluation between sessions and at the conclusion of sessions. Awareness regarding how effectively the activity met the desired objectives and goals will help lead you in choosing other activities for the group. These considerations often include examining both what went well and what could be altered or improved. Contemplate if you would use the activity again or if modification should be noted for future implementations.

Personal reflection on your own performance as a leader may also occur after a session. Champ, Okech, and Rubel (2013) discussed the importance of monitoring emotional reactivity not just in group members, but also in ourselves as leaders. They suggested group workers examine their own emotion regulation processes and develop strategies for managing emotion. It can be helpful after the session to think about what emotions the group has evoked in you, both as a leader and as a person. Co-leaders, colleagues, and supervisors are a good source of support through your debriefing process.

As master's degree students, we both participated in an experiential six week group as part of our Group Counseling course. This was an invaluable experience for gaining awareness of what new group members may be feeling as they go through the group process. Group work is challenging from both the leader and members' viewpoint; sharing experiences with others brings about a great deal of vulnerability and change. Not only did we talk about our experiences within the group, we engaged in classroom discussions and journaling as a way to further debrief. Processing and reflection are a leader's greatest assets when it comes to professional and personal development. As part of our continued development of group skills, we spend significant time reflecting upon and examining our experiences as group leaders. We would like to share some of those reflections with you, not only to assist in our own growth, but to perhaps provide some normalization of the struggles other beginning group leaders may encounter and offer some inspiration for your own reflections as new group leaders.

## Personal Reflections

In this final section, we'd like to share with you some of our personal reflections on our early group work experiences.

**Karen's Group Leadership Experience Reflections**

As a new group leader, I work predominantly with children and adolescents. My biggest challenge at this early stage in my career is time management. Sessions quickly pass and often many of the children still want to share or discuss something further. It is a challenge to successfully flow through a meaningful activity without interruption and allow ample time for processing. I have become more cognizant of my pacing and try to not rush the process. I have often prepared several weeks of group sessions at a time, only to find after the first two or three sessions that the members are in need of other exploration, self-discovery, or skills. Sometimes during sessions while I'm observing interactions, new ideas emerge, which I quickly jot down to revisit during my personal evaluation of a session. I have found that adaptability and recognizing the members' needs is essential to running successful groups.

A group leader has numerous tasks to fulfill during a session. I attempt to recognize members' feelings and subtle nonverbal cues, pace activities, and keep everyone engaged, all while allowing for spontaneity. One task I am currently focusing on is truly engaging in active listening and being present with the group. To be an effective active listener, the leader is not only listening to the content shared, but also paying attention to gestures, body language, and other underlying messages. Often my mind is distracted with worrisome thoughts about how much time is remaining, reading the nonverbal cues of members, thinking of how I can intervene, and making sure all participants are engaged. With a racing mind comes the potential to miss possible helpful intervention opportunities and serious emotional reactions that may be occurring within the group. I believe that good group leaders reflect feelings that members share and are able to clarify their intent, so not to misjudge a member's emotions. A helpful tip I like to use is checking in on members' emotions to make sure communication has not broken down. I may say something such as, "Please help me understand..." or "This may not be it, but are you maybe feeling like...?" This helps give the client ownership of the emotions presented without being too suggestive.

Once when leading a group with adolescent girls, I kept noticing a girl who either had her head down or hair covering her face. She previously spoke about a difficult friendship situation that she had experienced with two other girls in the group. Had I just let the group continue without acknowledging her body language and feelings at that time, she might have felt left out and uncompelled to share in the upcoming sessions. Instead, I asked the group to pause because I noticed the girl's body language seemed to change and I was curious to know how she was feeling. She immediately welcomed my acknowledgement and was able to further discuss the situation with the other two girls. This particular situation ended successfully. For me, this really solidified the idea that it is okay to be spontaneous and intervene when you see an opportunity. Take time to truly be present with your group and you will recognize opportunities where intervention is necessary. I feel confident saying that observing connections, personal awareness, and growth happen is worth every minute of the stress and anxiety that comes along with group work. I look forward to gaining more experience to shape my confidence as a group leader. In addition, I have set a personal goal to further assess the effectiveness of the groups I lead; I would like to specifically measure the extent of the skills taught in group to understand if months later, group intervention has impacted student's lives in a useful, meaningful way.

## Leslie's Group Leadership Experience Reflections

Initially, my first big challenge as a group leader was to find ways to use my strengths and overcome my fears. As an introvert and a planner, it was intimidating to think about managing a group, especially when things deviated from my plans. I had a strong support network of colleagues, professors, and even group members who believed in me, which gave me the courage to dive in to group counseling. I have honed my preparation and organization skills, but more importantly, I have learned how to be flexible and adapt in the moment if necessary.

When I focus on the here-and-now in a group, I can notice and attend to the things that may be steering the group into unexpected territory. Repeatedly, the most important development or poignant moments have occurred when the group work deviates slightly from what is planned. Instead of ruminating on things that fell flat, I reframe missed opportunities as learning experiences. I once planned an activity involving play-doh before knowing what room my group would use; we ended up in a room without tables or desk surfaces upon which the members could model. The group was still able to complete the activity in their chairs despite the inconvenience, and I have been more conscious of my group room setups ever since.

A common dilemma I encounter is what my role should be in leading an activity. Some exercises will require the group facilitator to participate as a leader or scorekeeper, though I sometimes give these types of roles to a group member if he or she can benefit from leading or if I believe my participation in that role may be less effective. As a leader, participating in the activity along with the members could be an opportunity to role model and build rapport with the group. If I find myself hesitant or unwilling to participate, I try to examine why and also use those feelings to generate empathy for group members. Even if observing and monitoring the group does not provide time to fully participate, I might do the activity beforehand (such as journaling ahead of time) to serve as an example or to better understand what the participants may be experiencing.

As I become more comfortable leading groups, I challenge myself to celebrate my successes and go deeper with my evaluation of the group process. My goals for future group work involve taking more time to explore my emotional reactivity with a supervisor and reevaluating the effectiveness of activities, psychoeducational materials, and assessments I use in my groups. While I have more practice leading groups with a substantial psychoeducational component, I am researching and preparing to initiate a more counseling-oriented group for those who have experienced trauma and addiction. In addition, I am expanding my knowledge of group process by training clients to lead or co-lead activities within the modified therapeutic community setting.

In conclusion, we hope that this chapter has provided you, as fellow beginning group workers, with some context and comfort as you pursue your group work-related endeavors. Despite the sometimes intimidating complexity of group process, continual self-reflection will enable you to gain confidence and increased awareness. We highly recommend examining your own experiences individually and with others. Challenges will not cease to occur, but be mindful of the progress made through previous challenges and how it informs your present work. It becomes easier to find a sense of assuredness rather than anxiety as we continue to practice group work. Support your early group learning by seeking out resources such as this book and exploring other media or trainings through associations like ASGW. We wish you the best of luck; hopefully our experiences shared here can assist you with your journey as beginning group workers.

References

Champ, J., Okech, J. E. A., & Rubel, D. J. (2013). Emotion regulation: Processes, strategies, and applications to group work training and supervision. *Journal for Specialists in Group Work, 38,* 349-368. doi: 10.1080/01933922.2013.834403

Thomas, R. V., & Pender, D. A. (2007). Association for specialists in group work: Best practice guidelines 2007 revisions. *Journal for Specialists in Group Work, 33,* 111-117. doi: 10.1080/01933920801971184

## Author Notes:

*Karen M. Eckert* recently graduated from Indiana University-Purdue University Fort Wayne with a Master's degree in School Counseling. She currently works as an Elementary School Counselor at Churubusco Elementary School. She enjoys leading groups with children and adolescents, and is specifically interested in working with groups that foster positive coping and emotion regulation skills. Additionally, she mentors counseling graduate students at Indiana University-Purdue University Fort Wayne, helping students develop essential skills in counseling.

*Leslie A. Malkemus* recently graduated from Indiana University-Purdue University Fort Wayne with a Master's degree in Marriage and Family Therapy and is licensed in the state of Indiana as Marriage and Family Therapy Associate. She works for Allen County Indiana Community Corrections as a mental health clinician providing individual, couple, family, and group therapy in a modified therapeutic community for men struggling with addiction, mental illness, and criminal offenses. She has a year and a half of group work experience facilitating groups in healthy relationships, conflict resolution, substance abuse, and relapse prevention. Additionally, she has led an experiential group for counseling graduate students as part of a Group Counseling course.

*Please direct questions or comments regarding this chapter to:*
Karen Eckert, (MS.Ed, Indiana School Counselor)
C/O IPFW Counseling Program
2101 E. Coliseum Blvd.
Fort Wayne, IN 46835
eckertkaren@gmail.com

# Considerations for Advanced Group Workers

## *Kerrie R. Fineran and Benjamin J. Houltberg*

If you have been around groups and group work for some time, you may wonder how an activity book like this one might be helpful to you in increasing your professional knowledge and group work competence. In fact, you may have quite a few group books that include activities sitting in your office bookshelf. Likely, you understand the tasks inherent in effectively choosing an activity for a specific group: you have considered the population, type, stage and needs of the group as well as the timing for activity implementation. You have likely reflected upon the following questions suggested by Jacobs and Schimmel (2009): *"Why am I doing this particular activity at this particular time?"* and *"What is it that I am hoping that the members, or the group as a whole, gain from participating in the activity?"* You are probably skilled in reflecting on ethical and cultural considerations in selecting group activities and formats. So again, the question becomes: what is the next step in your evolution as a group leader regarding using activities? First, we hope that this book provides you with some new ways of conceptualizing group activities, and that it serves as a springboard for the further development of creative and engaging activities with strong grounding in both theoretical knowledge and research. This book includes a great multitude of varying activities which we have categorized by population, topic, and type of activity.

We believe that the structure of organizing activities by population, topic, and type will assist group leaders in easily choosing activities that are designed with specific populations and topics in mind. Further, the type of exercises used in group activities may also be important to consider. Jacobs, Masson, and Harvill (2011) identified 14 types of exercises: 1) Written Exercises, 2) Movement Exercises, 3) Dyads and Triads, 4) Rounds, 5) Creative Props, 6) Arts and Crafts Exercises, 7) Fantasy Exercises, 8) Common Reading Exercises, 9) Feedback Exercises, 10) Trust Exercises, 11) Experiential Exercises, 12) Moral Dilemma Exercises, 13) Group-decision Exercises, and 14) Touching Exercises. They noted that although these types are often related and somewhat interchangeable, there may be times when one type of exercise may be more appropriate than another depending on the unique characteristics of the group. Almost all of these different types of exercises are represented in the activities included in this book, which we believe increases its utility for advanced group leaders. Several different types of exercises may also be used within one activity, and we have chosen to select the main type of exercise represented in the activity, however, it is important to note that activities may include exercises of more than one type. Descriptions of a few of the types and examples of the corresponding activities included in this book are outlined below.

Jacobs et al. (2011) noted that **Written Exercises** are those in which members answer questions in written form, make lists, record their reactions, fill out handouts or checklists, complete sentences, and so forth. They suggested that these types of exercises are beneficial in that members feel less pressure when asked to respond if they have pre-written responses and that it is often helpful to have written materials to take home at the conclusion of the group. Examples of Written Exercises in this book are *Values Clarification* (p. 342) and *Fear in a Hat* (p. 242).

Another kind of activity identified by Jacobs et al. (2011) is **Movement Exercises**. These involve activities in which members move around physically. Purposes for using these types of activities include involving all members equally, deepening the experience of an activity rather than just talking about it, and that movement may increase recall of group experiences. Examples of Movement Exercises in this book are *Life Stages and Group Stages: Asking the Existential Questions* (p. 272), *Do You Agree or Disagree?* (p. 162), and *Modified Polar Sculpture* (p. 288). Jacobs et al. also discussed **Dyads and Triads** as another type of group exercise. These give members an opportunity to interact in pairs or triads and often allow for skills practice. Examples of Dyads and Triads activities in this book are *Are You Listening?* (p. 38) and *Following Directions* (p. 245). Additionally, **Rounds** are exercises in which each member of the group responds to a prompt provided by the group leader. They may stand alone or be integrated into other activities. Rounds are frequently utilized by group leaders, are usually very useful to gather information, and are often extremely beneficial in that they encourage all members to participate while limiting members who tend to dominate. Examples of activities in this book that include Rounds are *Evaluating the Group Experience: A Check-In Exercise for a Substance Abuse Group* (p. 233), *Treasure Chest* (p. 73), and *Sharing Our HIV Diagnosis Experiences* (p. 308).

**Creative Props** and **Arts and Crafts** (Jacobs et al., 2011) are both types of exercises that encourage multisensory engagement of group members. These types of activities seem to generate member interest and engagement while providing new experiences and promoting self-expression. Examples of Creative Props Exercises in this book are *Rock Ice Breaker* (p. 194), *Time is on My Side* (p. 330), and *Lens of Perception* (p. 96). Arts and Crafts type activities include *The Mentor Map* (p. 326), *Group Work with African American Women: Using Vision Boards for Self-Reflection and Goal-Setting* (p. 250), and *Gratitude Garland* (p. 90).

**Fantasy Exercises** are those that invite members to imagine or envision themselves as an object, or as participating in a story-like scenario (Jacobs et al., 2011). The purpose of these exercises is often to assist members in exploring and developing awareness regarding their own emotional experiences or unexpressed ideas. An example of an activity that makes use of the fantasy exercise in this book is *I am a Coffee Mug* (p. 48).

**Common Reading Exercises** (Jacobs et al., 2011) are also often used as part of group activities, and examples of these in this book are *Planting Daffodils* (p. 295) and *Blue Goodbye* (p. 223). In Common Reading Exercises, members participate by reading or listening to short stories, poems, or other written materials. The goals of these types of exercises are typically focused on helping to develop a common frame of reference amongst group members, which may assist in focusing a topic, providing encouragement or inspiration, or prompting ideas.

One of the most noteworthy benefits of participating in group process is that the structure allows for significant giving and receiving of feedback to and from others. In **Feedback Exercises**, members (and often group leaders) share thoughts and feelings about one another in the group setting (Jacobs et al., 2011). This type of exercise may be used throughout all stages of the group process, but is often particularly helpful in the termination stage. An example of a Feedback Exercise in this book is *Reminders of What We Have Learned From Group* (p. 107). With these types of exercises it is very important that the group leader be observant and aware of the dynamics within the group to ensure that participating in the exercise results in a desired outcome. It is when group members have established a climate of honesty and trust in one another that these types of exercises are often most productive.

Of course, trust amongst members is a desired characteristic of most groups. In **Trust Exercises**, group members participate in some activity that helps them to focus on the issue of trust. The "trust fall" in which members fall backward, trusting others to catch them, is a typical and well-known exercise. Often, Trust and other types of exercises also fall under the category of **Experiential Exercises**. Many times, these are activities in which group members engage that are challenging and team-work oriented. They are often active and engaging exercises that are fun, which also challenges the group leader to ensure the exercise matches with the group goals and is thoroughly processed in a way that draws attention to the desired focus. Examples of Experiential Exercises in this book are *Breath & Being in the Present Moment* (p. 145) and *Nourishing the Body and Soul* (p. 355). **Touching Exercises** are those that utilize touch as a part of the activity. Clearly these types of activities require additional consideration regarding appropriate use. A Touching Exercise in this book is *The Handshake Activity* (p. 93).

**Group Decision Exercises** involve members working together to make decisions or complete a task (Jacobs et al., 2011). An example of this kind of activity is *Adventure: Magic Carpet Ride* (p. 31) in which members are asked to stand on a carpet or rug and turn it over without stepping off of it and while keeping their feet on the ground. Lastly, the **Moral Dilemma** type of exercises focuses on helping members identify morals, values, and priorities. They may involve stories or scenarios in which challenging decisions must be faced and made. Jacobs et al. (2011) noted that these types of exercises are often useful when working with groups of adolescents as they help to spark and facilitate engaged discussion.

In soliciting and reviewing submitted activities, we requested that submitting authors provide a detailed rationale for the use of the activity with their identified population. Although many authors included fantastic rationales for the use of these activities in group work with anecdotal evidence of success, few were able to provide empirical evidence related to the impact of the activity. We believe that this highlights a significant need in the area of group work, and with the use of activities in group settings. As a reader of this book, you are likely to share our belief that group work is an effective tool for promoting change and facilitating growth in diverse populations and contexts. But as Nitza (2013) noted, quite a bit as been published related to the utilization of activities in groups, but little empirical data has been presented that demonstrates the impact of these activities. This is particularly important to consider in today's managed care era where there is an increased need for demonstrating accountability and effectiveness. There will likely be a variety of readers that range in research involvement and experience but we believe that everybody can utilize research to enhance group activities and demonstrate the effectiveness of group work.

There has been a lot of dialogue about the importance of using evidence-based practices (EBP) and empirically supported treatments (EST) and the application of such approaches to community practice (APA, 2006; La Roche & Christopher, 2009; Lazarus & Rego, 2013).

Certainly, this area of research is important for establishing effectiveness of group work. However, the rigorous research methodology required for establishing ESTs and difficulties accessing these approaches make it challenging for practitioners to engage in this type of research (Stewart & Chambless, 2007). This does not suggest that this line of research is not important to the advancement of the field of group work. We applaud the efforts of those engaging in this research and challenge others who have the resources and capabilities to apply their skills in contributing to group work-related research. It is important for this line of research to be translated to practice and implemented more broadly. We also recognize that there are many practitioners who do not have the time or resources to conduct extensive research; however, we would argue that any participation, whether it be in consuming or producing research, is a valuable contribution in closing the research-to-practice gap.

Research may seem overwhelming for the group leader in practice as there is limited time and resources for conducting research to determine effectiveness of techniques. In addition, many masters' level graduate programs do not provide extensive training in research methods or program evaluation, but rather focus on strong clinical training. As they often have limited exposure to conducting their own research, it can be difficult for group leaders to utilize research in practice when they begin to work in the field. Thus, many group leaders may rely on experiential knowledge that has accumulated over the years or utilize approaches to which they were exposed during their educational experiences to determine what is effective in practice.

The idea of a *reflective practitioner* provides a model that integrates the importance of experience and continued knowledge of the relevant research in a synergistic fashion (Nelson & Neufelt, 1998). Reflective practice is identified as a standard of best practice in the Association for Specialists in Group Work's (ASGW) 2007 best practice guidelines (Thomas & Pender, 2008). Section C.2 reads, "Group workers attend to opportunities to synthesize theory and practice and to incorporate learning outcomes into ongoing groups" (p. 117). Thus, reflective group leaders do not rely solely on their own experiences but also acknowledge the importance of the integration of research and theory. Thus a reflective group leader is also a *research-informed practitioner* who utilizes current knowledge in the field to guide intervention and prevention efforts and conducts more progress or client-focused evaluation rather than group level or randomized clinical trials (RCTs) (see Karam & Sprenkle, 2010 for review).

The first part of being a research-informed practitioner is to be a consumer of empirical literature and apply this knowledge to practice in a meaningful way. One of the challenges that practitioners may face is gaining access to such research once they have completed their graduate work. However, there are several ways to stay up-to-date on current research such as belonging to professional organizations that provide you access to peer-reviewed journals (e.g. ACA, ASGW, APA), attending workshops or conferences, open access to peer reviewed online journals, or even providing clinical supervision to university graduate students. Many of our onsite supervisors express learning more about current research from their interns. Reading current research provides an opportunity to reflect on your experiences and evaluate therapeutic approaches.

In group work, you can draw upon research from multiple disciplines (e.g. developmental science, neuroscience, family science) to help guide you in applying group activities. For example, group work with adolescents could be informed by recognizing "deviancy talk" that has been shown to be a strong positive reinforcement for future adolescent antisocial behaviors (Dishion, Spracklen, Andrews, & Patterson, 1996). Despite much support against forming groups of only adolescents engaging in deviant behavior, many programs still operate this way because of practicality and economic cost (Dishion, Dodge, & Lansford, 2008). However, a research-informed approach to leading a group of adolescents who engage in deviant behaviors may involve implementing limits on talk that might incidentally train the other adolescents in becoming better at antisocial behaviors. Consulting a broad body of literature that applies to the clinical population that a counselor works with may also challenge other common practices and provide insight into better therapeutic approaches.

It is also important to utilize research to evaluate progress in group work. Smead (as cited in Gladding, 2003) has suggested that group leaders pose the following questions when considering how to evaluate the effectiveness of group: 1) *How do you plan to determine whether a member has changed due to the group experience?*, 2) *How are you going to determine whether your goals and objectives have been met?*, and 3) *How do you plan to evaluate leader performance?* (p. 16). These questions are an excellent place to start in evaluating the groups you lead and can help guide you as you plan to evaluate effectiveness.

After answering these questions you can then decide *what construct* you want to measure (e.g. group cohesion, leader performance, individual coping behaviors) and on *what level* you want to measure it (e.g. group leader, individual members, group process). For example, you might identify anger regulation (*construct*) as important to measure for each group member (*individual level*) when facilitating an anger management group for youth. Next, you could consider *how* you are going to measure (e.g. questionnaire, self-report, observational data), *who* will provide the information about the measure (e.g. parent, child, group leader, observer), and for what *length of time* (e.g. one session, one activity, over time). Consistent with the above example with anger regulation, you might have parents (*who*) report on their child's anger regulation ability utilizing an already validated measure (*how*). You could then have parents report on their children's progress at the end of the 8 week anger management program (*time*). Finally, it is important to reflect on the *meaning* of your evaluation for continual improvement. Was there improvement in anger regulation ability across the 8 week program? What does this mean? The sophistication of evaluating effectiveness depends on your familiarity with research methods and statistics. However, you can also utilize this approach to attain meaningful results for continual improvement without investing in the creation of a large-scale, sophisticated research project.

The same process can be used to evaluate group leader performance. For example, you may record a group session or have a process observer join the group with the purpose of evaluating the group leader or some group process. It important to note that many typical group work techniques are specifically designed to take advantage of the additive and synergistic effects of the group format which can pose some challenges for measuring effectiveness. Although in practice this is easily observed, in research, these same effects often create complications for statistical analysis. For example, as described by Marley (2010) the assumption of independence required for many typical statistical tests is typically violated by the very nature of group work. As group leaders and researchers ourselves, we fully appreciate that these challenges exist, but would argue that only continued, dedicated effort in meeting these challenges will result in achieving the goal of obtaining more empirical evidence supporting the use of group work, and specifically, supporting the use of activities such as those included in this book.

This book is an example of the integration of clinical experience and research-informed activities that may be a helpful tool for conducting group work. The reflective practitioner must consider his or her own experience and population with which these activities will be implemented. We encourage you to explore ways that you can engage in more research-informed approaches and progress evaluation within your own practice. In order to get you started, we would like to provide some brief suggestions for becoming more intentional in evaluating the use of specific activities in group work.

1) Begin by joining ASGW! Of course, as members of the organization, we are a little biased, but believe it to be an important step in the development of any group worker, from the beginning stages of a career to the more advanced stages. As a member, you will have the opportunity to meet and interact with others interested in group work though the annual national conference, state ASGW branches, and other group work-related events. You will receive The Group Worker newsletter and The Journal for Specialists in Group Work.

2) Form a research group with local colleagues who are also interested in group work. Plan to meet regularly to discuss relevant scholarly work and share ideas for applying this work to your practice. These meetings can be a valuable way to stimulate new ideas for practice and keep you accountable for keeping up with the latest information in our field. If local meetings are not plausible, consider creating or engaging in meetings online or through social networking. Connecting with other group work experts through the ASGW Facebook page or Twitter feed may be a good place to start in creating an online reading or research group! Information about these resources is available at the end of this chapter.

3) Re-dedicate yourself to reflective practice (see suggestions in previous chapter for more ideas). Conduct a brief literature review and reflect on ways that you are facilitating your own group. Record your preparations and thought processes as you select and lead activities. You may also wish to evaluate ways to improve on facilitating the group process. This could consist of recording group sessions and utilizing observational methods to collect data. It also can be helpful to ask a process observer to join your group.

4) Develop simple strategies for evaluating the impact of your activities. Look at one of the goals that have been outlined in this book and choose one or two constructs to measure. It can be helpful to find an already reliable and validated measure, but you can also create one of your own.

5) Connect with researchers interested in group work, who can often be found writing chapters like these in their offices at local universities. If you are already in one of those universities, make the effort to connect with local practitioners who are leading groups in their practices. These relationships are often beneficial in many ways, and are a great way to connect research and practice.

6) When you embrace the idea of evaluating the efficacy of the activities you use in groups, we suggest both examining the effectiveness of the activity as it is currently presented and devising new ways of engaging with the material on an empirical level. Perhaps it would be helpful to examine the cross-cultural applicability of a specific activity or consider the most appropriate ways to adapt the activity in a developmentally appropriate manner for another age group. Using the types of activities outlined, you can consider the population that it was designed for and reflect on the adaptations that are provided for other populations. You may be able to find further ways that these activities can be adapted to meet the needs of the people that you serve.

7) Share your work with others. This can be done in informal or formal ways but it is important that effective strategies and evaluation tools for group work are shared with the individuals who are facilitating these groups on a daily basis. The start of this professional dialogue is encompassed here and in the many related group activity books published by ASGW, however, let us not stop with this.

In conclusion, we anticipate that this book will serve as a valuable resource to you as you continue striving to increase your knowledge and skills as a group worker. Additionally, we hope and that you will consider utilizing research in meaningful, reflective ways and that you will share these ideas to enhance the group work community. We are humbled by the great work that many of you are doing in the field and feel honored to have been able to collect so many of your amazing ideas. We are sincerely grateful to everyone who shared their experiences, expertise, and creative knowledge in order to bring this book to fruition.

References

American Counseling Association. (2005). *Code of ethics*. Alexandria, VA: American Counseling Association.

American Psychological Association (2006). Evidence-based practice in psychology. *American Psychologist, 61*, 271-285. doi:10.1037/0003-066X.61.4.271

Dishion, T. J., Dodge, K. A., & Lansford, J. E. (2008). Deviant by design: Risks associated with aggregating deviant peers into group prevention and treatment programs. *The Prevention Researcher, 15*, 8-11. doi 10.1002/ab.21456

Dishion, T. J., Spracklen, K. M., Andrews, D. W., & Patterson, G. R. (1996). Deviancy training in male adolescent friendships. *Behavior Therapy, 27*, 373-390.

Gladding, S. T. (2003). *Group work: A counseling specialty* (4th ed.). Upper Saddle River, NJ: Merrill Prentice Hall.

Jacobs, E. E., Masson, R. L., & Harvill, R. L. (2011). *Group counseling: Strategies and skills* (7th ed.). Belmont, CA: Thompson.

Karam, E. A., & Sprenkle, D. H. (2010). The research-informed clinician: A guide to training the next-generation MFT. *Journal of Marital and Family Therapy, 36*, 307-319. doi: 10.1111/j.1752-0606.2009.00141

La Roche, M. J., & Christopher, M. S. (2009). Changing paradigms from empirically supported treatment to evidence-based practice: A cultural perspective. *Professional Psychology: Research and Practice, 40*, 396-402. doi:10.1037/a0015240

Lazarus, A. A., & Rego, S. A. (2013). What really matters: Learning from, not being limited by, empirically supported treatments. *The Behavior Therapist, 36*(3), 67-69.

Marley, S. C. (2010). Psychological measurement for specialists in group work. *The Journal for Specialists in Group Work, 35*, 331-348. doi: 10.1080/01933922.2010.514978

Nelson, M. L., & Neufelt, S. A. (1998). The pedagogy of counseling: A critical examination. *Counselor Education and Supervision, 38*, 70-88.

Nitza, A. (2014). Selecting and using activities in groups. In J. L. DeLucia-Waack, C. R. Kalodner, & M. Riva (Eds.), *Handbook of group counseling and psychotherapy (pp. 95-106)*. Thousand Oaks, CA: Sage Publications.

Stewart R. E., & Chambless D. L. (2007). Does psychotherapy research inform treatment decisions in private practice? *Journal of Clinical Psychology, 63*, 267-281. doi: 10.1002/jclp.20347

Thomas, R. V., & Pender, D. A. (2008). Association for Specialists in Group Work: Best practice guidelines 2007 revisions. *The Journal for Specialists in Group Work, 33,* 111-117. doi: 10.1080.01933920801971184

## Resources

**Association for Specialists in Group Work (ASGW) Website:** www.asgw.org

**ASGW Facebook page:** https://www.facebook.com/#!/pages/Association-for-Specialists-in-Group-Work-ASGW/345965228749278

**ASGW Twitter Feed:** https://twitter.com/GroupsWork

**American Counseling Association (ACA):** www.counseling.org

## Author Notes:

*Kerrie R. Fineran* and *Benjamin J. Houltberg* are both Assistant Professors of Counselor Education at Indiana University – Purdue University, Fort Wayne. Kerrie has more than 8 years of experience running groups related to adolescent development and school counseling, substance abuse and other addictions, mood and anxiety disorders, and dreamwork-focused groups. Kerrie's research is in the areas of school counseling, addictions, and suicide prevention/intervention. Benjamin is a licensed marriage and family therapist with extensive experience leading groups related to emotion regulation and problem solving skills, gang prevention and life-skills, and parent-child relationship focused groups in community settings, agencies, and schools. Benjamin's research focuses on understanding socialization factors across interacting systems that impact social and emotional development of youth and families that face adverse circumstances.

## Correspondence related to this chapter may be directed to:

Kerrie R. Fineran, Ph.D., NCC, PSC

IPFW Department of Professional Studies

2101 E. Coliseum Blvd.

Neff Hall 250L

Fort Wayne, IN 46835

finerank@ipfw.edu

# Building Friendship

*By Justina Gorman*

## Population:
This is most appropriate for children in kindergarten through third grade.

## Stage of Group:
Orientation

## Type of Group:
Counseling

## Rationale:

In school, children grow up in a social environment. Learning how to interact well with others and build friendships is a skill they will need throughout the rest of their lives. The activity also helps them identify actions that can hurt a friendship, and identifying them as a group can raise awareness about how certain actions (i.e. teasing, bullying) can make a person feel. The handout of the activity provides them a takeaway from the lesson to both share with their parents and serve as a personal reminder of it takes to build a friendship.

The students who have participated in this activity were able to readily identify actions that both build up and tear down friendships. It also appeared that they felt comfortable sharing in the group environment to the point of sharing specific times when they felt a friend was hurtful to them. At the end of the discussion, the students were able to reiterate what they had learned and excitedly colored their handouts. When the students were seen at a later date, they also enjoyed sharing the positive steps they had taken to being better friends.

## Goals:
Participants will:
1) identify how to build a friendship.
2) identify actions that may hurt a friendship.
3) identify specific actions they can take every day to show they're being a good friend.

## Materials:

1) Blank ship (i.e. no sails) – can be a posterboard cut-out or printed from the internet
2) Cut-out ships parts (sails, captain's wheel, anchor) and rough water
3) Laminating plastic
4) Dry erase marker

5) Wipes
6) "Friend" Ship Handout
7) Crayons

## Time Allotment:

20-30 Minutes
As the group leader facilitates the conversation, time can generally be kept at this allotment. Some groups may be more or less talkative than others, but the group leader can gauge group members' level of participation and respond accordingly (i.e. by thanking members for their suggestions, but moving on to the next part of the activity).

## Directions:

*Preparation*
1) Find desired ship, ship parts, and rough water for activity (author used images 1-4)
2) Print out pieces at desired size (8.5" x 11" paper should be fine for a small group)
3) Cut out pieces and laminate

Step:
1) Introduction: Ask if anyone has been sailing. When someone says yes, ask what the thing is that they sail on. Keep asking until someone says "ship." State that you brought a ship with you today- a very special ship called the "Friend Ship."

2) The ship you show will be the blank one. Ask if it looks like it is ready to go on the water. When they say no, ask them if they can help you build your "friend" ship. (It is a good time to use processing question #1). Generally, you will have an idea of the kinds of qualities you would like represented- keep asking until you have enough diverse answers. Write their answers on the laminated pieces with the dry erase marker.

3) Once all of the pieces to the ship are filled out, state that you have one more piece (the rough water). Ask if that looks like nice, smooth water they want to be sailing on. When they say no, say that this rough water is kind of like the things that you don't like people to do to you- it can damage the ship and make you not feel well. (Now use processing question #2).

4) Repeat some of the words they come up with for the rough water, and ask what it feels like when someone does those things to them. They will likely say mad and sad. You can start a conversation about "treating others the way you want to be treated."

5) Ask processing question #3, and after their suggestions, take away the rough water saying that all their suggestions make it seem like they won't hit too much rough water.

6) Thank them for helping you build your strong "friend" ship. Pass out the "friend" ship handout for them to start coloring. You can let them color for a few minutes in case

questions come up. While they are coloring, you can use processing question #4 to close.

## Processing Questions:

1) What makes a good friend? (ship parts)
2) What kinds of things would you not like a friend to do to you? (rough water)
3) What are some things you could do today to show your classmates you know how to build a good friendship?
4) At the end, ask as a reminder "What did we learn how to build today?"

## Special Considerations:

None were identified by the author.

## Adaptations:

1) Questions can be adapted to be appropriate for each grade level.
2) Older students can write the stated qualities of friendship on their handout rather just watching the facilitator write.
3) Time can be extended with further discussion on bullying
4) Activity may be adapted for older populations in counseling groups working on social skills or relationship-building. Visuals and questions may both be modified to be age-appropriate.

## References:

Image 1: http://www.clker.com/clipart-9585.html

Image 2: http://flickrcomments.wordpress.com/2011/12/21/night-day/

Image 3: http://www.clker.com/clipart-lime-green-anchor.html

Image 4: http://www.clker.com/clipart-wave-2.html

## Author Notes:

*Justina Gorman* is a Graduate Student at Walsh University who expects to graduate in December 2014 with degrees in both School and Mental Health Counseling. She has worked with grade school students as well as students in the introductory counseling class at Walsh.

## Correspondence:

Questions and comments related to this activity may be directed to:

Justina Gorman
Walsh University
2020 East Maple Street
North Canton, OH 44720
justinagorman@walsh.edu

# You: The Car

*By Laurel Malloy*

## Population:
Children and Adolescents, ages 8 – 17

## Stage of Group:
Orientation

## Type of Group:
Psychoeducational, Counseling

## Rationale:
In William Glasser's Choice Theory (1998) total behavior is defined in terms of a car, with the front wheels being thinking and acting and the back wheels being feeling and physiology. Having group members identify themselves with a specific type of car facilitates participant introduction and allows for teaching of total behavior concepts.

## Goals:
Participants will:
1) introduce themselves in a non-threatening and fun manner.
2) understand the components of total behavior.
3) recognize how choices are part of total behavior.

## Materials:
1) Three-inch toy vehicles of all sorts of styles, including emergency vehicles, cars and trucks
2) Handout on total behavior (Glasser, W. 2005)

## Time Allotment:
45 – 50 minutes, 10 minutes as ice-breaker only

## Directions:
Step:
1) Seat group in a circle. Vehicles should be in the center of the group arranged randomly. Invite group member to each select a vehicle that they believe best fits them without indicating to other group members their choice. Stress that they are not to touch the vehicles, and it will be acceptable for more than one person to

choose the same vehicle. The leader might say, *"Look at these vehicles and without touching any of them, decide which one is most like you. More than one person may select a vehicle, so do not worry about that."*

2) After assuring that all group members have selected a vehicle, ask the participants to introduce themselves by holding their selected vehicle and talking about how it represents them. The leader may say, *"Now that everyone has selected a vehicle, we will go around the circle. When it is your turn, go ahead and pick up your vehicle. Tell the group what about the vehicle made you think it was like you. When you are done, put the vehicle back with the other ones."*

3) Once each group member has introduced him/herself ask the following:
    a) What did you learn about each other because of the vehicles chosen?
    b) Was there a vehicle, color or style missing that you would have preferred to pick?
    c) If another person chose the same vehicle as you, how did that impact what you said about your choice? Did anyone change their choice because their vehicle was "taken?" How did you come to that decision?

4) Bring out the handout on total behavior to teach the concept to the group. Depending upon the age of the group, you may say, *"Total Behavior is a Choice Theory concept which describes how people meet their basic emotional needs (survival, love and belonging, power and worthwhileness, freedom, fun and pleasure). At all times our Total Behavior is powered by those needs – the engine of the car. Meeting these needs is not always conscious, but always involves the four parts of behavior – acting, thinking, feeling and physiology. These are the tires of the car. A person can consciously choose to think or act on a certain need, but feelings and physiology are subconscious."* Point to the various parts of the handout as you are explaining, and simplify the vocabulary for groups with younger (twelve and under) members.

5) Proceed to discuss examples of total behaviors. For example, eating an apple: *"A person may recognize the physiological signal that says, 'I am hungry.' The person may then think, 'Hmm, what would I like to eat? I think I'll eat an apple.' She gets up; goes to the refrigerator and gets the apple. After eating the apple, the person may think, 'That was just what I needed. I feel satisfied and happy.' Sometimes total behavior is not that easy to detail. A person may feel grouchy (feeling). He may think that he's angry, but he may actually have shoes that are too tight (physiology). Going home from work and taking off his shoes (action), may result in feeling better, and he may never realize (subconscious thinking) that he was grouchy because of the shoes."* Encourage students share a behavior they are concerned about and walk the group through discovering the Total Behavior behind the recognized behavior (Glasser, W. 2000).

6) Proceed to processing questions.

## Processing Questions:

1) How does learning about Total Behavior influence your choice of car? Would it change, and how? Why or why not?
2) What was the most interesting thing you learned about another group member?

## Special Considerations:

Be aware that the use of emergency vehicles may trigger memories in individuals with traumas attached to those vehicles.

## Adaptations:

For use with any counseling theory as an ice-breaker, team builder: end after step 3.

## References/Credits:

Glasser, W. (1998). *Choice theory: A new psychology of personal freedom.* New York: HarperCollins.

Glasser, W. (2000). *Counseling with choice theory.* New York: HarperCollins.

Glasser, W. (2005). *How the brain works* [chart]. Chatsworth, CA: The William Glasser Institute.

## Author Notes:

*Laurel Malloy* is a Professional School Counselor in Northside ISD in San Antonio, TX. She has 15 years experiencing in designing and facilitating groups on topics including reducing at-risk behaviors, school success, grief, transition, substance abuse prevention/intervention, and LGBTQQ issues.

## Correspondence:

Questions and comments related to this activity may be directed to:

Laurel Malloy, M. Ed, CSC, LPC
10106 Sandbrook Hill
San Antonio, TX 78254
laurelmalloy@sbcglobal.net

# Adventure: Helium Stick

*By Bobbi Beale & Azra Karajic Siwiec*

## Population:

Children and adolescents

## Stage of Group:

In the transition stage group is working on building cohesiveness and this activity would in turn emphasize to group members the value of each member's work/effort.

## Type of Group:

Psychoeducational and counseling

## Rationale:

This activity is very helpful with groups consisting of children and teens, especially when they are struggling with communication and role within the group. The use of adventure based activities allows group members to problem solve and build cohesiveness while also increasing frustration tolerance. Participants get to focus on task-at hand and move away from focusing on the particular issues that brought them to counseling. Adventure-based activities engage participants on cognitive, affective and/or behavioral levels (Gass, 1999; Gass, 2001; Gass, Gillis, & Russell, 2012).

## Goals:

Participants will:
1) improve communication.
2) engage in teamwork and cooperation.
3) increase problem solving skills.
4) increase frustration tolerance.

## Materials:

Long, thin lightweight rod, at least 6 feet in length.  Tent poles are ideal.

## Time Allotment:

30-45 minutes for 6 to 8 physically able-bodied group members

## Directions:

Step:
1) Introduction by the group leader: *"We get to use a stick which is filled with helium. Soon you will witness that. First, everyone line up facing one another and extend both hands out in front of you.*

*Be aware that you all vary in height so when this stick is passed on to you, you all have to agree on the height that you will start, which should be about chest high. Point your index finger away from you and your thumbs up. The helium stick rests upon your finger at all times."*

2) Lay the tent pole down on their fingers, providing gentle pressure down on the stick as they get arranged. Get the group to adjust their finger heights until the Helium Stick is horizontal and everyone's' index fingers are touching the stick. Group leader should stand near the center and hold the Helium Stick steady.

3) Next, tell them: *"Now, the challenge is to work together and lower this stick to the ground. Be aware that everyone's index fingers must be in contact with the Helium Stick at all times. Pinching or grabbing the pole is not allowed - it must rest on top of your fingers."*

4) Group leader then releases the stick.

5) The catch: Paradoxically, the stick will rise as they attempt to keep their fingers in contact with it.

6) Reiterate to the group that if anyone's finger is caught not touching the Helium Stick or pinching it, the task will be restarted. *"Let the task begin...."*

## Processing Questions:
1) What happened? Why did the Helium Stick keep rising?
2) Was your group successful? What strategies or skills were helpful?
3) What skills did you see others use?
4) Did a leader emerge? How was he or she helpful?
5) What did each member in the group have to do to make it successful?
6) How can you apply the skills from this activity to other areas of your lives?

## Special Considerations:
Some groups or individuals after 5 to 10 minutes of trying may be inclined to give up, believing it is impossible or that it is too hard. The facilitator should stop the group if the frustration level gets too high. The facilitator can offer hints or suggest the group discuss their strategy, and then try again.
This activity can also be used with adult group members who do not have limited mobility because of the need to stand and extend arm and also bend down to put the "stick" down.

## Adaptations:
This activity can be used with adults who are able-bodied also.

# References:

Gass, M. A. (1999). Lowering the bar. *Ziplines: The Voice for Adventure Education, 39*,25-27.

Gass, M. A. (2001). Lowering the bar. In: S. Priest & K. Rohnke (Eds.) *101 of the best corporate team-building activities we know!* Dubuque, IA: Kendall/Hunt.

Gass, M., Gillis, L., & Russell, K. (2012). *Adventure therapy: Theory, research, and practice.* New York: Routledge.

# Author Notes:

*Bobbi Beale* is a Group Programs Director working for Child and Adolescent Behavioral Health in Canton, Ohio. She has had 20 years of group work experience using adventure therapy with kids teaching them how to improve behavioral and emotional self-regulation and social competence.

*Azra Karajic Siwiec* is an Assistant Professor of Counselor Education at Walsh University. She has four years of group work experience ranging from inpatient based to school based group therapy.

# Correspondence:

Questions and comments related to this activity may be directed to:

Bobbi Beale, PsyD.
919 Second Ave NE
Canton OH 44704
bbeale@childandadolescent.org

# Adventure: Magic Carpet

*By Bobbi Beale & Azra Karajic Siwiec*

## Population:
Children and teens

## Stage of Group:
Transition

## Type of Group:
Psychoeducational and counseling

## Rationale:
This activity can be helpful with groups who are struggling with communication and roles. The use of adventure based activities allows participants to problem solve together in an engaging and non-threatening manner. Participants get to focus on the task-at hand and move away from focusing on the particular issues that brought them to counseling. Adventure-based activities engage participants on any or all of these levels, avoiding resistance: cognitive, affective and/or behavioral (Gass, Gillis, & Russell, 2012).

## Goals:
Participants will:
4) engage in teamwork.
5) increase problem solving skills.
6) improve communication

## Materials:
A small tarp, tablecloth or blanket, approximately 6x6, upon which all of the members of the group can stand when spread open; something not too soft, so it won't tear.

## Time Allotment:
30-45 minutes for 6 to 8 physically able-bodied group members

## Directions:

Step:

1) Introduction by the group leader: *"You lucky people are going to enjoy a magic carpet ride! Everyone get onboard for your trip."* Once everyone is on the carpet, remind them that they are flying 20,000 feet in the air, so obviously they must remain on the carpet at all times. Stepping off the carpet will require restarting the activity.

2) Let the group know that the carpet is malfunctioning because it was boarded upside down. *"Oh, no! That turbulence that you feel is because your carpet is upside down. You will need to flip it right side up WITHOUT stepping off of the carpet or touching the ground around it. Safety regulations require all flyers to keep at least one foot on the tarp at all times (no climbing on backs or shoulders)."*

## Processing Questions:

1) What happened? What did your group do together?
2) What did you accomplish? What strategies or skills were helpful?
3) What skills did you see others use?
4) Did a leader emerge? How was he or she helpful?
5) What did each member in the group have to do to make it successful?
6) How can you apply the skills from this activity to other areas of your lives?

## Special Considerations:

1) The facilitator should allow the group to struggle and be frustrated. It is important that the group leader not coach members to the solution; they will learn more and "own" the problem solving skills only if you let them accomplish the task on their own.
2) Facilitators must be diligent about monitoring for safety in this activity. Group members will want to lift each other off the ground or climb onto each other. If the group gets frustrated or stuck, offer a brainstorming break, then restart the activity.

## Adaptations:

This activity can also be used with able-bodied adults.

Adaptation 1: For groups of 12+, use multiple tarps so everyone can participate at once. Place the tarps near each other, but not adjacent. Some groups may discover that a long step or short leap allows them to move from one tarp to another without violating the rule and touching the ground. This provides ample space for a smaller number of group members to easily flip the carpet and invite the flyers to climb back on.

**Adaptation 2:** Have the group write on a piece of masking tape goals they have for the future. Place these pieces of tape on the bottom side of the tarp. Then have them write 'barriers' or 'obstacles' to achieving these goals on different pieces of tape and tape them to the top side of the tarp. Then explain the rules and have them Turn over a New Leaf.

**Adaptation 3:** Revolve your discussion around working through challenges and obstacles to achieve your goals.

## References:

Gass, M., Gillis, L., & Russell, K. (2012). *Adventure therapy: Theory, research, and practice.* New York: Routledge.

Gass, M. (1993). *Adventure therapy: Therapeutic applications of adventure programming.* Dubuque, IA: Kendall/Hunt Publishing Co.

## Author Notes:

*Bobbi Beale* is a Group Programs Director working for Child and Adolescent Behavioral Health in Canton, Ohio. She has had 20 years of group work experience using adventure therapy with kids teaching them how to improve behavioral and emotional self-regulation and social competence.

*Azra Karajic Siwiec* is an Assistant Professor of Counselor Education at Walsh University. She has four years of group work experience ranging from inpatient based to school based group therapy.

## Correspondence:

Questions and comments related to this activity may be directed to:

Bobbi Beale, PsyD.
919 Second Ave NE
Canton OH 44704
bbeale@childandadolescent.org

# Am I Someone Who...

*By Jill Fetterolf*

## Population:

Children and adolescents

## Stage of Group:

This group activity is most appropriate for the Transition Stage, or for groups with members at different stages.

## Type of Group:

This group activity is most appropriate for Counseling and/or Therapy Groups.

## Rationale:

Many people think they understand who they are and what they believe. However, when faced with providing an explanation-not everyone can truly verbalize the reasons. The questions, situations, and decisions that people have to face are unlimited. Many of these will never be faced or even thought about by most people. This activity gives group members an opportunity to look inward and make decisions based on their own morals, values, opinions, and ideas. In addition, many members in the Transition Stage may be defensive and questioning can be counterproductive. By wording the statements as "I" statements, the members are provided more of an opportunity for self-reflection versus focusing on what other members would say. (Corey, Corey, & Corey, 2010).

## Goals:

Participants will:
1) discuss ideas and beliefs about self that are related to specific statements.
2) develop greater self-awareness about morals, values, opinions and/or ideas.
3) consider and evaluate various questions, thoughts, ideas, and situations that apply to self.
4) integrate thought process into every day choices.

## Materials:

1) List of questions as compiled by facilitator
2) Pencils or pens

## Time Allocated:

The time needed for this group would typically take 45-60 minutes.

## Directions:

Step:

1) Compile a list of closed-ended questions that would begin with "Am I Someone Who....?" which are specific to the group population. Make sure that the questions are varied and challenge the thinking and decision-making of the members. For example, "Am I someone who believes everything I see on television?" or "Am I someone who feels the people at your work/school know me well?" or "Am I someone who would be comfortable speaking in front of a crowd of people?"

2) Explain to group members to read and think about each of the questions on the questionnaire and decide if it is something that would apply to them individually. For example, group leader could state, "*Please read the following statements and determine if the statement applies to you. There are no right or wrong answers, and some might apply more than others.*"

3) Have group members indicate their decisions for each one by noting a "Y" for yes, "N" for no, and "M" for maybe on each line.

4) When finished-the group leader may read each statement or choose specific ones to discuss with the group.

5) During discussion about a specific statement, and when a member reveals their answer, ask the group members if they have agreed or disagreed and their individual reasons for choosing their answer. Additionally, questions can be asked to facilitate further self-awareness and group discussion. Some examples for group discussion questions would include:

   a) Which statements were easiest to determine?

   b) Which ones were more difficult?

   c) From the statements that you chose "Maybe"...what made it hard for you to decide?

## Processing Questions:

1) What have you learned about yourself after completing this and discussing your answers?
2) What statements and answers surprised you and why?
3) How honest were you with yourself and your answers and how can your answers help you in the counseling process?

## Special Considerations:

Group members may have strong disagreements due to the emotional nature of questions in this activity. It is important for group leaders to be aware of group characteristics and adjust questions according to their particular group. It would be particularly important to create an environment that allows for disagreement and for the group leader to anticipate any problems that may arise from particular statements that could be emotional for group members.

## Adaptations:

For populations of younger children or individuals with limited attention and/or reading skills- the group can be adapted. For these groups, hang three signs in separate areas of the room. One sign will be labeled "YES," one will be labeled "NO," and the other one will be labeled "MAYBE." Choose selected appropriate questions suitable to the specific group and ask them to go stand under the appropriate answer. Follow through with the questions as indicated previously.

## References:

Corey, M.S., Corey, G., & Corey, C. (2010). *Groups: Process and practice* (8th ed.). Belmont, CA: Brooks/Cole.

## Author Note:

Jill Fetterolf earned her Bachelor of Science degree in Administration of Justice at The Pennsylvania State University. She is currently a Master's Student at The Pennsylvania State University in the Counselor Education Program with a focus in Clinical Mental Health Counseling. She has over two years' group work experience in a variety of settings including adult corrections, juvenile justice, and a psychiatric hospital.

## Correspondence:

Questions and comments related to this activity may be directed to:

Jill Fetterolf, BS
Graduate Student-The Pennsylvania State University
Counselor Education-Clinical Mental Health Counseling
1173 William Penn Highway
Mifflintown, PA 17059
jillfetterolf@gmail.com

## Am I Someone Who?

Please read the questions and answer Y-yes, N-no or M-maybe. There are no wrong answers and some of the questions might apply to you more than others.

1. Needs to be alone?_____
2. Would kill in self-defense?_____
3. Would let my child drink or smoke pot?_____
4. Is apt to judge by appearance?_____
5. Can receive a gift easily?_____
6. Is afraid to be alone?_____
7. Is afraid to be alone in a strange place?_____
8. Will order a new dish in a restaurant?_____
9. Will publicly show affection to another person?_____
10. Will probably never give up smoking?_____
11. Is capable of handling opinions different from my own?_____
12. Responds with compassion when others suffer misfortune?_____
13. Thinks interracial marriage is acceptable?_____
14. Reads the comics in the newspaper first?_____
15. Would die for my beliefs and values?_____
16. Is easily swayed by the latest fads and gimmicks?_____
17. Believes everything I read?_____
18. Volunteers for jobs that are necessary but unpleasant?_____
19. Would want to design and build my own home?_____
20. Would marry for money and prestige?_____
21. Enjoys playing games rather than watching television?_____
22. Spends a lot of time worrying about things without doing anything about them?_____
23. Tries to do everything as perfectly as possible?_____
24. Often drives over the speed limit?_____
25. Believes in the live-to-eat philosophy?_____
26. Finds it difficult to praise someone for a job well done?_____
27. Considers loyalty to a friend or a cause more important than honesty?_____
28. Tries to understand respect others opinions?_____
29. Likes conformity rather than diversity?_____
30. Would rather fight than quit?_____
31. Would like to hitchhike through Europe?_____
32. Falls in love right away?_____
33. Has ever felt lonely, even in a crowd of people?_____
34. Has had such bad problems that I wished I could die so I would not have to face them?_____
35. Thinks that women should stay home and be wives and mothers?_____
36. Would like to make some changes in my life?_____
37. Would like to jump from an airplane with a parachute?_____
38. Would like to have a secret lover?_____
39. Could invite someone I could not stand to my home?_____
40. Has ever wanted to really hurt someone for what they did to me?_____

# Are You Listening?

*By Marcey Mettica*

## Population:

Children and adolescents with communication struggles in relationships. Possible adaptations for other populations can be found in the adaptations section.

## Stage of Group:

Transition or Working

## Type of Group:

Psychoeducational

## Rationale:

Communication skills are a critical part of interpersonal relationships. Understanding how to communicate more effectively and the importance of non-verbal cues are critical life skills that are vital for human interaction. Effective communication skills are necessary to get needs met and for relationships to flourish. Nonverbal communication or body language is a crucial component of interactions, delivering more of the message than words alone. Empirical research supports the notion that effective communication skills are an important facet of every relationship.

## Goals:

Participants will:
1) identify effective communication skills.
2) demonstrate the importance of nonverbal communication.

## Materials:

1) White board or flip-chart and markers.
2) Simple sketches (see attached examples).
3) Writing instrument and paper for each group member.

## Time Allotment:

One hour.

## Directions:

Step:
1) Welcome participants and begin to explore goals of communication. Sample script for group leader: *"What are the goals of communication?"* Write group members'

comments on the board.  Two primary goals of communication are to establish mutual understanding and find a solution to a problem.

2) Explain effective communication skills. Sample script for group leader: *"What are some good communication skills?"* Write group members' comments on the board.  Good communication skills include, but are not limited to:  picking the right time, defining the topic, speaking clearly, asking for what you want, using good manners, using "I" statements, emphasizing the positive, using visual cues, listening, and patience.

3) Discuss what to do when inevitable conflict arises in relationships. Group leader sample script: *"What should you do when conflict arises?"* Write group members' comments on the board.  Possible answers include: stay focused on the present problem without bringing up the past; avoid saying "never", "always", and "forever"; listen and reflect back what the other person is saying; be respectful; try to see the other' person's point of view; respond to criticism with empathy; own what is yours; use "I" messages instead of "You" messages; look for a win-win solution; take a time out if needed but don't give up; and ask for help if you need it.

4) Explore nonverbal communication. Group leader sample script: *"What is nonverbal communication?"* Write group members' comments on the board.  Examples could include body language, gestures, personal space, the way we sit/stand, voice inflection, tone, volume, eye contact,  and touch. Nonverbal communication provide confirmation or contradiction to our words and can accentuate or complement our words.  Group leader sample script: *"If our words don't match our nonverbal signals, what is believed?"* Give examples such as frowning or smiling when saying *"You look nice today"* (contradiction or confirmation), pounding desk when saying *"I'm so mad!"* (accentuate) or patting someone's back when saying *"I'm proud of you"* (compliment).

5) Teach how much of the intended message is delivered through nonverbal communication. Group leader sample script: *"How much of communication is our words?"* There are various statistics available on this, but our words constitute very little of what we communicate with an estimated 7% being words, 38% being voice inflection, and 53% being facial expressions and body language.

6) Instruct group members to choose a partner and sit back to back.  Give one person in each pair a drawing (sample drawings attached). Group leader sample script: *"If I gave you a drawing, your role is to describe the picture to your partner without showing it to them. The other person's role is to draw what they are told without any nonverbal communication. When you have completed the drawing, you may then compare pictures with your partner."*

7) Each dyad is given another picture to complete the activity again. Group leader sample script: *"If you drew the picture the last time, this time you will explain the picture and your partner will draw it."*

8) Encourage group participation to discuss what communication barriers interfered with accuracy. Group leader sample script: *"What made this activity difficult? What would have made this activity easier?"*

## Processing Questions:

1) What did you learn from this activity?
2) What will you do differently because of what you learned today?
3) How might participating in this group today impact your relationships?

## Special Considerations:

Drawings should be adjusted in complexity to meet the developmental level of the group members.

## Adaptations:

This activity can also be used with adults during couple's counseling or family therapy to help build stronger communication skills within struggling relational dynamics.

## References:

Ten Effective Communication Skills. Retrieved from: http://www.life123.com/relationships/communication/effective-communication

Nonverbal Communicating: Improving Nonverbal Skills & Reading Body Language. Retrieved from: http://helpguide.org/mental/eq6_nonverbal_commuication.htm

## Author Notes:

*Marcey Mettica* is the owner of a private practice, **First Street Counseling and Consulting, PLLC**, specializing in the treatment of children, adolescents, and families. She is a Doctoral Student at Texas Women's University in the Family Studies program. She has worked as a group therapist with survivors of childhood sexual abuse, psychiatric inpatient adolescents, children's social skills groups, and parent groups.

## Correspondence:

Questions and comments related to this activity may be directed to:

Marcey Mettica, M.S., LPC, RPT
First Street Counseling & Consulting, PLLC
3067 Falcon Road, Suite 100
Prosper, TX 75078
marceymettica@yahoo.com

# Broken Flower Pot

By Katrina Cook & Mary G. Mayorga

## Population:

This activity is designed for group members who are grieving over the loss of a loved one. Group members can be in late childhood, adolescence, or adulthood.

## Stage of Group:

Working or termination

## Type of Group:

Counseling, therapy

## Rationale:

Participation in interpersonal counseling groups can be beneficial for members who are grieving the loss of a loved one, providing them with opportunities for exploring feelings related to the loss and experiencing catharsis (Para, 2009). The use of props in counseling sessions has been promoted as a method to help group members give concrete form to vague concepts or analogies (Harvill, Jacobs, & Masson, 1984). This activity uses the prop of a broken flower pot to demonstrate a healing process as participants learn to cope with their loss.

## Goals:

Participants will:
1)  recognize that they are changed as a result of the loss they experienced.
2)  realize that something beautiful can develop from the "broken" pieces of their hearts.
3)  experience a sense of hope for the future.

## Materials:

1)  One small flower pot for each group member
2)  Markers
3)  Glue (carpenter's glue)
4)  Potting soil
5)  Small plants ( one for each group member

## Time Allotment:

In general, this session would take an hour to complete. Allow extra time for younger participants who may need help gluing their pots back together. Wait between sessions to add the dirt and the plants so the glued pieces have an opportunity to dry.

# Directions:

Note: This activity has three stages.

## Stage 1: Breaking the pot.
Step :

1)  Invite each group member to select a pot and break it by throwing it on the ground.

2)  Ask the participants to gather the pieces of their pots and look at them.

3)  Ask each participant to compare how the broken pieces of the pot resemble how they feel after the loss of their loved one (i.e. life is shattered, family is scattered, heart is broken, etc.).

4)  Facilitate a discussion by asking the following questions.
    a)  What was it like for you to break the pot?
    b)  How does the broke pot resemble your life after your loss?

## Stage 2: Putting it back together.
Step:

1)  Ask participants to glue the pot back together as best they can.

2)  Once the pots are glued, discuss how they will always miss their loved ones, but they can take the broken pieces of their hearts and rebuild them. Their lives will never be the same after the loss, but they can still function, just as the pot that is glued back together can continue to function.

3)  Facilitate a discussion by asking the following questions.
    a)  How does the glued pot resemble your life now?
    b)  Will the pot ever be the same as it was before it was broken?
    c)  What kind-of support would the pot need to grow something?
    d)  What kind-of support do you need in order to continue to grow and thrive?

## Stage 3: Planting.
Step:

1)  Give each participant some dirt and a plant to plant in his or her pot.
    *The growth of the new plant is a symbol of new life and hope that evolves from their pain and the broken pieces.*

# Processing Questions:

1)  What was this activity like for you?
2)  What are some things you learned about the other group members that you did not know before?
3)  What do you feel hopeful about?

## Special Considerations:

1) Determine a group member's readiness to engage in this activity. It may not be as effective with those group members experiencing a very recent loss.
2) Participants may want to wear gardening gloves when handling sharp shards of pottery to prevent the possibility of cutting themselves.

## Adaptations:

Young group members may need assistance in breaking and regluing the pot. This group can also be used with persons experiencing other losses, such as the loss of a pet, a job, or a significant relationship.

## References:

Harvill, R., Jacobs, E. E., & Masson, R. L. (1984). Use of props in counseling. *Personnel and Guidance Journal, 62.* 419-431.

Just for me! Healing activities for grieving children and teens. (n.d.). Retrieved October 2, 2012 from http://campbell.k12.va.us/tes/wpuckette/media/justforme.pdf

Para, E. A. (2009). Group counseling for complicated grief: A literature review. *Graduate Journal of Counseling Psychology 1*(2), 100-112.

## Author Notes:

*Katrina Cook* is an Assistant Professor of Counselor Education at Texas A&M University – San Antonio. She has had twenty-nine years of group work experience, including facilitating groups with children and adolescents.

*Mary G. Mayorga* is an Assistant Professor Of Counselor Education at Texas A&M University – San Antonio. She has facilitated groups related to substance, abuse, couples and family, juvenile justice and conflict resolution.

## Correspondence:

Questions and comments related to this activity may be directed to:

Dr. Katrina Cook, Ph.D., LPC-S, LMFT-S, CSC
Texas A&M University – San Antonio
One University Way, Mailing Address
Katrina.cook@tamusa.tamus.edu
One University Way, San Antonio, Texas, 78224
Katrina.cook@tamusa.tamus.edu

# Group Work with Military Children: Feeling Explorations

*By Stephanie Lewis & Katie Lopolito-Meyer*

## Population:

The identified population for this activity is children aged 8 years old to 12 years old who have a parent or a family member serving in the military in the past, present, or future.

## Stage of Group:

Working Stage

## Type of Group:

Counseling

## Rationale:

Military children experience a wide variety of obstacles without many outlets to describe, experience, and display their emotions regarding the situation. Greenleaf, Thompson-Gillespie and Wood (2012) identify some common reactions among students of deployed parents such as "decline in academic performance, increased absenteeism from school, loss of interest in peers, having a short temper, outbursts of anger, feelings of anxiety, depression, loss of control, and difficulty concentrating and learning, rise in health-related issues, and creating violent drawings or writings in personal journals." (p. 2). Many of these effects are caused by repeated and extended separation from their parents and by relocating typically three times more than their non-military peers. This then becomes compounded by the everyday stressors of living in a military home.

Due to the lack of predictability concerning the military family member(s), military children need additional assistance in overcoming the challenges and obstacles experienced at home which may require the support and consistency of group work. Furthermore, Kim, Kirchhoff, and Whitsett (2011) have described how expressive art therapy can be used to address a wide range of therapeutic material and meet the developmental needs of this age group while allowing it to be offered to a diverse group of children. Group work with these children can provide an opportunity to process and integrate a wide range of emotional experiences, while also providing social support, intrapersonal learning, and promoting hope.

## Goals:

Participants will:
1) Prepare for deployment through preliminary consideration of what deployment often entails for military families.
2) Experience normalization of feelings.
3) Set emotional goals for deployment.
4) Build self-esteem.

## Materials:

1) Old Magazines
2) Scissors
3) Poster Board
4) Glue Sticks
5) Markers/Colored Pencils

## Time Allotment:

This activity can be completed in one hour with 15 minutes for pre-discussion, 30 minutes for making the collage, and 15 minutes for post-discussion.

## Directions:

Step:
1) Ask the group members if they have thought about their deployment expectations. Discuss thoughts and feelings. Say *"Today we will be exploring what it's like to have a parent or family member who is deployed."*

2) Summarize what took place in earlier sessions regarding initial expectations and fears.

3) Ask the group members to think about some of their own personal thoughts and feelings regarding deployment. Below are some prompt questions to use to help get the conversation going
   a. *What are some feelings you have about deployment?*
   b. *What is a main concern for you?*
      i. *What will my role be within the family?*
      ii. *How will life be different?*
      iii. *How long will my family member be gone?*
      iv. *Will my family member forget about me?*
      v. *How much control will I have in making decisions?*
      vi. *How often will I get to talk to my family member?*
   c. *What are your plans for dealing with some of these concerns?*
   d. *Has anyone ever had a friend he/she has not seen in a while? What was it like to be away from him or her?*

4) After the discussion, explain the activity. Say *"we are now going to make a group collage that helps us portray our feeling about deployments... A collage is a group of cut-out pictures or words that helps express what is going on inside of you to others."*

5) Have group members look through the magazines for pictures or words that correspond with their feelings of deployment and have them glue them onto the big poster board you've placed at the front of the room. Tell the group members *"now I would like you to each look through these magazine and find pictures or words that describe, to you, your feelings about deployment. Feel free to discuss these thoughts and feeling with your fellow group members while you work. Once you cut out all your pictures and words, you can glue them on to the large poster board I've placed at the front of the room. When we have all had a chance to glue some items onto the board you will have the opportunity to share with your fellow group members why you chose a certain picture or word."*

6) After the group members have created their collages, they can display their collage to the group and discuss some of the following:
   a. What picture or word is most significant to you?
   b. What commonalities do you see?
   c. Were there things that you had not thought of? Tell us about them.

7) Summarize the main points and commonalities among members. Let the group members know that *"Adjusting to deployment will take patience, time, and understanding, but we are all here to support one another through this process."*

## Processing Questions:
1) What did you learn about yourself by creating this collage?
2) What did you learn about your fellow group members while creating this collage?
3) How was the experience of creating the collage for you?
4) How do you feel after doing this?
5) What was said that impacted you most?
6) What might members think, feel, or do differently as a result of what they learned from this activity?

## Special Considerations:
1) When conducting this activity, group leaders should carefully monitor the direction of the conversation. It can be easy, especially with a frightening topic like military deployments, for children to get caught in a negative spiral when discussing fears about this experience. Although it is certainly important to discuss and process negative feelings and fears related to deployment, it may be important to avoid negative emotional spirals and focus heavily on coping skills and utilizing the group for support.
2) When conducting this activity, group leaders should be aware of any motor (fine or gross) disabilities and make adaptations accordingly such as helping the child cut or allowing the child to share from his/her seat.

3) Since children will be using scissors to cut out the pictures from the magazines, group leaders should make sure that they discuss safety with sharp objects or have pre-cut items available.

## Adaptations:

This activity can be adapted to correspond with any family crisis by enabling children to normalize and discuss their feelings. This activity can also be adapted to working with adolescents by changing verbiage and expectations such as writing their own poetry and drawing their own pictures to create a collage to be shared with the group.

## References:

Greenleaf, A. T., Thompson-Gillespie, L, & Wood, S. M. (2012). Promising practices for school counselors working with military families. *Counseling Today.* Retrieved from http://ct.counseling.org/2012/08/promising-practices-for-school-counselors- working with-students-of-military-families/.

Kim, J. B., Kirchhoff, M. & Whitsett,S. (2001). Expressive arts group therapy with middle-school aged children from military families. *The Arts in Psychology 55,* 356-362.

National Military Family Association (2003). *Working with military children: A primer for school personnel* (NGB). Arlington, VA: US Government Printing Office.

## Author Notes:

*Stephanie Lewis* is currently pursuing her master's degree in counseling at Indiana University Purdue University Fort Wayne. She is currently employed at SCAN (Stop Child Abuse and Neglect) Inc. in Fort Wayne, Indiana where she works with families. Stephanie grew up in a military town and is a spouse of a United States Marine, which has significantly influenced her interest in working with Military Families.

*Katie Lopolito-Meyer* is currently pursuing her master's degree in counseling at Indiana University-Purdue University and is also employed as a middle school teacher at Summit Middle School in Fort Wayne, Indiana. Katie's interest in working with military families is related to her experience being the child of a United States' Army helicopter pilot. She desires to share her knowledge with others to encourage understanding of the unique needs of military children.

## Correspondence:

Questions and comments related to this activity may be directed to:
Stephanie Lewis
Indiana University Purdue University Fort Wayne
IPFW Counseling Program
2101 East Coliseum Blvd.
Neff Hall 250
Fort Wayne, IN 46835
Srlewis129@gmail.com

# I am a Coffee Mug

*By Kristin Meany-Walen*

## Population:

This activity is intended for outpatient adolescents and adults with mental health disorders. Modifications can be made for use with other populations (see Adaptations Section).

## Stage of Group:

Orientation Stage (but could be adapted to work well in any stage).

## Type of Group:

Counseling

## Rationale:

One of the primary goals of the orientation phase is for group members to begin to build cohesion (Schneider Corey, Corey, & Corey, 2010). Cohesion has several benefits, a few of which are increased self-disclosure and better individual outcomes (Yalom, 1995). During this phase, group members are assessing other members for values, similarities and differences in order to build relationships and are monitoring the safety of the group (Schneider Corey, Corey, & Corey, 2010). Expressive arts, and similar activities such as the one described here, can be a useful strategies to increase self-disclosure and participation, and reduce anxiety and resistance (Gladding, 2005). Therefore, *I am a Coffee Mug* serves to increase participation and cohesion and reduce barriers to the group counseling process.

## Goals:

Participants will:
1) learn about one another.
2) gain insight through the process of sharing.
3) begin to develop group cohesion.

## Materials:

Materials are supplied by the group members based on the items they regularly bring to group sessions. The leader does not need to bring supplies for this activity. For example, group members my use any of the following materials: water bottle, keys, purse or wallet, shoe, pen, rubber band, driver's license or other identification card.

## Time Allotment:

Approximately 3-5 minutes per group member.

## Directions:

Step:

1) The group leader will introduce the activity. The following is an example of what a leader might say: "*Individually, you will introduce yourself to the group by describing yourself as an item you have brought with you (or find in the room). As you describe yourself, you must speak in first person as if you ARE that item.*" Provide a few minutes for group members to select an item.." The leader may give an example to start the process. For example, the group leader may say," *I will start….I am a coffee mug. I am thick and sturdy. This helps me to stay balanced and protects others from my contents. I can be dropped and banged with little permanent damage. However, I can be hurt and even brake if I am treated too poorly. I am useful in a number of ways. I can do my intended job, holding hot liquids, or I can do a variety of other tasks such as hold pens or candy, be a paper weight, or be used to trace circles. For some people, I am a decoration and used to remind them of a specific event or time in their life. For other people, I am a mere convenience and useful item. I have boundaries and keep my contents contained. I have also been known to overflow at times when I ignore my limits.*"

2) After the leader provides an example and an introduces himself/herself, the group members take turns introducing themselves as their chosen object. The leader will redirect members to use first person rather than talking about the item. After each member shares, the leader can acknowledge the group member by making a reflection or observation about the group member's item and description. For example: "*Ruth, you chose your purse and described how it keeps important and useful things. I'd guess that being practical and responsible are important qualities to you.*" The group leader may also make connections amongst group members based on their chosen items and/or descriptions. For example: "*Jack and LaKesha both used writing utensils to describe themselves. It seems the two of you have something in common!*"

## Processing Questions:

1) In what ways are you similar/dissimilar to your description of your item?
2) How do those characteristics contribute to your problems/successes in life?
3) What similarities/differences exist between members of the group?
4) How could you improve your item?
5) How will the group activity impact your life outside of group?

## Special Considerations/Cautions:

No risks exist outside of the typical group counseling experience with this activity.

## Adaptations:

This activity can be used in a number of settings: schools, community agencies, private practice, or hospitals. Processing questions may be adapted or changed based on the purpose of the group, cognitive ability/development of the group members, and stage of the group process.

# References:

Schneider Corey, M., Corey, G., & Corey, C. (2010). *Groups: Process and practice* (8th ed.). Belmont, CA: Brooks/Cole.

Yalom, I. (1995). *The theory and practice of group psychotherapy* (4th ed.). New York, NY: Basic Books.

# Author Notes:

*Kristin Meany-Walen* is an Assistant Professor of Counseling at University of Northern Iowa. She has several years of experience working with a variety of groups including substance abuse recovery groups, social skills groups for children and adolescents, sibling and family groups, parent training and teacher training groups.

# Correspondence:

Questions and comments related to this activity may be directed to:

Kristin Meany-Walen, Ph.D., LMHC, RPT, NCC
Assistant Professor
University of Northern Iowa
227 Latham Hall
University of Northern Iowa
Cedar Falls, IA 50614
Kristin.Meany-Walen@uni.edu

# Icebreaker Activity

## Population:

This group activity will work in most any population. It has been used in a psychiatric hospital with the children, adolescent, adult, and stabilization units.

## Stage of Group:

Orientation

## Type of Group:

Counseling and/or Therapy

## Rationale:

This activity provides the opportunity for group members to think of themselves and their individual lives through creative means, and allows them to express ideas in a non-directive manner. It has been my experience that asking someone to respond to a question structured in an abstract or creative manner can actually generate some thought-provoking responses. Many of these responses may provide more information indirectly than that group member would have been willing and possibly able to provide directly. For example, some of the quotes included can lead a person to talk about their personal values and views without specifically asking the question asking them to identify them. Also, the questions/quotes included can assist with providing someone a starting point to express their personal views. The explanations of why they chose a specific answer can actually provide additional information in an indirect manner. These things are important in the Orientation/Initial Stage of a group. It is during this stage when members are just learning to express thoughts and feelings and attempting to establish goals. The information that they learn from their answers may assist in each of these areas. (Corey, Corey, & Corey, 2010)

## Goals:

Participants will:
1) develop greater self-awareness.
2) share information about their self with the group.
3) identify thoughts and emotions in regards to certain topics and possibly connect them to their own personal wellness.

## Materials:

1) Icebreaker questions and quotes (see compiled list for example)
2) Scissors
3) Basket or something to place slips of paper into.

# Time Allocated:

The time needed for this group would typically take 45-60 minutes.

# Directions:

Step:

1) Cut Icebreaker questions and quotes into separate papers with one per paper. Explain to group members that you have various questions, quotes, etc. on separate papers. The group leader may state further directions such as, "Each member will select one slip of paper. Each paper will have either a question, statement, or quote listed to be read to provide a response.

2) Ask the group members to randomly choose one and provide a response. For example, if a group member choses a paper stating, "Two wrongs do not make a right-unknown" Ask the group member if they have ever heard the saying before? Do they agree with the statement-why or why not? And how might they apply that to their own life-past, present, or future.

3) As each person chooses one and responds, ask other members of the group to reflect about the same question/saying and discuss. Examples of questions for reflection could include:

   a) How would anyone else respond to this same question/quote?

   b) What similarities to this member's response would you have in your response?

   c) What would be different with your response?

   d) How has this question/quote applied to anyone else's life?

4) Continue to ask for volunteers until either time is up or every one of the papers has been chosen.

5) Questions to encourage further discussion about the activity could also be used towards the end of the group time. For example:

   a) Which questions/quotes were easiest for you to respond?

   b) Which ones were more difficult?

   c) What specifically made them easy or difficult?

   d) What other questions/quotes would you add to the activity?

## Processing Questions:

1) What have you learned about yourself during this activity?
2) How comfortable were you during this activity?
3) How will you look at questions/quotes differently after this activity?
4) What information from this activity can you apply to your counseling process?

## Special Considerations:

There are several less intense questions and sayings on the attached sheet. These questions could also be good transition when the group appears to be struggling in additional stages other than the Orientation Stage of group. The group members will typically still provide important information about themselves in the process, but perhaps the method is less threatening to them.

## Adaptations:

For populations of younger children or individuals with limited attention and/or reading skills- the group can be altered. For these groups, choose appropriate statements according to the specific group. Follow through with the questions as indicated previously.

## References:

Corey, M.S., Corey, G., & Corey, C. (2010). *Groups: Process and practice* (8th ed.). Belmont, CA. Brooks/Cole.

## Author Note:

*Jill Fetterolf* earned her Bachelor of Science degree in Administration of Justice at The Pennsylvania State University. She is currently a Master's Student at The Pennsylvania State University in the Counselor Education Program with a focus in Clinical Mental Health Counseling. She has over two years' group work experience in a variety of settings including adult corrections, juvenile justice, and a psychiatric hospital.

## Correspondence:

Questions and comments related to this activity may be directed to:

Jill Fetterolf
Graduate Student-The Pennsylvania State University
Counselor Education-Clinical Mental Health Counseling
1173 William Penn Highway
Mifflintown, PA 17059
jillfetterolf@gmail.com

# Icebreaker Questions & Quotes

1. What would you pick for a mascot for your life? Explain.
2. What song would you name as the theme song for your life? Explain.
3. What piece of candy best represents you? Explain.
4. What movie title would be the best representation of your life story? Explain.
5. What video game best represents you? Explain.
6. Which one of the four season's best represents you? Explain.
7. If you were writing a book about your life what would the title be & what chapter are you in? Explain.
8. What cartoon character would best represent you? Explain.
9. If you could pick a license plate to tell your life story what would it say? Explain.   (limit of 7 letters/numbers)
10. What make and model car would best represent you? Explain.
11. What one thing in nature would best represent you and your life? Explain.
12. What type of building would best represent you and your life? Explain.
13. What toy would best represent you? Explain.
14. You can do anything-If you want it bad enough, and you work hard enough-unknown
15. Two wrongs do not make a right-unknown
16. Learn from the mistakes of others, you can't live long enough to make them all yourself-Eleanor Roosevelt
17. To handle yourself, use your head, To handle others, use your heart-Eleanor Roosevelt
18. Anger is only one letter short of danger-Eleanor Roosevelt
19. Great minds discuss ideas-Average minds discuss events-Small minds discuss people-Eleanor Roosevelt
20. Today is the first day of the rest of your life-Charles Dederich/Abbie Hoffman

# Identifying Strengths among Immigrant Youth with Cultural Artifacts

*By Ana Estrada*

## Population:

This activity is appropriate for immigrant youth (age 9 and above) and the group constellations identified below.

## Stage of Group:

Orientation

This activity promotes self-disclosure in a structured and safe way with each new member regulating her/his sharing in the group. It will also facilitate the discovery of shared and non-shared cultural backgrounds, immigration histories, identities and experiences among the members as the group forms.

## Type of Group:

Task, Psychoeducational, Counseling

This activity has been used with a variety of groups of immigrant youth including Task/Work and Psychoeducational groups. Additionally, depending on the level of functioning of members, it can be used in the orientation phase of Counseling, and Therapy groups.

## Rationale:

Developing a sense of identity, belongingness, meaning and purpose are all developmental tasks that are prone to disruption among immigrant and undocumented youth, and require particular attention, understanding and support (Gonzales, Suárez-Orozco, & Dedios-Sanguineti, 2013). Understanding group members' cultural background, country of origin, identity and differences including but not limited to age, race/ethnicity, culture, gender, immigration, acculturation, nationality, sexuality, spirituality, sexuality, class family history, disabilities, and physical characteristics or limitations is consistent with the 2007 updated Best Practices Guidelines of the Association for Specialists in Group Work (ASGW; Thomas and Pender, 2008).

Beginning the group with the sharing of one's cultural history and artifacts can create an affirming opportunity for the group to view each other in their cultural contexts, and for members to share the complexity of their multiple and intersecting identities and journeys in their families of origin and communities with their peers. This is particularly important for immigrant youth whose stories of their family background, ancestry and immigration are often lost or disparaged in the increasingly hostile political climate which permeates the national discussion of immigration reform and has escalated in southern California and the southwest border regions of the U.S.

# Goals:

Participants will:
1) increase awareness of members' and the group's countries of origin, immigration experiences, cultural values, identity, and the strengths that derive from these identifications.
2) highlight the strengths and intersectionality (e.g., the intersection of immigration history, gender, sexuality and ethnicity) of members' backgrounds and identities.
3) increase awareness of the impact of these above factors as members develop their identities, affiliations, and connections with peers and their community.
4) be encouraged to join in the group process by bringing valued parts of themselves, literally and figuratively, to the group.

# Materials:

Members are invited to bring an object from home that represents their cultural and immigration background. Examples of items have included a piece of clothing, musical instrument, artwork, graduation stole, family photograph, and (playing) a piece of music.

# Time Allotment:

Time needed for this activity depends on the size of the group. Each member of the group can share their item within a 5-7 minute period, including questions.

# Directions:

Step:
1) During the first meeting, members are invited to bring a "cultural artifact" to the second meeting to share with the group. A "cultural artifact" is defined as a special object that reflects one's cultural, family or individual values, immigration history, beliefs, or traditions.

2) The member will have an opportunity to share their story related to their artifact.

3) After sharing, group members will have an opportunity to view the artifact and ask a few questions about the cultural artifact and its significance.
    a. Why is this artifact important to you? To your family?
    b. (If appropriate) Did you make this artifact?
    c. How does this object reflect you? Your culture? Your family? Your community?
    d. How do these artifacts represent your immigration journey or experience?

# Processing Questions:

1) What did you learn about yourself?
2) What did you learn about the other members of the group?

3) Can you identify some commonalities and differences among members?
4) What does this experience mean for the group?
5) How will your learning impact your work together as a group?

## Special Considerations:

Given the special and personal significance of the objects and immigration stories, it is important for the group leaders to facilitate and at times moderate the questions that emerge from the group to ensure that group inquiries are respectful, and not excessively intrusive or time consuming. I suggest the group leaders also complete this exercise and share first so that they model sharing their cultural artifact appropriately with the group. Finally, the sharing of artifacts is a rich opportunity for the group leaders to facilitate the joining and connections in the group as a whole.

## Adaptations:

For larger groups or highly active groups that engage in extended sharing, it is suggested that the leaders divide the sharing of cultural artifacts across a couple of sessions. This also allows the group to accomplish other tasks during the sessions in which the sharing occurs.

## References:

Gonzales, R. G., Suárez-Orozco, C., & Dedios-Sanguineti, M. C. (2013). No place to belong: Contextualizing concepts of mental health among undocumented immigrant youth in the United States. *American Behavioral Scientist*, 57(8), 1174-1199.

Thomas, V. R., & Pender, D. A. (2008). Association for Specialists in Group Work: Best Practice Guidelines 2007 Revisions. *The Journal for Specialists in Group Work*, 33 (2), 111-117.

## Author Notes:

*Ana Estrada* is the Counseling Program Director at the University of San Diego. She has over 25 years of experience in facilitating and coaching children, adolescents, adults, and family groups largely comprised of racial/ethnic minority, immigrant and Spanish Speaking youth and families.

## Correspondence:

Questions and comments related to this activity may be directed to:

Ana Ulloa Estrada, Ph.D., LMFT
Associate Professor and Director of Counseling Program,
Department of School, Family and Mental Health Professions (SFMHP)
School of Leadership and Education Sciences (SOLES)
University of San Diego
5998 Alcala Park
San Diego, CA 92110
estradaa@sandiego.edu

# Magnificent Creation

*By Kristin Meany-Walen & Natalya Lindo*

## Population:

This activity is intended for outpatient children and adolescents with mental health and/or behavior concerns. Modifications can be made for use with other populations (see Adaptations Section).

## Stage of Group:

Working

## Type of Group:

Counseling

## Rationale:

The working stage of groups is a time when group members are reflective, working toward their goals, and aware of the group dynamics (Schneider Corey, Corey, & Corey, 2010). According to Piaget, children are concrete learners and learn best by being actively involved with tangible materials in order to best understand and apply new information (Piaget, 1962). Moreover, children between the ages of middle childhood and early adolescence are interested in discovering their capabilities, how they belong with others, and ways in which they contribute to the world (Erikson, 1968). This activity aligns with the group and developmental literature by creating an opportunity for group members to participate in small teams with a tangible task. Members will be guided to reflect upon their roles in the group and their contribution to their assigned team.

## Goals:

Participants will:
1) improve interpersonal skills by participating in the joint efforts of an activity.
2) increase self-esteem through recognizing positive ways in which one contributes to others/tasks.
3) increase appropriate social behaviors through teamwork, feedback, and leader direction.

# Materials:

Materials can vary based on availability and group leaders' preferences. Examples of materials may include:

1) pom poms
2) pipe cleaners
3) colored paper
4) foil
5) glue and/or tape
6) dry noodles
7) glitter
8) feathers
9) empty egg carton
10) toilet paper or paper towel roll
11) a variety of craft materials

# Time Allotment:

Approximately 10 minutes for the activity; 20 minutes for processing

# Directions:

Step:

1) In groups of 3 or 4, members will make a "magnificent creation" out of the materials provided. The following is an example of how a group leader might introduce the activity to the group. *"Today you are going to work as in small groups to make a magnificent creation. I will divide you into small groups. You can use all of the materials in most of the ways you wish. You cannot use the materials in a way that is hurtful to yourself, each other, or the room. Aside from this, there are not 'rules' about the final product. Be creative and have fun. You have 10 minutes* (time can vary depending on the group) *to complete this activity."* Directions are left intentionally vague in order to allow group members to work through ambiguity and navigate through the process of making the final creation.

2) Group leader(s) avoid giving more directions to group members who want more clarity. Examples of responses to these members might be, *"You and your group can decide what to create. There is no right or wrong way to do this."* Or *"I know it's challenging when you're not given a lot of directions, but I know you can figure out what to do."*

3) Group leader(s) should be open to the process and product of this activity. Within each group, members may work together to create one magnificent creation, or each member of the smaller groups might create his or her own magnificent creation. The small groups might decide to work together and make a combined magnificent creation. The process and group members' interpretation of the activity becomes "grist for the mill."

4) The group leader(s) will inform the group when 5 minutes remain and when 1 minute remains.

## Processing Questions:

1) How did your group decide what you were going to make?
2) In what ways was your creation different than you had pictured in your mind?
3) How did you help your group in the creation?
4) How would other group members describe your role in this activity?
5) How was your role in this group similar or different than your role in other groups (i.e. class, family, sports).

## Special Considerations:

Materials must be safe for the age and development of the participants. Because of the active nature of this activity, consideration for members' physical ability will be necessary.

## Adaptations:

Adaptations can be made to use this activity with multiple types of groups and populations (i.e. family groups, adults, consultation groups, students, counselor-in-training supervisees). Changes to processing questions might be made to accommodate specific group needs such as population, stage, or type of group.

Group leaders may choose for the small groups to work together to combine each magnificent creation into one large group magnificent creation. Among other ideas, the leader(s) may process with the group how the smaller parts contribute to the bigger creation.

School counselors may want to use this with students in counseling or guidance lessons. For example, this could be an "outside" activity by instructing group members to collect items at the park or in nature.

Examples may include:
1) leaves
2) sticks
3) gravel
4) broken bird eggs
5) flowers
6) tree bark
7) litter or other findings

*The leader may still want to include tape, glue or other materials.

## References:

Schneider Corey, M., Corey, G., & Corey, C. (2010). *Groups: Process and practice* (8th ed.). Belmont, CA: Brooks/Cole.

Erikson, E. H. (1968). *Identity: Youth in crisis.* New York, NY: Norton.

Piaget, J. (1962). *Play, dreams, and imitation in childhood.* New York: Routledge.

## Author Notes:

*Kristin Meany-Walen* is an Assistant Professor of Counseling at University of Northern Iowa. She has several years of experience working with a variety of groups including substance abuse recovery groups, social skills groups for children and adolescents, sibling and family groups, parent training and teacher training groups.

*Natalya Lindo* is an Assistant Professor of Counseling at University of North Texas. She has led several groups that incorporate didactic and expressive techniques to engage members in the interpersonal and intrapersonal process of groups. Natalya's specific interests include leading parent- and teacher-training groups and facilitating groups with culturally diverse membership.

## Correspondence:

Questions and comments related to this activity may be directed to:

Kristin Meany-Walen, Ph.D., LMHC, RPT, NCC
Assistant Professor
University of Northern Iowa
227 Latham Hall
University of Northern Iowa
Cedar Falls, IA 50614
Kristin.Meany-Walen@uni.edu

# Masks

By Jill Fetterolf

## Population:
Children and adolescent inpatient populations

## Stage of Group:
Working

## Type of Group:
Counseling and/or Therapy Groups

## Rationale:
People often hide their true selves with a "mask." A mask often alters a person's identity and hides feelings and emotions. When others see this mask they form an opinion of a person that might not be accurate. Also, some people struggling with low self-esteem, lack of self-identity, and/or an inability to express emotions believe that others see them differently than they see themselves. Identifying these differences and allowing and accepting a true self to emerge is a vital part of a group member's counseling process. This is important during this working stage in group therapy. Members are at a point where they put themselves at risk and test the trust of other members. When the members disclose information such as their ideas behind their masks, they are actively putting trust in other members. This trust can enhance further self-exploration. (Corey, Corey, & Corey, 2010).

## Goals:
Participants will:
1) explore interpretation of true self versus perceived self.
2) develop greater self-awareness.
3) enable reflection of self and identify thoughts and emotions.

## Materials:
1) Mask poem/story of your choice-specific to the group population (there are many poems sites online to search)
2) Paper masks (either drawn free-hand, traced from an actual mask, or printable masks can be obtained free online)
3) Blank masks (may be purchased at craft and party stores)
4) Pencils, pens, crayons, & markers
5) Glue, sequins, glitter, feathers, paint, foam shapes, gems, and various other craft materials

## Time Allocated:

The time needed for this group would typically take 45-60 minutes or longer.

## Directions:

Step:

1) Ask group members if they know any reasons why a person might wear a "mask."

2) After brief discussion, read poem/story to group members about masks.

3) Tell group members to consider their life and any "masks" they might wear. Group leaders could explain as follows, "They might not always be the same. Sometimes people portray a certain character and/or wear a particular mask during a specific time, place, or with certain people."

4) Ask group members to decorate a mask with the outside of their mask on how they think others see them and the inside of the mask on how they see themselves. Group leaders might explain, "*Think about your life (now or in the past) and determine how you see yourself and how others see you. Try to show this in the creation of your masks.*"

5) Upon completion of masks, take turns asking people to show their masks and explain their decorations inside and out. After all group members have shown their masks, ask and discuss the following:

   a) Which side was more difficult to decorate and share and for what reasons?

   b) Explain any similarities or differences between the two sides.

   c) What has your mask helped you learn about yourself and how do you think you can work at making both sides match more closely?

## Processing Questions:

1) Consider the changes that you mentioned in trying to match the sides of the mask, and tell me how those changes might help you in the counseling process?
2) Have you ever considered that you were portraying someone other than your true self?
3) How can this activity help you with goals for your future?
4) How might this activity help with your interaction with others in general?

## Special Considerations:

Depending on the population, location, and situation of the group, safety might be a significant factor. The materials used and types of masks used should take safety into consideration.

## Adaptations:

For financial reasons, safety reasons, populations of younger children, or individuals with limited skills-the group can be altered. Instead of reading the poems, the definition of masquerade may be read and discussed. Also, instead of actually decorating a real mask, the group members can decorate two paper masks. One mask can represent how they think others see them and one can represent how they see themselves.

## References:

Corey, M.S., Corey, G., & Corey, C. (2010). *Groups: Process and practice* (8th ed.).Belmont, CA. Brooks/Cole.

## Author Note:

*Jill Fetterolf* earned her Bachelor of Science degree in Administration of Justice at The Pennsylvania State University. She is currently a Master's Student at The Pennsylvania State University in the Counselor Education Program with a focus in Clinical Mental Health Counseling. She has over two years' group work experience in a variety of settings including adult corrections, juvenile justice, and a psychiatric hospital.

## Correspondence:

Questions and comments related to this activity may be directed to:

Jill Fetterolf
Graduate Student-The Pennsylvania State University
Counselor Education-Clinical Mental Health Counseling
1173 William Penn Highway
Mifflintown, PA 17059
jillfetterolf@gmail.com

# Picture My Life

*By Marcey Mettica*

## Population:

Children and adolescents with emotional or relational difficulties. Possible adaptations for other populations can be found in the adaptations section.

## Stage of Group:

Transition or Working

## Type of Group:

Counseling or Therapy

## Rationale:

The purpose of this activity is to help group members verbalize feelings about themselves and other people in their life using meaningful metaphoric objects as a vehicle. The use of symbolic metaphors may remove inhibitions to explore and express more painful, difficult, or suppressed emotions. The verbal expression of emotions has neurological responses that improve mood through the benefit of the labeling experience (Tamir & Mitchell, 2012). Group members' self-disclosures will provide an opportunity to increase emotional understanding and normalize difficult feelings and relationships. This activity will promote insight into faulty thinking and repetitive patterns of interactions with family and friends.

## Goals:

Participants will:
1) Identify important people in the group member's life.
2) Develop increased awareness of self.
3) Explore group member's social connectedness.
4) Express feelings through the symbolic representation of self in relation to others.
5) Assess and explore causes of such feelings that may be manifesting in dysfunctional family dynamics, anger, anxiety, insecurity or depression.
6) Examine increased self-awareness.

## Materials:

1) Large sheet of paper for each group member.
2) Markers.
3) Clip art picture cards (approximately 10-15) in a thematic category (e.g., sports, musical instruments, shoes, animals, etc.) for each group member (see attached example).
4) Glue stick for each group member.
5) Paper and pen for journaling.

## Time Allotment:

One hour for five or fewer group members. Larger group sizes may need two sessions to allow all group members time to fully participate.

## Directions:

Step:

1) Print clip art pictures from thematic category that may be meaningful to the group (e.g., boys' group—sports; children's group—animals; adolescent girls' group—shoes)

2) Make appropriate number of copies of clip art picture cards for every group member.

3) Distribute markers, paper, and glue stick to each member.

4) Begin the activity. Sample script for group leader: *"Write the word, 'ME' anywhere on the paper to represent yourself. Then, write the names of other people in your life anywhere on the same sheet of paper. These can be people you like or dislike; people you see frequently or do not see often; people you get along well with or people you do not. Please write down as many names as you would like anywhere on the paper."*

5) Distribute a clip art picture packet to each group member.

6) Instruct everyone to select an object from the picture packet that reminds them of each person, including him or herself. Sample script for group leader: *"Now, select a picture for each person on your paper that reminds you of that person. After you have selected a picture for everyone, including yourself, please glue the picture next to the person's name. Continue until every person has an object glued next to it."*

7) Once everyone is done, ask for volunteers to share. Sample script for group leader: *"Please tell us about each of the people on your sheet, what object you selected for the person, and why you selected it."* Important items and questions to consider at this point:

a) Whom the group member chose to write down. This will provide useful information about the group member's current world and who the important people are in it.
   i. *Did the group member choose only people they liked or only people they disliked?*
   ii. *Did they choose only family members or only friends?*
   iii. *Did they choose anyone they did not get to see very often?*

b) The placement of the group member and the other names in relation to himself or herself.
   i. *Is the group member in the center with everyone else circled around him or her?*
   ii. *Is the group member off in an area separate and away from the rest of the people?*
   iii. *Are there several people grouped together either near or far away from the group member?*
   iv. *Is the group member close to some but far from others?*

c) Which object they chose to represent each person and why. This could be very insightful in exploring the feelings the group member has about each of the objects chosen and why they picked that particular one for that person. Note: Seemingly obvious meanings should not be assumed to be accurate (e.g. a polar-bear represents coldness, a mouse, meekness or a lion, braveness). The group member assigns the meaning to the object they have chosen to represent each person.
   i. *What characteristics about the object selected remind the group member of the person?*
   ii. *How do these characteristics impact the group member's relationship with this person?*
   iii. *Are any relational patterns clarified or elucidated?*

8) Once everyone is done presenting, ask the group members to journal. Sample script for group leader: *"Please write down what you learned about yourself during this activity."*

## Processing Questions:

1) What did you learn about yourself by doing the activity? This may be done individually and privately by encouraging group members to journal their thoughts after the activity to encourage deeper self-awareness and reflection.
2) What did you notice about other group members?
3) Is there anything you would like to say to another group member?

## Special Considerations:

1) Due to the symbolic nature of the activity, the cognitive development of the group member should be considered to ensure they are capable of abstract thought.
2) Participants will be asked to verbalize their feelings so a capacity for expression is also required.
3) For larger group sizes, the activity may need to be continued to future group sessions to allow all members to share and process.

## Adaptations:

Any symbolic category can be used for the specified population. Possible categories include, but need not be limited to: sports equipment, shoes and boots, animals, musical instruments, insects, etc. This activity can also be used in individual or family therapy sessions, with selection of a symbolic category that is meaningful to the individual or family.

## References:

Tamir, D. I. & Mitchell, J. P. (2012). Disclosing information about the self is intrinsically rewarding. *Proceedings of the National Academy of Sciences, 109*, 8038–8043.

## Author Notes:

*Marcey Mettica* is the owner of a private practice, **First Street Counseling and Consulting, PLLC**, specializing in the treatment of children, adolescents, and families. She is a doctoral student at Texas Women's University in the Family Studies program. She has worked as a group therapist with survivors of childhood sexual abuse, psychiatric inpatient adolescents, children's social skills groups, and parent groups.

## Correspondence:

Questions and comments related to this activity may be directed to:

Marcey Mettica, M.S., LPC, RPT
First Street Counseling & Consulting, PLLC
3067 Falcon Road, Suite 100
Prosper, TX 75078
marceymettica@yahoo.com

# Transition is the Mission

*By Jacqueline J. Young, Adrienne E. Ahr, & Lisa L. Schulz*

## Population:

Children in early and middle childhood. Children diagnosed autism spectrum disorder (ASD) and social (pragmatic) communication disorder (SCD) with the developmental ages ranging between 5 and 8 years old. This can include any child in early and middle childhood, as well as adolescents and adults diagnosed with ASD or SCD.

## Stage of Group:

Working stage

## Type of Group:

Psychoeducational

## Rationale:

When working with children diagnosed with ASD and disorder SCD, the child may struggle with various forms of transition. Whether getting into the car to go to school, getting dropped off at school, moving from one school activity to another, going to the restroom, or struggling with life adjustments, such as moving and divorce, the difficulty in transitioning to a new circumstance can cause emotional distress (American Psychiatric Association, 2013; Cox, 2008). This activity is designed for a small group work setting and may need to be repeated due to challenges with generalization learning in order for the group members to fully understand and accept transitions (Sowden, Perkins, & Clegg, 2011).

## Goals:

Participants will:
1) reduce anxiety provoked by transitions.
2) increase effective coping skills.
3) increase awareness of group member's own reactions to transitions.

## Materials:

1) One 50 to 100 piece puzzle for ages 5 and up. Note: Often children with ASD and SCD are more visually oriented, so the difficulty of the puzzle may need to be increased.
2) One container of bubble solution with wand for each group member.
3) A stop watch or clock to keep track of time.
4) A space large enough to divide the room into two halves, one activity per half. The room needs to be large enough so group members cannot reach or be distracted by the other activity.

# Time Allotment:

25 - 30 minutes for both activities
Time may vary due to size of group and how group members respond to one another. Potential disruptive behaviors may occur within the group, due to lighting, sound, anxiety, or possible over or under stimulation.

# Directions:

Step:

1) Set up two activity stations in opposite corners of the room, making sure the activities are far enough apart so the group members cannot easily reach the other activity.

2) Choose two activities that are developmentally appropriate for the group. Select one activity that is more easily accomplished by the group and one that is more difficult. For this example, the difficult activity will be a group effort to assemble a 100 piece puzzle, and the easier activity will be blowing bubbles.

3) Introduce the activity by saying: *"We will be doing two activities today. We will start by doing a puzzle together and when I tell you, we will switch to a new activity".* Note: It can be difficult at times to stop one activity before it is finished or before members may want to stop and begin the other activity. Acknowledge that this process is meant to be hard but will only last 10 minutes.

4) Ask the group to start one activity, and state to group members it will last for five minutes. The group facilitator will track and reflect throughout the activity.

5) Give a one minute warning before switching to the next activity. State: *"We will be going to the next activity in one minute."*

6) Move the group to the new activity. State: *"We will be here for five minutes."* Continue to track and reflect throughout the process.

7) Announce when there is one minute left in the activity.

8) Ask the group members to return to their seats.

9) Group facilitator will help members process their experiences with the activities paying particular attention to both the successes and challenges they encountered when transitioning.

10) Repeat the same process the following session. Consider switching the order of the activities or introducing different activities, one being more difficult than the other.

## Processing Questions:

1) How hard was this for you?
2) What did you see other people doing?
3) When have you done something like this before?
4) What was similar or different?
5) What could make this easier for you?

NOTE: Given the questions may be difficult for children diagnosed with ASD and SCD, the facilitator is encouraged to state observations and reflections noted while the members were involved in the activity, identifying specific accomplishments and difficulties. For example:

1) *I noticed you all switched from one activity to the other as a group.*
2) *I noticed one person really wanted to stay in the puzzle activity and not move with the others to go to the bubbles.*
3) *I noticed some of you chose not to move.*

## Special Considerations:

1) Use caution when selecting a setting in order to reduce unwanted distraction and interruption.
2) Be mindful of lighting and noises. Research suggests that repetitive movements and sounds tend to draw the attention of those diagnosed with ASD (National Institute of Mental Health, n. d.). Some children may be sensitive to harsh lights and sounds such as a whistle or a bell intended to gain their attention or initiate transition.
3) It is appropriate to increase the frequency of tracking and use repetitive phrases and reflections when working with this population.

## Adaptations:

Each group member may have different transitional needs to work on, in which case you may start with smaller changes such as décor, sitting position, light, or sound quality. In addition, using visual cues may benefit children who struggle with auditory processing or are non-verbal. These cues may be pictures of children performing the activities that you use. This activity supports neuro-typical groups experiencing major changes in their environment (i.e., a new school, new living situation). When working with older children or adolescents, you may introduce additional activities balancing "difficult" and "easy". Consider lengthening the duration of each activity as well as the time for processing. When working with adults, you may choose to increase the duration and number of activities. Also, consider transitions between locations to meet the group's needs. Gaining awareness of each group member's developmental level of functioning when making decisions for this activity will increase its potential effectiveness, members' willingness to interact, and social engagement.

# References:

American Psychiatric Association. (2013). *Diagnostic and statistical manual of mental disorders* (5th ed.). Arlington, VA: American Psychiatric Publishing.

Cox, A. J. (2008). *No mind left behind: Understanding and fostering executive control - The eight essential brain skills every child needs to thrive.* New York, NY: Penguin Group.

National Institute of Mental Health. (n.d.). Retrieved from http://www.nimh.nih.gov/health/topics/autism-spectrum-disorders-pervasive-developmental-disorders/index.shtml

Rossiter, A. (1988). A model for group intervention with preschool children experiencing separation and divorce. *American Journal of Orthopsychiatry, 58*(3), 387-396. *This group activity is an adaptation of this program designed by Rossiter.

Sowden, H., Perkins, M., & Clegg, J. (2011). Contexts and communication strategies in naturalist behavioral intervention: A framework for understanding how practitioners facilitate communication in children with ASD. *Child Language Teaching and Therapy, 27*(1), 21-38.

# Author Notes:

*Jacqueline J. Young* is a new professional working in the Dallas-Fort Worth metroplex and a graduate of the University of North Texas counseling program. Her group work experience includes co-leading a psycho-social group for children diagnosed with ASD, group play therapy, parent filial group for parents with children diagnosed with ASD, and sibling support group for siblings of children diagnosed with ASD.

*Adrienne E. Ahr* is a graduate of the counseling program at the University of North Texas and a new professional in the Dallas-Fort Worth metroplex. She has group work experience co-leading a psycho-social group for children diagnosed with ASD, group play therapy, parent filial group for parents with children diagnosed with ASD, and sibling support group for siblings of children diagnosed with ASD.

*Lisa L. Schulz* is a Clinical Assistant Professor in the department of Counseling and Higher Education, University of North Texas. Dr. Schulz has facilitated multiple groups in K-12 settings with a specific focus on bicultural identity development. She has also facilitated multiple groups focused on domestic violence and empowerment for Latino men and women.

# Correspondence:

Questions and comments related to this activity may be directed to:
Jayde Young, M.S., NCC
University of North Texas
1705 Quail Grove Drive Fort Worth, TX 76177
jayde.young8@gmail.com

# Treasure Chest

*By Jill Fetterolf*

## Population:

Children

## Stage of Group:

Termination

## Type of Group:

Counseling and/or Therapy Groups.

## Rationale:

Everyone has people, places, things, events, feelings, etc. that they treasure. Those treasures are vital factors in a person's life. Not everyone is aware and considers these treasures on a regular basis, nor do they realize what a big part of life they are. This activity brings those valuable strengths to recognition, and helps the group members place these "treasures" into perspective of importance in relation to their individual life's journey. This activity is best suited for the termination stage of the group as members have to evaluate what they have learned in group and attempt to apply it to their behaviors, relationships, and lives after group. Members will no longer have the safe environment of the group setting or the direct support of other group members. Identifying some of these "treasures" outside of group before actually leaving the support of the group is an appropriate and necessary task. (Corey, Corey, & Corey, 2010)

## Goals:

Participants will:
1) reflect on personal beliefs of other group members.
2) identify personal beliefs about values.
3) identify personal strengths.

## Materials:

1) Slips of paper
2) Pencils or pens
3) Treasure chest (purchased or self-constructed)

## Time Allocated:

The time needed for this group would vary on number of group members and their number of "treasures" submitted, but would typically take 45-60 minutes total with opening discussion, reflection and writing time, and processing time.

# *Directions:*

Step:

1) Begin by asking group members to reflect on what they might "treasure" in their lives.

2) Explain to group members that you would like them to write down the different treasures and place them in the treasure box. Further explain that you will randomly read one out loud for group discussion.

3) On separate slips of paper-have group members write what they treasure. Members may identify as many or as few as they like. In order to generate a deeper discussion on important issues, add in other treasures ahead of time. Some examples could be independence, ability to learn, freedom, my loyalty, music, my honesty, and laughter.

4) When finished-the group leader will draw one treasure out of the treasure chest at a time to present. If the person who submitted the treasure chooses to identify him/herself, the group leader will ask for explanation for choosing that particular treasure.

5) Group members that submitted the treasure have the choice to claim it at this point. If the treasure is claimed, the person is asked to discuss the meaning of this particular treasure.

6) The group leader can then ask other group members if they also identify with this particular treasure as follows:

   a. Has anyone else written the same treasure and how specifically does it apply to you as well?

   b. If you did not think about this treasure but would now write it for yourself-please explain.

   c. If you thought about this treasure but did not write it-please explain.

7) If no group member chooses to claim the treasure then the group leader must facilitate the discussion around the unclaimed treasure-asking if other members can identify with the treasure or if the treasure has an alternate meaning to any members.

8) Discussion questions for the group can also help facilitate further exploration of the meaning of treasure for group members. Examples could be as follows:
   a. Which treasures did you think of more quickly and why?

   b. What was the most difficult to think of and why?

   c. What did you learn about what your treasures were?

   d. What are the reasons this information is important for you?

## Processing Questions:

1) What did you learn today about your own treasures and how can it apply to your daily life?
2) How does what you learned today about your treasures apply to your goals in counseling?
3) How does your treasure align with how you are living your life?

## Special Considerations:

Some group member may not feel comfortable speaking in the group setting but would still like to identify the treasure that they submitted. This could be done by allowing the group members to raise his/her hand without having to speak. This will provide more information to the group leader and possibly even empower the group member.

## Adaptations:

Younger children or group members with limited writing abilities could draw a picture of what they treasure in life on quarter sheets of paper. The group leader can generate more discussion by adding in a few pictures such as a heart, smiley face, house or cat.

## References:

Corey, M.S., Corey, G., & Corey, C. (2010). *Groups: Process and practice* (8th ed.).Belmont, CA: Brooks/Cole.

## Author Note:

*Jill Fetterolf* earned her Bachelor of Science degree in Administration of Justice at The Pennsylvania State University. She is currently a Master's Student at The Pennsylvania State University in the Counselor Education Program with a focus in Clinical Mental Health Counseling. She has over two years' group work experience in a variety of settings including adult corrections, juvenile justice, and a psychiatric hospital.

## Correspondence:

Questions and comments related to this activity may be directed to:

Jill Fetterolf
Graduate Student-The Penn State University
Counselor Education-Clinical Mental Health Counseling
1173 William Penn Highway
Mifflintown, PA 17059
jillfetterolf@gmail.com

# Blooming Toward Change

*By Colleen Sweeney-DelZotti*

## Population:

This activity is most appropriate for older adolescents and adults

## Stage of Group:

Termination

## Type of Group:

Counseling

## Rationale:

The termination phase is a vital process which provides members an opportunity to evaluate their own and each other's growth, to identify areas in need of continued work, and to develop plans for continuing without the group (Berg, Fall, & Landreth, 2013).

Based on anecdotal evidence this activity gives members a chance to review and share progress or changes made throughout the course of group. Group members may also use the activity to discuss steps they will take or continue to take after group ends to achieve their goals. This activity is designed to generate supportive and encouraging discussion among the group members.

## Goals:

Participants will:
1) recognize progress or changes each member has made to resolve their issues.
2) offer words of support and encouragement to fellow group members.
3) identify issues each member wanted to resolve and/or minimize during the course of group counseling.

## Materials:

1) 1 glass or plastic vase
2) Brown construction paper
3) Markers
4) Pipe cleaners of various colors
5) Daisy paper cut out
6) Tape

## Time Allotment:

30 minutes

## Directions:

Step:

1) Cut brown construction paper into strips large enough to fit a sentence or two. Make sure to cut enough strips so each member has three.

2) The daisy paper cut outs should be purchased or premade by leader prior to group.

3) To save time the leader can tape the pipe cleaner to each daisy cut out beforehand.

4) Begin the activity by placing the vase in the middle of the group circle. Say, *"Today, we will be doing a group activity. I will give each of you three strips of brown paper. On each strip I would like you to write issues you had at the beginning phase of group."*

5) After giving members a few minutes to write, say, *"I would like each of you to read your issues aloud, crumble up the strips of paper and put in the vase."*

6) After the vase is filled with the crumbled strips of paper, say to the members, *"I will give each of you a daisy paper cut out and a pipe cleaner (flower stem) to tape to the back of your daisy cut out."*

7) Provide markers for the members to write on their daisy petals. Instruct the group members by saying, *"I would like you to use these markers to write on your daisy petals steps you took or are taking to overcome your issues."*

8) Give the group members a few minutes to write on their daisy petals, and then say *"I would like each of you to share what you wrote on your daisy petals, and then place your completed flower in the vase."*

9) At the closing of group, members have the option of taking their flower home

## Processing Questions:

1) What parts of this activity were difficult?
2) What parts of this activity were easy?
3) What kind of feelings and/or thoughts did you have while crumbling up and throwing your weaknesses into the vase?
4) What were some thoughts and/or feelings you had when you were writing on the daisy petals?
5) What have you learned about yourself in this exercise?
6) If you choose to take home your daisy, where might you keep it to remember what you have learned and accomplished in group?

## Special Considerations:

Some members may need physical assistance to complete this activity

## Adaptations:

This activity can also be used with cognitive behavioral group therapy. Group members can write their past irrational thoughts or beliefs on the strips of construction paper and write their new rational thoughts or beliefs on the petals.

## References:

Berg, R. C., Landreth, G. L., & Fall, K. A. (2013). *Group counseling: Concepts and procedures* (5th ed.). New York, NY: Routledge.

## Author Notes:

*Colleen Sweeney-DelZotti* is a Graduate Student in the clinical mental health counseling program at Northern Kentucky University. She has had two years of group work experience, specifically working with clients diagnosed with co-occurring disorders.

## Correspondence:

Questions and comments related to this activity may be directed to:

Colleen Sweeney-DelZotti
Northern Kentucky University
Office of Graduate Programs
302 Lucas Administrative Center
Highland Heights, KY 41099
csweeney380@gmail.com

# Chaos

*By Sharon Thompson*

## Populations:
Adolescents

## Stage of Group:
Orientation or Working Stage, depending upon the level of processing

## Type of Group:
Counseling

## Rationale:

The purpose of this activity is for participants to explore, experientially, the chaos in their own lives and how they are addressing it. As they try to juggle various items thrown at them by another group member, they will later process how this is similar to juggling all of the activities, commitments, etc. in their lives. This activity is a high-energy activity. This has proven to be extremely useful with resistant groups. Participants are able to easily let down walls and begin to communicate. There is a lot of laughter and fun, as well as focus.

In addition, this activity is cost-effective, as the facilitator can utilize materials on hand, or that are easily obtained. Medrick (1974) provides a practical basis for the general adventure based counseling model pioneered by Project Adventure. This "counseling on the run' based model describes a counseling protocol that stresses therapeutic progress through physical activity and metaphor. This model of experiential counseling has also been utilized successfully by Outward Bound, as well as many school based and residential therapeutic programs.

## Goals:

Participants will:
1) utilize thrown physical objects simulate the effect of all that participants may feel is "thrown" at them as they juggle their busy lives.
2) identify the chaos in one's life, and prioritizing accordingly.
3) identify communication patterns in the midst of stressful life events and learning to improve upon them.
4) identify strengths and weaknesses that an individual might demonstrate in the midst of an addiction or other challenge.
5) Identify couple communication patterns.

## Materials:

1) 20-30 "soft items" for throwing (for a group of 8-10). Generally, you need 2-3 items per person.

2) The more novel the items you choose, the better the activity will go due to the element of surprise.
   a. Examples include: small stuffed animals, dog toys, rubber chickens, nerf balls, duct-taped toilet paper (adolescent boys love this!), rubber flying discs, soft balls, plastic food.
3) You need a laundry bag or stuff sack for storage and handling of your items.

## Time Allotment:

20-45 minutes, depending on your group.

## Directions:

1) Gather participants in a large circle

2) Place the bag of "soft items" for throwing next to you, the facilitator

3) Throw a ball to someone across the circle from you, calling that person's name as you throw it to him or her.

4) Instruct that person to then throw it to someone else.

5) After each person has thrown the ball, he or she will sit down or step back to indicate that he or she is no longer a candidate for receiving the ball.

6) Instruct individuals to remember whom they threw the ball to and whom they received the ball from.

7) The last person to receive the ball will throw it back to you.

8) Instruct participants to stand up and rejoin the circle.

9) Instruct participants to point to the person that they threw the ball to.

10) Now, instruct participants to look to see if the correct person is pointing to them.

11) Repeat the same sequence of throwing the ball---exactly the same order.

12) When you have finished, say, "keep going and don't drop anything" and add objects, throwing them to the person you threw your ball to.

13) Continue until you have thrown all of your objects at least twice.

14) Applaud loudly. Well done!!

## Processing Questions:

1) What was this activity like? (Crazy, chaotic, wild, etc.)

2) What did you have to do to be successful in this activity? (Focus, pay attention, listen, look at what was coming next, look at my partner, etc.)
3) How is this activity like your life/your addiction/parenting in today's world/your marriage? (Chaotic, crazy, so much coming at us, hard to focus. drop things sometimes)
4) How is what you did to be successful in this activity like what you need to do to be successful in your life/your addiction/parenting in today's world/your marriage, etc.? (Focus on priorities, primary relationships, being present/paying attention, etc.)

## Adaptations:

If time allows, have participants place sticky notes on objects to visually label stressors/activities/commitments. Then, they could list them in their own priority order on a sheet of paper and use this for goal setting. Addictions groups could list coping skills for juggling life demands minus their addictive behavior. Parenting groups can talk about stressors/commitments of the family and how those line up with their value system. A way to do this is to ask," If I had said "No matter what don't drop the chicken', would you have played the game differently? What is the 'chicken' for your family value system? Maybe it is your faith, education, or time with family. How reflective is it in the actual time spent in the activities of your family schedule? What can you to differently this week to insure you do not drop the chicken?"

## References:

Medrick, R. (1979) *Confronting passive behavior through outdoor experience.* Hamilton, Massachusetts: Project Adventure.

Rohnke, K. & Butler, S. (1995). *Quicksilver: Adventure games, initiative problems, trust activities, and a guide to effective leadership.* Dubuque, Iowa : Kendall/Hunt Pub. Co. GV 362 .R5671 1995

Schoel, J., Prouty, D., & Radcliffe, P. (1988). *Islands of healing.* Hamilton, Massachusetts: Project Adventure.

## Author Section:

*Sharon Thompson* has been a licensed clinician working with adolescent, parenting, psychoeducational and general counseling groups for over 17 years. In addition, she is a Faculty Member at Troy University Pensacola teaching group counseling, facilitation, and multicultural counseling.

## Correspondence:

Questions and comments related to this activity may be directed to:
Sharon Thompson, Ph.D., NCC, LMHC, LPC, Licensed School Psychologist
Lecturer, Troy University, Pensacola, FL
Troy University 21 N. New Warrington Rd, Pensacola, FL 32507
soaringdrt@aol.com

# Communication Blocks

*By Melanie Bullock*

## Population:

Adolescents
This exercise has been successfully used with individuals from adolescence to adults of different genders, cultures, and in different settings.

## Stage of Group:

Orientation, transition, working

## Type of Group :

Psycho-educational, counseling, therapy

## Rationale:

The ability to communicate effectively impacts the quality of our lives. This engaging exercise demonstrates the complexity of communication. Participants' will learn about various variables present in effective communication and increase awareness of their personal communication style.

This exercise was introduced during a couples counseling session that I observed. I have found it to be an effective activity with individuals striving to enhance their professional and personal relationships. Participants have reported insight into their communication styles. One client stated "I thought my partner just wasn't listening to me. Now I realize I was not communicating my thoughts clearly."

This approach fits with Adlerian and Cognitive Behavioral approaches.

## Goals:

Participants will:
1) Demonstrate the complexity of verbal communication.
2) Identify various components that influence effective communication.
3) Gain awareness of personal communication style.

## Materials:

1) Megabloks (80 Pc Large classic Bag for ages 1-5)
2) Sheet or blanket to protect group members' clothes.

## Time Allotment:

Generally 10 minutes for the exercise portion, 10 minutes for exercise processing per pair.

Please leave 15 minutes at end of group for final processing.  With large groups you may run 3 to 4 exercise pairs.

## *Directions:*

**Preparation:**

    1)  Place chairs in a circle with a large open space in center.

    2)  Spread sheet/blanket in center.

    3)  Separate blocks into two identical piles (color, size, and number of blocks).

    4)  Place a pile of blocks on opposite sides of sheet/blanket.

**Exercise:**

    1)  When group begins, tell members that we will be doing an exercise.  Ask for two volunteers.

    2)  Instruct volunteers to sit in center of sheet/blanket, back-to-back.

    3)  Explain that one member will build a structure from the blocks sitting in front of him or her.

    4)  The second member will listen to the instructions given and build the same structure using their blocks. S/he may not turn to look and may not ask any questions.

    5)  Group members that are observing are to remain silent.  They do not make comments or provide assistance to either volunteer.

    6)  When the builder has used all his/her blocks, or tells leader they wish to stop, the group leader begins processing the experience.

    7)  Volunteers may compare structures at this time.

    8)  Exercise Processing:  Group Leaders be aware of how each volunteer participated in the exercise.  Did they organize blocks by color and size?  Do they repeat instructions several times? Be aware of the listener's nonverbal communication. How do they demonstrate frustration?  How quickly do they become frustrated?  How do they respond to the frustration? Did the group members continue building or want to quit?

**Ask volunteers:**

    1)  What was it like to give directions?
    2)  What was it like to receive?
    3)  Ask the observers - what did you notice?

## Processing Questions:

1) What variables influence effective communication? (emotions, personality, tolerance, gender, culture, etc.).
2) What have you learned about your communication style today?
3) What steps will you take to become a more effective communicator?

## Special Considerations:

In situations where the mobility of a member is limited, the group leader may build the structure previous to the start of the activity. The group member with limited mobility will verbally give instructions, while the able-bodied group member builds the structure.

## Adaptations:

This exercise has been successfully used with individuals from adolescence to adults of different genders, cultures, and in different settings.

## References:

Satir, V. (1988). *The new peoplemaking.* Palo Alto, CA: Science and Behavior.

Satir, V., Gomori, M., & Gerber, J. (1991). *The Satir model: Family therapy and beyond.* Palo Alto, CA: Science and Behavior.

## Author Notes:

*Melanie Bullock* is an Assistant Professor of Counselor Education at Lamar University. She has had ten years of group work experience with adjudicated youth, perpetrators and victims of relationship violence, as well as college/university students.

## Correspondence:

Questions and comments related to this activity may be directed to:

Dr. Melanie Bullock
Lamar University
College of Education
Department of Counseling
Beaumont, TX 77710
mbullocl@lamar.edu

# Family Changes
## (In response to grief after loss from deployment)

*By Brandie Oliver, Alyson Bradley, Courtney Clements, Darin Landers, Amy Moran, & James Spears*

## Population:

This grief group is targeted for adolescents who have lost a loved one during deployment. The group will consist of two group leaders who will act as co-leaders and up to 10 adolescents, but may be modified for use with other populations (please see adaptations section).

## Stage of Group:

Working

## Type of Group:

Psychoeducational, Counseling

## Rationale:

The purpose of this activity is to explore how the family roles change after the death of a loved one while s/he is serving abroad in the armed forces. The objective of this group will be to help the group members explore feelings of grief, provide them with coping strategies, understand family changes and realize that they are not alone. The death of a loved one while that loved one is deployed may result in complicated grief or traumatic bereavement (Perschy, 2004). This loss is ambiguous and inherently traumatic because the inability to resolve the situation causes pain, confusion, shock, and distress (Boss, 2006).

Grief group participation can be beneficial to an adolescent who has suffered the loss of a loved one while that loved one is deployed. The supportive, relational aspects of group counseling (Jordan & Neimeyer, 2003) can be helpful to assist in the 'normalizing' of grief, giving information, and empowering grieving group members to take control of their lives (Parkes, 1980). According to Walz and Bleuer (1992) 64% of youth stated that their involvement in a peer support group had made a major, positive difference in their lives.

## Goals:

Participants will:
1) start a dialogue about how their families have changed since the death of the loved one and how their families are adapting and coping with the roles changing.
2) be able to identify what roles in their family units have changed and to identify ways they as individuals can cope with the changes.
3) be able to both identify and express changes that have occurred because of death.

4) be able to talk about feelings and their responses to change.

# Materials:

1) Paper
2) Pens/Pencils
3) Question Basket (i.e., gift bag, hat, box, etc.)
4) Markers
5) Magazines
6) Glue

# Time Allotment:

45-60 minutes

# Directions:

Step:

1) Review group rules and confidentiality.

2) Start by asking if there is anything the group would like to talk about regarding their changed families. Allow group members the opportunity to share "change" through their own respective lenses.

3) Now & Then Activity
   a) Hand out paper/writing tool and invite each member to draw a line down the middle of the page.
   b) Instruct group members to draw/paste (from magazines or other items available) pictures, words, phrases, characteristics of their family before and after death.
   c) Allow time to individually reflect on questions:
      i. *What has changed?*
      ii. *What is the same?*

4) Process activity being mindful to draw connections of both challenges and strengths heard among group members.

5) Introduce the "Question Basket" Activity as way to synthesize information shared and continue the discussion and processing of changing family roles after the death. This activity could also be implemented at another group session if time does not allow.
   a) A basket holding the pare-written cards is passed around the group.
   b) A card is picked and read out loud. Each person may respond to the question.
   c) When everyone has had a chance to respond, the basket is passed to the next person and the process continues.

**Sample Questions for Question Basket**

1) Before the death, my biggest responsibility was.... Today it's _____.
2) Before the death, my most loved possession was _____. Today my most loved possession is _____.
3) Before the death, my biggest fear was _____. Today my biggest fear is _____.
4) What about you has changed lately without your permission?
5) If you could change how you were told of the death, what would you do differently?
6) How do other members of your family express their grief?
7) How do you feel when someone says, "I know just what you're going through?"
8) How has your success in school been influenced by this death?
9) If you could change parts of the funeral, what would you do differently?
10) Describe one of the most special sympathy cards or letters you received?
11) When you feel like expressing your grief, who do you choose to be with and why?
12) What advice have you received that was helpful for you in coping with your grief?
13) Anger is a common response to loss and grief. Give a recent example of such anger in your life.
14) In what ways have your hopes and plans for the future changed as a result of the death?
15) Describe what it is like for you to visit the cemetery.
16) Complete this statement: "When I feel like crying, I _____."
17) What advice would you give a funeral director or minister in terms of helping grieving people, especially young people?
18) What do you wish other young people would do or say to assist in your grieving process?

Optional Homework: Have each group member bring in a photograph of the lost loved one for next session.

## Processing Questions:

1) Explore the loss: How has your role in your family changed? What is the same?
2) How has the role of others in your family changed? How does that affect you?
3) How have your expectations and opportunities been impacted by the loss?
4) How will participating in this group today impact what you do next?

## Special Considerations:

When mourning is complicated, the mourner may attempt to repress, deny, or avoid aspects of the loss (Perschy, 2004). A teen experiencing complicated grief may benefit from individual counseling; seeking a grief group as a second form of treatment (Pershchy, 2004). When considering a grief group, it is essential to evaluate if the adolescent has moved through the trauma sufficiently to profit from the grief group's emphasis on the loss aspect of the complicated mourning (Perschy, 2004). Structured activities may take the pressure off reticent members who are reluctant to share, however it is imperative the group leader is flexible and willing to focus on what members bring with them to each group session (Perschy, 2004). These can include, but are not limited to, writing, drama, guided imagery and art (Walz & Bleuer, 1992).

## Adaptations:

This group activity is also appropriate for group members experiencing grief due to other types of loss.

## References:

Jordan, J., & Neimeyer, R. (2003). Does grief counseling work? *Death Studies, 27*, 765-786.

Parkes, C.M. (1980). Bereavement counseling: does it work? *British Medical Journal*, 5 July, 3-6.

Perschy, M. K. (2004). *Helping teens work through grief* (2nd ed.). Brunner-Routledge: New York.

Walz, G. R., & Bleuer, J. C. (Eds.). (1992). Helping students cope with fears and crises. *ERIC Clearinghouse on Counseling and Personnel Services.* Retrieved from eric.ed.gov/PDFS/ED340987.pdf

Johnson, S. (2012) *Teen Grief Groups: An eight-week curriculum*. Retrieved from http://griefed.files.wordpress.com/2010/01/teen-grief-curriculum.pdf

Ryan's Heart. (2009). *Just for Me*. Presque Isle, ME: Author.

* Special Note: Dr. Brandie Oliver teaches the Group Counseling course within the Butler University School Counseling program. This lesson has been adapted from a course project developed for use in a high school setting.

## Author Notes:

*Brandie Oliver* is an Assistant Professor of Counselor Education at Butler University. She has over six years of running groups specific to professional school counseling.

*Alyson Bradley* is a licensed School Counselor and recent graduate of the Butler University school counseling program.

*Courtney Clements* is a current graduate student in the school counseling program at Butler University.

*Darin Landers* is a licensed School Counselor and a recent graduate of the Butler University school counseling program. He has had one year of experience running groups specific to professional school counseling.

*Amy Moran* is a licensed School Counselor and recent graduate of the Butler University school counseling program.

*James Spears* is a licensed School Counselor and recent graduate of the Butler University school counseling program.

## Correspondence:

Questions and comments related to this activity may be directed to:

Brandie Oliver, Ed.D., NCC
Butler University
4600 Sunset Avenue
Indianapolis, IN 46208
bmoliver@butler.edu

# Gratitude Garland

*By Amy Williams*

## Population:

Adolescent (with or without family member participation) and adult substance abuse groups

## Stage of Group:

Transition or Working Stage

## Type of Group:

Psychoeducational

## Rationale:

Wood, Froh, and Geraghty (2010) report that orienting toward and expressing gratitude is connected with improved mood and affect, greater life satisfaction, and improved emotional functioning. The authors also identify a connection between orientation toward gratitude and improved social relationships and reduced frequency of psychopathology. The composition of gratitude lists, an intervention aligned with Positive Psychology, is an intervention often used both in gratitude research and as a clinical intervention (Wood, Froh, & Geraghty, 2010).

This activity, a variation on the gratitude list, allows participants to express gratitude in a tangible way. By providing participants with the experience of linking individual pieces of gratitude together into a paper chain, this activity allows participants to see that there are things they are grateful for, and that these things are more bountiful than they may appear to be in times of stress. By providing a tangible reminder of gratitude that participants can see and add to on their own, this activity encourages gratitude as a regular practice to support balance and perspective in coping with stressors.

## Goals:

Participants will:
1) verbalize gratitude by identifying specific things for which each participant is grateful.
2) identify benefits of incorporating expressing gratitude into daily life.

## Materials:

1) Construction paper strips
2) Glue sticks
3) Magazines, rubber stamps, markers, etc. (to create words and/or images on paper strips)
4) Stapler and/or tape to attach strips to one another in garland form

## Time Allotment:

60 minutes; less time may be needed for smaller groups (5 or fewer people) and younger adolescent groups (age 13-15); additional time may be needed for large groups (greater than 12 people)

## Directions:

Step:

1) Explain that expressing gratitude is a coping skill that participants can use to help maintain perspective and remain positive in situations that are not ideal.

2) Ask participants what gratitude means to them. Explore participants' thoughts and feelings surrounding the importance of expressing gratitude on a regular basis. When is it easy to express gratitude? When is it more difficult? Why is this so?

3) Explain activity: Creating a Gratitude Garland. Participants will use paper strips to model things they are grateful for. Instead of simply writing words, participants may use stamps, cut letters out of paper to spell the words, or create artistic representations (i.e. pictures) of what they are grateful for on the paper strips. Each paper strip should contain one thing the participant is grateful for.

4) Give participants time to create their paper strips.

5) After participants have created their strips, allow them to share what they put on each strip and why they are grateful for this thing. As participants share their strips, tape or staple the strips into circles to form a paper chain for each participant.

6) After all participants have shared, explore participants' responses to creating their Gratitude Garland. How did it feel to focus on things participants are grateful for? Was it difficult or easy? How can focusing on gratitude help participants to cope with stressors?

7) Explore how participants might use the technique of expressing gratitude in their daily lives to support coping with stressors. Help individuals to connect focusing on gratitude with maintaining a positive outlook in other areas of life.

8) Explain to participants that they can keep their Gratitude Garland, and encourage participants to add to their garlands at home if they so choose.

9) Encourage participants to attend to their feelings of gratitude and to integrate the expression of gratitude into their daily and weekly routines.

## Processing Questions:

1) When is it easy to express gratitude? When is it more difficult? Why is this so?
2) How did it feel to focus on things participants are grateful for? Was it difficult or easy?
3) How can focusing on gratitude help participants to cope with stressors and triggers?
4) How might you identify and express gratitude in the next week?

## Special Considerations:

1) This activity should be used with caution with stressors triggering strong emotions or crisis in a group member, as the group member may become overwhelmed or have difficulty containing emotions related to stressors. This can be managed by checking in with group members briefly prior to initiating activity to determine whether a more pressing clinical issue must be addressed and by providing appropriate clinical assessment and support to a group member in crisis.

## Adaptations:

When using this activity with family groups, families can create one garland to represent the family unit instead of individual garlands for each family member.

## References:

Wood, A. M., Froh, J. J., & Geraghty, A. W. (2010). *Gratitude and well-being: A review and theoretical integration.* Clinical Psychology, 30, 890-905.

## Author Notes:

*Amy Williams* is a Current Student in the PhD in Counselor Education program at The College of William and Mary. She has two years of group work experience designing and facilitating art-based stress-reduction groups and facilitating substance abuse groups for adults, adolescents, and families.

## Correspondence:

Questions and comments related to this activity may be directed to:

Amy E. Williams, M.Ed., NCC
The College of William and Mary
P. O. Box 6396, Williamsburg, VA  23188
aewilliams@email.wm.edu

# Handshake Activity

*By Brandy Schumann & Josh Hawkins*

## Population:

This activity should be used for adolescents seeking help with social skills. Because this activity requires higher level processing skills, specific to insight into one's own comfort level with touch, and likely requires abstract thought it is recommended for preadolescents and older.

## Stage of Group:

Working Phase

## Type of Group:

Psychoeducational, Counseling, Therapy

## Rationale:

Many people struggle to understand appropriate versus inappropriate touch (Berg, Landreth, and Fall, 1998). They may be too aggressive, too weary, use touch to show anger, or avoid touch without knowing it. This activity helps group members collaboratively understand boundaries and decide what kind of touch is appropriate for self and group.

## Goals:

Participants will:
1) Develop an understanding of appropriate touch and how it is conversely defined.
2) Increase group problem solving skills by facilitating a situation where group members are challenged to come to an agreement together.

## Materials:

No materials required.

## Time Allotment:

This activity takes 30 minutes. Group size can add on additional time. Post processing may add additional time depending on group's comfort with sharing and members' perceived feelings of group safety.

## Directions:

Step:

1) The leader asks the group to design their own group handshake.

2) Each participant is encouraged to contribute a piece to the group handshake. For example, if there are six members, each member adds their own type of shake to the sequence of the handshake.

3) After electing the full six pieces the group members can enjoy practicing the handshake sequence.

## Processing Questions:

1) How was this for you?
2) Reflect on who jumped in and took the lead of the activity and who had apprehensions towards the activity.
3) Reflect on any observed discomfort with the final handshake.
4) What reactions did you have while making this handshake?
5) If you could change anything about this handshake what would it be?

## Considerations:

There are a couple considerations to be aware of with this activity. If someone in the group has severe anxiety, specifically social anxiety, this activity may pose discomfort. Also, if someone has been sexually or physically abused the use of touch could serve as a trigger (Rothschild, 2000).

## Adaptations:

This activity can be used as a psycho-educational tool with younger children. Another adaptation to consider is using this activity during the orientation phase of group to work as a way to bring the group together. This activity can also be used for preadolescents and adults.

## References:

Berg, C. R., Landreth, L. G., Fall, A. K. (1998). *Group counseling: Concepts and procedures* (3rd ed.). Philadelphia, PA: Accelerated Development.

Rothschild, B. (2000). *The body remembers: The psychophysiology of trauma and trauma treatment.* New York, NY: W.W. Norton and Company.

## Author Notes:

*Brandy Schumann* has more than a decade worth of experience delivering group therapy services to children, preadolescents, adolescents, adults and parents. Servicing the public from her private practice, Therapy on the Square in McKinney, TX, she provides groups to address self-esteem, divorce, social skills and parenting needs.

*Josh Hawkins* has specialty training and experience in delivering group therapy services to children, preadolescents, adults, parents and grandparents. He currently provides services to build social skills and teach relationship skills to parents at Therapy on the Square in McKinney, TX.

## Correspondence:

Questions and comments related to this activity can be directed to:

Brandy Schumann, Ph.D., LPC-S, RPT-S, NCC
Therapy on the Square
114 E. Louisiana, St. #201
McKinney, TX 75069
DrBrandy@tots.pro

# Lens of Perception

By Jill Packman & Shannon Morrow

## Population:

This activity is ideal for adolescents whose development at this age is focused upon identity and social awareness. Identity is a concept developed in context (Rogers, 1951). As adolescents is a time when children are trying on many hats (or glasses), this activity gives adolescents the opportunity to try new things and receive feedback from their peers (the most influential group for this age) in a safe, therapeutic environment with a counselor.

## Stage of Group Work:

Working Stage

This activity is best for the working stage of a group. Members must be comfortable enough to wear silly glasses in front of each other, and the process could stimulate discussion around perception, self-perception and the perception of other members' perceptions. In this activity, group members are asked to reflect upon how they perceive themselves and how they believe they are being perceived. Without group cohesion, group members may not be willing to be vulnerable enough to effectively process how perceptions affect them.

## Type of Group:

Psychoeducational, Counseling

This activity can be used for different types of group. In a counseling/therapy group, the activity could bring awareness to projections members make that effect how they believe they are being perceived. In a psychoeducational group, learning around how we judge and perceive others could be discussed.

## Rationale:

The purpose of this group activity is to demonstrate how perceptions differ from person to person, and how these differences influence self-perception. O'Mahoney (1984) stated that it is commonly accepted that our perceptions of ourselves influence our perceptions and interactions with others. This activity provides experiential awareness of this intuitive reaction. Through this activity group members can observe the relationship between the way we perceive ourselves and the way we believe others perceive us. As we become more aware of how others perceive us and how we interpret their reactions, we gain a broader perception of ourselves (O'Mahoney, 1984). Our internal perception of ourselves influences how others perceive us, and the way others perceive us influences our self-perception. In adolescence, the developmental task according to Erikson (1950) is the fleshing out of one's identity. As we often compare ourselves to others socially, the knowledge of others' perceptions allows us to determine our real selves (Rogers, 1951). Perceptions of self are created and modified in interactions with others. As we interact and discover how others see us, we are given the opportunity to amend, accept, or reject the perceptions of others. This activity provides the opportunity for adolescents to see and hear how others' perceive them. This knowledge and experience facilitates the development of self-perception or identity.

## Goals:

Participants will:
1) increase awareness about the way group members perceive themselves and others.
2) gain insight into the relationship between how they think about themselves and how others' perceive them.
3) gain awareness into how members read and are read by others. With this awareness, members can choose to accept or reject these perceptions.

## Materials:

1) Silly glasses from toy stores. (Jumbo sunglasses, Charlie Chaplin nose/eyebrow glasses, drooping eyes, bug-eye glasses, alien eyes, etc.) If one or two pairs are difficult to see through, this can provide a powerful covert metaphor. Have enough glasses for each person to have one pair plus a few extra.
2) One handheld mirror.

## Time:

This activity requires approximately 30-45 minutes.

## Directions:

Step:
1) Put the glasses in the middle of the group, saying, *"Okay, here are some fun glasses, and you can each choose a pair, but please wait to put them on."* It can be helpful to observe who had an easy time choosing and who had a more difficult time choosing.

2) Ask members to put on the glasses saying, *"go ahead and put the glasses on."* This can be done one at a time or altogether. If done one at a time, you can ask for volunteers or ask the person who chose his or her glasses first to go first. As members put on the glasses, the group leader should observe the reactions of both the wearer and the observers.

3) Go around (or as members put on the glasses, if having them do it one at a time), asking *"how do the glasses you're wearing affect the way you perceive all of us?"*

4) After reflecting what the member says, ask the person wearing the glasses, *"how do the glasses you're wearing affect the way you think we are perceiving you?"* or *"when you put the glasses on, what do you think we think of you?"*

5) During this time, the group leader should reflect and link members' responses.

6) Repeat steps 2-4 with all members. During this process, ask members to keep the glasses on.

7) Once everyone is wearing glasses and has responded or participated, bring out the handheld mirror. (Keep it hidden until now.) Say, *"now you get to see what you look like!"* The mirror is to be passed from one member to the next. As members look at themselves in the mirror, have them hold the mirror low enough so that the others in the group can perceive individual member's reactions.

8) Reflect and respond during this process. As the group leader, it may be helpful to provide a summary of each member's reaction prior to moving to the next individual. For example, saying *"you seem embarrassed with those glasses on!"* or *"you don't like the way you look in those."*

9) After the mirror has gone around the group, members may remove their glasses observing discomfort created by awareness of how they looked in their glasses (Observe the behavior in taking off glasses. Do some take them off quickly? Are others more comfortable and playful with how they look?)

10) As the group leader, again reflect and respond to reactions as members remove their glasses.

11) Begin to process how others responded and reacted to the member wearing the glasses and how that reaction and response affected the glasses wearer. Say to the group, *"How do others' opinions or perceived opinions affect us?"*

## Processing Questions:
1) What did you observe as you watched (name) in the mirror? What do you think he/she was thinking? How is that different from what you thought?
2) How much are you aware of others' reactions to you?
3) How do those reactions affect you?
4) Do you let others know their reactions affect you? How or how not?
5) When people were looking in the mirror at themselves, whose reaction surprised you?
6) How do others' opinions mirror or not mirror your own opinions of you?
7) How do others' reactions to themselves affect your opinion of yourself? Of them?
8) After completing this activity, what realizations did you have about how you see yourself or others? How will this affect your interactions with others?

## Special Considerations/Cautions:
Group members wearing their own glasses will need to remove them to put on their silly glasses. If a group member can't see without his/her regular glasses, some of the silly glasses may fit over

prescription glasses. Giving these members first choice of glasses may accommodate this limitation. Some silly glasses distort vision, which may make a member uncomfortable. This is when extra glasses would be an asset.

## Adaptations:

This group could be easily adapted to work in schools. Additionally, this activity can be used with young adults or adults who could benefit from being less influenced by perceptions. Families could also benefit from this activity because it demonstrates how parents' or siblings' beliefs about other family member may influence behavior.

## References/Credits:

Erikson, E. (1950). *Childhood and Society*. New York: Norton.

Jacobs, E., Masson, R., Harvill, R., Schimmel, C. (2012). *Group Counseling: Strategies and Skills* (7th ed.). Belmont, CA: Brooks/Cole.

O'Mahoney, J. (1984). Knowing others through the self—Influence of self-perception on perception of others: A review. *Current Psychology, 3*(4), 48-62.

Rogers, C. (1951). *Client Centered Therapy*. Boston: Houghton Mifflin.

## Author Notes:

*Jill Packman* has been in the counseling profession for 20 years. During this time, she has led groups in schools with elementary students, middle school students, and high school students and college students both graduate and undergraduate. She has also led groups in private practice and community settings. These groups have focused on self-esteem, team building, parenting, personal growth, behavioral changes, and academic achievement, to name a few. She teaches the group counseling course for master's students at the University of Nevada, Reno. Packman is trained in adventure based counseling, group play therapy, activity therapy, and filial therapy.

*Shannon Morrow* is a Graduate Student in the Counseling and Educational Psychology Program at the University of Nevada, Reno. His group work experience includes creating and leading a men's group.

## Correspondence:

Questions and comments related to this activity may be directed to:

Shannon Morrow, Graduate Student
Counseling and Educational Psychology Program
University of Nevada, Reno
P.O. Box 341
Reno, NV 89504  shannon.morrow@gmail.com

# Marshmallow/Toothpick Activity

*By Christy W. Land*

## Population:

Elementary or middle school students in a stress or anger management group.

## Stage of Group:

Termination Stage

## Type of Group:

Psychoeducational or Counseling

## Rationale:

This activity may be utilized during the termination phase of an anger or stress management small group. This culminating activity allows the group members to further discuss their anger/stress triggers and identify which coping mechanism they will use to manage the situation. This activity was constructed utilizing a Cognitive Behavioral theoretical framework. CBT focuses on identify and changing behaviors that may cause stress, anxiety, or anger (Anxiety and Stress Management Center, 2013).

## Goals:

Participants will:
1) be able to identify anger/stress triggers.
2) be able to identify coping mechanisms to manage trigger situations.
3) be able to apply specific coping mechanisms to specific trigger situations.

## Materials Needed:

1) Styrofoam Ball
2) Toothpicks
3) Large Marshmallows

## Time Allotment:

Approximately 30-40 minutes- group size and age of participants may impact time needed.

## Directions:

Step:

1) Each group member will be given a small Styrofoam ball and five toothpicks.

2) In a round robin style the group members will share a situation where they have become angry/stressed or a situation that could potentially provoke feelings of anger or stress.

3) Group members should share one situation at time while placing one toothpick in their Styrofoam ball, going around the group, until all group members have shared five situations.

4) After each group member has shared five situations and have five toothpicks sticking out of their Styrofoam ball the group leader will facilitate a discussion about how the toothpicks feel. The group leader may start with saying *"they feel prickly...not good...they hurt...much like feelings of anger or stress feel if not handled appropriately"*.

5) The group leader will then give each group member five large marshmallows.

6) In round robin style the group members will share a healthy coping mechanism that they can use for each of their anger or stress situations/triggers while placing the marshmallow on top of the toothpick.

7) Group members should share one coping mechanisms at a time, going around the group, until all group members have shared five coping mechanisms.

8) After each group member has shared five coping mechanisms and has five marshmallows on top of each of the toothpicks the group leader will facilitate discussion about how the marshmallows feel. The group leader may start with saying *"they feel softer...better...fluffy... much like our feelings of anger or stress can feel OK if we handle them appropriately."*

## Processing Questions:

1) What does anger or stress feel like when it gets out of control?
2) Why is it important to manage our anger or stress?
3) What are some things that we are going to do to help manage our anger or stress?

## Special Considerations/Cautions:

Group leaders should question whether any group member has any allergies they could be triggered by contact with a marshmallow.

## Adaptations:

The activity may be adapted to use with a topic other than anger or stress. Further, this activity may be adapted for use with adults by verbally discussing triggers and appropriate coping mechanisms. A ball of play dough may be used instead of a Styrofoam ball.

## References/Credits:

Anxiety and Stress Management Center (2013). *Cognitive Behavioral Therapy.* Retrieved from: http://www.anxietyandstressmanagement.com/cbt.html.

## Author Notes:

*Christy W. Land* is in her eleventh year as a Professional School Counselor and facilitates several small counseling and psychoeducational groups each year on a variety of topics to address the academic/personal/social, and career needs of my students and parents.

## Correspondence:

Questions or comments related to this activity may be directed to:

Christy W. Land, Ed.S, LPC
Professional School Counselor
Cobb County School District
1811 Mirraview Drive
Marietta, Georgia 30066
Christy.land@cobbk12.org

# Personalized Stress Ball

*By Joseph Graham*

## Population:

Originally designed for adolescent males and females dealing with stress, anxiety, and/or anger issues, this activity may be modified for use with other populations (see adaptation section).

## Stage of Group:

Transition stage

## Type of Group:

Counseling

## Rationale:

Although experiencing stress is commonplace, stress can become overwhelming and interfere with one's life activities. The cathartic effect of squeezing stress balls is widely accepted (Abbott, Shanahan, & Neufeld, 2013). This activity serves the dual purpose of normalizing anger/stress/anxiety and of individualizing each participant's experience of anger/stress/anxiety. Creative arts interventions have been shown to reduce stress (Walsh, Martin, & Schmidt, 2004). The personalized stress ball serves as a reminder that although what provokes anger/stress/anxiety may be beyond our control, we have power over how we react and control our emotions.

## Goals:

Participants will:
1) experience normalization of anger/stress/anxiety.
2) experience cathartic effects.
3) create a personalized stress ball to be utilized in and out of session.

## Materials:

Scissors (for group leader)
For each group member:
1) Sheet of paper
2) Writing implement
3) Container of Play-Dough
4) White or Light-Colored Balloon
5) Decorative materials (e.g., glitter glue, markers), if applicable

# Time Allotment:

45 minutes to 1 hour.

# Directions:

I like to conduct this activity without informing the group members that we are making a stress ball and waiting until its completion to point out what they created. The directions will be for anger management groups, but this activity can be adapted for stress and anxiety as well.

Step:

1) Instruct group members to write down everything that they can think of that makes them angry on the sheet of paper. Say, *"Take a moment to think about what kinds of things or people make you angry and write down as many of them on your paper."*

2) Ask group members to share what they have written (other group members might want to add to their lists) by saying, *"I'd like to invite each of you to please share your lists with the group."*

3) Reflect and process what the group members have shared. Sample questions include, *"Did you hear anything you'd like to add to your list?,"* or *"What is like looking at your list?"*

4) Ask group members to come up with one word that summarizes everything on their lists and write that word as large as possible on their sheet of paper.

5) Process the writing of the single word with the group. A sample question might include, *"How did you determine your word?"*

6) Instruct group members to shred the sheet of paper into the smallest pieces possible and make a pile. Say, *"Now, with your hands, tear up the paper into the smallest pieces you can and make a pile."*

7) Reflect what you observed as group members did this and process by asking questions like, *"What was it like tearing up your sheet?"*

8) Give group members a container of Play-Dough and instruct them to flatten it (I enjoy processing the aroma of Play-Dough as it can bring up childhood memories). Instruct the group members by saying, *"Next, take out the Play-Dough and flatten it like a pancake."*

9) Instruct group members to use the Play-Dough to pick up every shred of paper; this usually requires several folding attempts but it can be done. Say, *"Place the Play-Dough on top of your shredded paper and fold the paper into the Play-Dough. Don't worry, it will pick up all the pieces."*

10) Give group members a balloon and instruct them to put the Play-Dough inside; this usually is done in tandems.  Say, *"Next, select a partner to help you put the Play-Dough into the balloon.  Usually, one person will use their thumbs to open the balloon and the other will insert the Play-Dough."*

11) Instruct group members to shove the Play-Dough as far into the balloon as possible, tie off the end, and cut off the balloon tail that develops.

12) Reflect and process with questions like, *"What is it like holding all of your stressors in your hand?,"* and/or *"When do you see yourself using your stress ball?"*

13)  Instruct group members to decorate their balloon in any fashion they desire. (Optional)

## Processing Questions:

1)  What is it like seeing all the things that make you angry right in front of you?
2)  What are some of the things you all have in common?
3)  How did you determine your one word?
4)  What is like holding all of the things that make you angry in the palm of your hand?
5)  What do you think is the purpose of this activity?
6)  How will you use today's activity for the rest of the week?

## Special Considerations:

Scissors are potentially dangerous and group leaders should exercise caution and good judgment if considering giving group members scissors.  Group members with physical limitations for completing the activity should be accommodated.

## Adaptations:

This activity, although originally designed for adolescent group members, can be adapted to any age population.  Any group that can benefit from listing stressors will benefit from this activity.  Also, this activity is adaptable to individual counseling

## References:

Abbott, K. A., Shanahan, M. J., & Neufeld, R. W. J. (2013). Artistic tasks outperform nonartistic tasks for stress reduction. *Art Therapy: Journal of the American Art Therapy Association, 30*(2), 71-78. doi: 10.1080/07421656.2013.787214

Walsh, S. M., Martin, S. C., & Schmidt, L. A. (2004). Testing the efficacy of a creative-arts intervention with family caregivers of patients with cancer. *Journal of Nursing Scholarship, 36*(3), 214-219. doi: 10.1111/j.1547-5069.2004.04040.x

## Author Notes:

*Joseph Graham* is a Doctoral Student at the University of Central Florida. Currently, Joseph operates a private practice that includes several groups and is earning his PhD in Counselor Education. Also, Joseph teaches a Group Counseling course to master's level counselors-in-training.

## Correspondence:

Questions and comments related to this activity may be directed to:

Joseph M. Graham, Jr., MA, RMHCI
University of Central Florida
PO Box 161250
Orlando, FL 32828-1250
Joseph.Graham@ucf.edu

# Reminders of What We Have Learned From Group

*By Janice DeLucia-Waack, Maureen Brett, & Sara Wahila*

## Population:

Adolescents (but may be modified for use with other populations --see adaptations section).

## Stage of Group:

Termination

## Type of Group:

Psychoeducational

## Rationale:

It is important in termination to help group members assess what they have learned and how they will use it in the future (DeLucia-Waack, 2006). Nitza (2014) stated that "key issues in the termination stage include consolidation of learning.... Activities that help members identify what they have learned and how they learned it are beneifical....as well as activities that help members express what they learned from each other" (p. 100). Concrete objects help group members remember inspirational message from the group and what they have learned.

## Goals:

Participants will:
1) clearly identify what they have learned from the group.
2) identify how they have helped each other.
3) be provided with a concrete reminder of the group experience to take home.

## Materials:

1) a piece of paper for each group member (with a list of group members and three things I learned from this group are...)
2) a set of stones (or beads, rocks, or stickers) for each person in a different color or shape (e.g., if there are 8 group members and a group leader, there would be 9 different stickers or 9 different colored stones each – so 81 pieces)
3) containers (or something to affix stickers or string beads) for each group member to take home
4) email addresses for members (optional)

# Time Allotted:
30 to 40 minutes

# Directions:

Step:

1) The week before the last group session, tell the group to think about the following questions:

   a) What new ways of thinking, behaving, and feeling have you learned?

   b) How did you learn these new skills?

   c) What did we do in group to help you learn this?

   d) What did people say or do to help you?

   e) When you remember this group, what positive instructions do you want to give yourself to keep up your new skills?

2) Say: "*Next week is the last session of group and one of the things that we need to do is to assess what we've learned as a group and how each group member has contributed to our learning. So we are going to do this in several steps.*"

3) Hand out the pieces of paper with each group member's first name written on it and **Three things I have learned from group.** Ask them to take them home and spend some time writing down at least three things they have learned from group. Additionally, ask them to make some notes about things that other group members have done that have helped them learn something new in this group. Ask them to be as specific as possible. Give them examples, such as, "*when Scott said that this was hard for him too, it made me not feel alone.*"

4) If possible, email group members the last during the week or check with them informally to make sure they still have **Three things I have learned from group** handout.

5) At the beginning of the last session as members come in, check to see if they have filled out the list. If not, give them another one and suggest that they quickly jot things down. Reassure them that they have probably been thinking about it on some level all week so some ideas will come to them.

6) At this point, take the beads, stones, rocks, or stickers out and put them in like piles (e.g., a pile of 8 blue stones, 8 blue beads, or 8 blue silly bands). Pick one pile (sometimes the largest stone or bead to signify you as the group leader) and explain why you chose that object and how it represents you. Explain in such a way that the group members will remember that this is your stone (e.g., blue is my favorite color and it reminds me to keep calm). Then state at least one important skill you want them to remember from

this group. Have them write down the color or shape you chose next to your name and also what you want them to remember (be brief and focus on the positive). I usually say *"blue is my favorite color and it reminds me to be calm so when you see this stone I want you to think of group and ways we learned to be calm."*

7) One at a time, ask group members to pick out a set of objects that resembles them in some way. Have them do this in some random order such as by order of birthdate.

8) After each group member has chosen his/her set of objects, ask each of them to briefly explain to the group why their object resembles them and the most important thing they learned from group.

9) As each group member shares, ask the other members to write down next to the group member's name the object (name, color or shape) and the most important thing they learned from group (you can make one list and copy it quickly if the group members are too young to write quickly or neatly).

10) Then say: "*Now, we are going to talk about how other group members helped us learn what we've learned. Oftentimes, we think that others know how much we appreciate their help and support, but they don't know that. This is true in life as well. So let's tell other group members how much they've helped us to learn in this group and practice a new skill that we can use with family and friends as well. You should have one stone for each group member. Look at your list on your paper and then think for a minute about what you want to say thank you to this person for, things like helping me to see that others have problems, caring about me, making me smile. Be as specific as you can. Be direct and use I statements if you can. If you can't be specific, just say 'Thank you for being in group' or 'Thanks for being a good group member' or 'Thanks for caring.' That's ok to say. Let us now get into a circle that intermingles so that as you walk, you are facing another person. When you come face-to-face with another group member, hand him or her a stone and say: Thank you for _____.*"

11) Finally, when all group members have passed out all of your stones, sit down.

12) If you are putting the stones in a container, you may have group members decorate the container (e.g. basket, jar, box, bag) to remind them of group. Have them put their list of names and skills to remember at the bottom with the beads on top.

## *Processing Questions:*
1) What was it like for you do to identify what you've learned in group?
2) What are you going to do differently as a result of this group?
3) Where are you going to keep this kit to remind you of what you've learned and what you are going to do differently?
4) How hard was it for you to identify people who helped you in group?
5) What was it like to share how another member helped you with that member?
6) What was it like to receive feedback from the other members?
7) Were you surprised by any of the feedback?

## Special Considerations:

1) Focus the group members specifically on how they were helped by other members so that there are no negative comments at this time. A member may indicate that a particular person has not been helpful to him or her; I usually respond that everyone has been helpful by being present and a part of the group and thus, has influenced the group, so it is ok to thank him or her for just being here and/or being a part of the group.
2) If members are not mobile or moving around may be disruptive to the group, the group leader may distribute the objects while the group members talk to each group member.

## Adaptations:

This activity may be used with younger adolescents and children. Stickers and foam board work well with elementary-aged children.

## References:

Adapted from:

DeLucia-Waack (2006). Closing: Thanking others. In J. L. DeLucia-Waack, K. H. Bridbord, J. S. Kleiner, & Nitza, A. (Eds.), *Group work experts share their favorite activities: A guide to choosing, planning, conducting, and processing* (Rev. Ed.)(pp.155-159). Alexandria, VA: Association for Specialists in Group Work.

*Leading Groups with Adolescents (DVD).* (Dr. Janice DeLucia-Waack and Dr. Allen Segrist).

DeLucia-Waack. J. (2006). *Leading psychoeducational groups.* Thousand Oaks, CA: Sage.

Nitza, A. (2014). Selecting and using activities in groups. In J. DeLucia-Waack, C. Kalodner, and M. Riva (Eds.) (2nd Ed.), *Handbook of group counseling and psychotherapy* (pp. 95-106). Thousand Oaks, CA: Sage.

## Author Notes:

*Janice DeLucia-Waack* is an Associate Professor and School Counseling Program Director at the University at Buffalo, SUNY. She is a Fellow in ACA, ASGW, and APA Division 49. Janice has also served as editor of the *Journal for Specialists in Group Work* and President of the **Association for Specialists in Group Work.**

*Maureen Brett* is a Middle School Counselor in Lancaster, NY. She is NYS certified as a School Counselor and her master's degree is from University at Buffalo, SUNY.

*Sara Wahila* is a High School Counselor in Susquehanna, NY. She is NYS certified as a School Counselor and her master's degree is from University at Buffalo, SUNY.

## Correspondence:

Questions and comments related to this activity may be directed to:

Dr. Janice DeLucia-Waack, Ph.D.
Associate Professor and School Counseling Program Director
University at Buffalo, SUNY
409 Baldy Hall
Buffalo, NY 14260
jdelucia@buffalo.edu

# Tearing Down Obstacles

*By Brandie Oliver, Susan Kleinman, Pamela Nixon,
Matthew Stach & Lara Pastore*

## Population:

High School Students; See Adaptations section below for additional populations for which this activity might be useful.

## Stage of Group:

Working Stage

## Type of Group:

Psychoeducational

## Rationale:

The professional school counselor can be a powerful factor in a comprehensive strategy to maximize high school graduation rates. A great deal of research reviews best practices and counseling methods and theories for students who are at risk of dropping out. Counselors can provide the support and advocacy that can create change in school climates and directly impact students at risk of dropping out. One protective factor in schools contributing to decreased likelihood of school dropout is degree of social support, including peer support. Research shows that providing social support for students during early adolescence is a valuable intervention (White, 2010). Counselors can also implement peer "buddy" systems and programs that involve teachers as advisors. Studies have shown that both of these strategies can increase the degree of social support for students in schools (White, 2010).

This activity is designed to help at-risk students develop problem-solving skills to deal with their obstacles using logic and adaptation. By preparing them for setbacks, the activity helps students gain a realistic view of the challenges they face in the journey to high school graduation. Once they have a set of skills and a plan in place to overcome the obstacles, they will have an increased chance of overcoming the obstacles.

## Goals:

Participants will:
1) think proactively about the obstacles that may appear in their way and come up with plans to deal with setbacks.
2) name obstacles to that may interfere with graduation.
3) brainstorm ways to overcome these obstacles.
4) create a plan for success to overcome obstacles.

## Materials:

1) Two column sheet of paper
2) Blue ink pen
3) Pencil
4) Large boat drawn on large paper and stuck to wall
5) 25 small construction paper submarines
6) 5 medium size construction paper submarines
7) Giant gray toolbox drawn on giant art paper

## Time Allotment:

90 minutes (Consider incorporating this activity into a group offered after-school)

## Directions:

Step:

1) Icebreaker: Begin the activity by asking students to list the only two items they would take with them if they knew they were going to be stranded on a deserted island for exactly one year. They may also share why they chose the items. Use this icebreaker to transition to the activity by pointing out that in life, we can be faced with obstacles and we must have tools to overcome our obstacles.

2) Review group rules and confidentiality.

3) Pre-assessment: brainstorm obstacles and tools to overcome them. Students will be provided a two-column sheet of paper. One column is titled, "Obstacles" and the other "Tools to Overcome". Allow students to individually brainstorm and record obstacles in their lives that have impeded their abilities to feel successful in high school. Introduce the activity as follows: *"Today we will explore some of the obstacles that can create challenges in students' success in school. Please take a few moments to think about the challenges and road bumps that you have experienced. Please list these challenges in the left side column on the paper. In addition to obstacles, please include any solutions or 'tools' you may have used to assist you to overcome the obstacles. Don't worry if you do not have many ideas at this time. The goal of our group today is to add to this side of the column."*

4) Explain to the group that the boat on the wall represents a student traveling through high school. High school is like an ocean, and it is the only way to get from one continent (middle school) to another (graduation and postsecondary plans).

5) Based on the pre-assessment brainstorming, ask the students to individually write the three obstacles that they think are most troublesome on their three small submarines, one on each submarine.

6) Invite group members to share why they decided those three were most important and invite them to stick their submarines on the board to show that obstacles are trying to sink the student's success while traveling toward graduation and

postsecondary plans.

7) Allow the group to discuss the obstacles and why they are particularly worrisome.

8) When students are done sharing, open the group in a discussion of which 5 of the obstacles they felt were most unanimously challenging. As the group leader, begin to reflect the connections and common themes heard as group members shared their obstacles. At this point, invite the group members to brainstorm the top five most common obstacles they have discussed thus far. The group leader will write the top five obstacles on the five medium-sized submarines and post on the board.

9) Then, invite students to take turns sharing their thoughts on how each of the obstacles could be overcome. Write the suggestions in the toolbox that is also pasted near the boat. Be sure to encourage students to think outside the box and decide whether a strategy is a possibility before discarding an idea.

10) Discuss how the problem-solving tools can be put into play with the obstacles.

11) Situational reframing: Explain this concept to students as follows: *"It is important that we take some time to change the way we look at these obstacles that we have discussed today. When we are faced with challenges, we need to expand the way we view these challenges...what I call, expanding our lens. When we expand our lens, we allow ourselves to see multiple perspectives and possible solutions to these obstacles."*

    The group will practice reframing obstacles. For example, if an obstacle is that studying and homework are too time consuming, students will discuss that particular obstacle and turn the benefits of completing studying and homework into a different perspective.

12) Open up the remainder of the 90-minute time block and ask students to discuss anything that has been covered so far and how they feel about the group experience, about dropout obstacles, etc. By this time, since the group is more familiar with one another, a discussion will be more fluid.

13) Post-assessment: Instruct students to take out the two-column list they started earlier. The students will now add tools to the obstacles they listed previously. Add additional tools to their two-column list.

14) Closing: Suggest that students spend some time this week thinking about what their postsecondary goals are now that they have the tools to get there.

## Processing Questions:

1) What did you hear about commonalities of obstacles that were shared?
2) How do you think you can best be supported to overcome these obstacles?
3) What can you do to help yourself add tools to overcome these obstacles?
4) When thinking and visualizing your success, what do you see? How are you feeling at that successful moment?

## Special Considerations:

1) Students may not want to admit that they are at risk for potential obstacles or share obstacles within a group setting. For example, a student who is engaging in unprotected sex may be choosing to ignore the health consequences, but may not have heard about the academic consequences that could follow while balancing pregnancy and/or parenthood with school.
2) By this point in the group process, some group members may have grown tired of the intense focus on graduation. They may have lost interest since graduation is such a long-term concept.

## Adaptations:

1) Perhaps it would be helpful for the students to stop and think about possible situations that have led to obstacles or challenges. Students will be encouraged to share their ideas. Each time a student says, "That won't happen to me," ask the group whether they know anyone for whom the obstacle led to dropping out of high school.
2) Other populations that would be appropriate for this activity include:
   a) students/group members with English as a second language
   b) pregnant teens,
   c) students/group members struggling with addictions.
3) This activity can also be adapted for use in peer-led mentoring groups.

## References:

White, S. (2010). The school counselor's role in school dropout prevention. *Journal of Counseling and Development, 88,* 227-235.

# Author Notes:

*Brandie Oliver* is an Assistant Professor of Counselor Education at Butler University. She has over six years of running groups specific to professional school counseling.

*Susan Kleinman* is a licensed School Counselor and recent graduate of the Butler University school counseling program actively pursuing her mental health license.

*Pamela Nixon* is a licensed School Counselor and a recent graduate of the Butler University school counseling program.

*Matthew Stach* is a current Graduate Student in the School Counseling Program at Butler University.

*Lara Pastore* is a current Graduate Student in the School Counseling Program at Butler University.

# Correspondence:

Questions and comments related to this activity may be directed to:

Brandie Oliver, Ed.D., NCC
Butler University
4600 Sunset Avenue
Indianapolis, IN 46208
bmoliver@butler.edu

# The Line in the Sand

By Joseph M. Graham Jr. & Olivia Uwamahoro

## Populations:

Adolescent substance abusers but could be used with any age group with substance abuse issues.

## Stage of Group:

Transition Phase/Working Phase

## Type of Group:

Counseling Group

## Rationale:

The rationale for The Line in the Sand activity comes from the necessity for providing group work for substance abuse group members that extends beyond psychoeducation. The activity includes several therapeutic factors: (a) universality, (b) cohesiveness, (c) existential factors, (d) interpersonal learning, (e) instillation of hope, and (f) self-understanding. The activity highlights that over the span of our lives we consistently adjust "the line in the sand," or the limit to what we will participate in. For example, a group member who abused cocaine and marijuana might have heroin as her line in the sand. The activity points out to group members that the line in the sand has been adjusted over time and it can be adjusted again perhaps in the direction toward recovery.

Rationalization is a major component of persistent addiction (Chai & Cho, 2011; Kleinjan, van den Eijnden, & Engels, 2009; Ward & Rothaus, 1991) that serves to maintain stagnancy toward behavior change (Prochaska, DiClemente, & Norcross, 1992). Under the Stages of Change model (Prochaska & Norcross, 2001), this activity assists group members between precontemplation and contemplation and between contemplation and preparation. The activity emotionally elicits past and present rationalizations designed to perpetuate addictive behaviors.

## Goals:

Participants will:

1) experience illumination of the process of accelerating one's substance abuse behavior
2) experience instillation of hope that change is possible
3) experience normalization of the process of becoming a group member who abuses substances.

## Materials:

1) 10 strings of different colored yarn each measuring 3 feet in length.
2) 10 sheets of construction paper
3) Markers

## Time Allotment:

1-2 hours, depending upon depth of processing. Depending on the size of the group, this activity can be completed in one session or it may carry over into a second session.

## Directions:

Note: This activity is conducted one person at a time and the other group members are encouraged to remain silent until each participant completes the activity.

Step:

1) As a group, participants create 10 categories of substances (e.g., hallucinogens) or specific substances (e.g., LSD, mushrooms) until there are 10 in total. On sheets of white construction paper the group leader writes one category or substance per sheet with a marker.

2) The group facilitator places the 10 strings on the floor with at least one foot between each string.

3) The first volunteer is then asked to rank the ten substances in order from least harmful to most harmful by placing the sheet of paper between the strings. Here is an example:

| Nicotine | Alcohol | Marijuana | Prescriptions | Ecstasy | LSD | Mushrooms | Cocaine | Heroin | Crystal Meth |
|---|---|---|---|---|---|---|---|---|---|
|  |  |  |  |  |  |  |  |  |  |

4) The participant is asked to stand directly behind his or her current line in the sand, or the substance that he or she currently will not ingest. For instance, a participant might stand in "mushrooms" because she will not touch cocaine, heroin, or crystal meth.

118

5) Process the current line in the sand and how the participant plans to maintain it. Some possible questions could be:
   a) How have you been able to maintain your current line in the sand?
   b) What would it take to change directions and move the line backwards?

6) Next, the participant is asked to remember where he or she was five years ago (or an appropriate amount of time, the point is for the participant to move to a new square).

7) Process how the participant made the decisions to move the line in the sand over time.
   a) What is it like recalling your past lines in the sand?
   b) How did you decide to move your line?
   c) Tell me about a time when you decided to not move the line.

8) Repeat the process for all (willing) participants.

9) Process as a group.

## Processing Questions:

1) What was that experience like for you?
2) What did you learn from this experience?
3) What feelings emerged during this activity?
4) What was it like watching the other group members?
5) Whose experience was the most similar/different to yours?
6) What is your take away from this activity?

## Special Considerations/Cautions:

Considering the potential depth of disclosure of group members, group leaders must be cognizant of confidentiality, both in relation to the parents of the group members and between the group members. This activity is best conducted with cohesive and respectful groups, and is therefore not appropriate for every group. Since this activity requires group members to be quiet for an extended period of time while observing the active group member, group leaders are advised to find a method to maintain attention. One example would be a memory contest of the different orders that group members placed their drugs. This activity is designed to be emotionally charged. Therefore, proper supervision and practice is highly suggested before performing.

## Adaptations:

Adaptable to individual counseling. If space permits, this activity can be conducted in full. However, if there is not enough floor room, the activity can be adapted to a drawing activity whereby a sheet of paper is divided into ten sections with the different drugs filled in by the group member. Any game piece or object that represents the group member can be used and moved about in a manner similar to a board game. Considering the depth of self-disclosure and self-awareness necessary to properly conduct this activity, group leaders are advised to assess for appropriate developmental levels of participants.

# References/Credits:

Chai, S., & Cho, Y. (2011). Cognitions associated with recovery from alcohol dependence. *Japanese Psychological Research, 53*(3), 327-332. doi: 10.1111/j.1468-5884.2011.00473.x.

Kleinjan, M., van den Eijnden, R. J. J. M., & Engels, R. C. M. E. (2009). Adolescents' rationalizations to continue smoking: The role of disengagement beliefs and nicotine dependence in smoking cessation. *Addictive Behaviors, 34*(5), 440-445. doi: 10.1016/j.addbeh.2008.12.010.

Prochaska, J. O., DiClemente, C. C., & Norcross, J. C. (1992). In search of how people change: Applications to addictive behaviors. *American Psychologist, 47*, 1102-1114.

Prochaska, J. O., & Norcross, J. C. (2001). Stages of change. *Psychotherapy, 38*, 443-448. doi: 10.1002/jclp.20758.

Ward, L. C., & Rothaus, P. (1991). The measurement of denial and rationalization in male alcoholics. *Journal of Clinical Psychology, 47*(3), 465-468.

# Author Section:

*Joseph Graham* is a Doctoral Student at the University of Central Florida in counselor education. Currently, he operates a private practice that includes several groups and teaches a Group Counseling course to master's level counselors-in-training.

*Olivia Uwamahoro* is a Doctoral Student at the University of Central Florida in counselor education. She has experience facilitating many types of groups with adolescents during her training and as a mental health counselor. In addition, Olivia has facilitated groups with master's level counselors-in-training.

# Correspondence:

Questions and comments related to this activity may be directed to:

Joseph M. Graham, Jr., MA, RMHCI
University of Central Florida
PO Box 161250
Orlando, FL 32828-1250
Joseph.Graham@ucf.edu

# The Shape Sorter, Meaning Maker

*By Aubrey Uresti*

## Population:

This activity was initially designed for a grief group for adolescent boys. The activity explores universal themes that are relevant for children, adolescents, or adults (refer to "Adaptations" for activity modifications and suggestions for various populations).

## Stage of Group:

Transition, Working
Although this activity could work at any stage of group, it is especially useful in the shift from the Transition to the Working stage.

## Type of Group:

psychoeducational, counseling, therapy

## Rationale:

Drawing inspiration from the concept behind the shape sorting toys popular for children—where wooden pieces fit into matching holes as children learn their shapes—this activity encourages group members to sort through and identify key people, issues, and/or themes (represented by the various shapes) in their lives and assign meaning to these. The activity facilitates a deeper level of self-disclosure for group members and the opportunity for peer feedback and connection between members. While the categories for disclosure are the same for all group members, individuals have the ability to make intentional decisions about the information they actually reveal and to what degree they share (i.e., the level of vulnerability). The categories designed in this activity tend to be common topics in many types of groups. The themes, in that they are introduced, discussed, and processed by all members, also contribute to the possibility for normalizing member experience through universality and building cohesion through risk-taking (Corey, 2012; Corey, Schneider Corey, Callanan, & Russell, 2004; Hazler, 2007; Meier & Davis, 2011; Yalom & Lescz, 2005).

## Goals:

Participants will:
1) engage in individual reflection and meaningful self-disclosure.
2) clarify values and goals.
3) increase group cohesion.

# Materials:

One of each of the following items for every member of group:
1) Paper or cardstock
2) Scissors (optional)
3) Colored pens, pencils, or markers
4) Baggies, envelopes, or paper clips
5) Shape Sorter Template (author created, see below)

# Time Allotment:

Time will depend primarily on the size and stage of group. For smaller groups, less than six people, 90 minutes could be sufficient to complete the entire activity. With a larger group, the activity might require two sessions. However, the activity could easily be tailored by the facilitator to fit within a particular timeframe by adjusting the number of cutouts used for the activity. Finally, the stage of group may be a consideration when planning for adequate time.

# Directions:

Step:
1) This activity can be prepared in advance by the facilitator, or during group by the members. If the facilitator prepares beforehand, the shape sorter template should be copied (1 per group member) and the shapes cut out. A baggie, envelope, or paper clip can be used to organize the pieces into sets. If set-up occurs during group, scissors should be available for members to use and each member should be provided with a template handout. Members are instructed to cut out each shape from the template, making their own set of shapes. In either event, each group member ultimately has an identical pile of shapes.

2) A key with the shapes and their corresponding definitions (see below) can be set up with the materials so that group members can remember what each shape represents without needing to ask the facilitator to repeat this information during the activity, in order to allow for space, reflection, and quiet processing.

3) Pens, pencils, and/or markers are made available and can be shared among group members.

4) Group members can be given an open prompt that allows for individual interpretation and meaning making. For example, a prompt like, *"Today, I would like to invite you to participate in an activity designed to promote individual and collective reflection. Everyone has a series of shapes before them. Use the cutouts to share the things that matter to you"* would allow a group member to write and/or draw a response.

5) Group leaders should use verbs like *share, show, represent, create,* or *make* in order to allow for member creativity and expression. For example, a leader may say, *"Represent on the shapes what you value most."*

6) Once members have sorted through their shapes and decided upon a meaning for each one, they are invited to share.

7) The group leader can use the key below to guide initial discussion, followed by processing questions about the activity.
   8) Key: Shape Definitions and Facilitator Questions
      a) The stick figure can be used to identify a significant person (or people) in the group member's life. *"Who matters to you?"*
      b) The exclamation is used to indicate a noteworthy event in one's life. *"When was an important moment for you?"*
      c) The heart is for love. *"What do you love?"*
      d) The question mark corresponds to an area of uncertainty. *"What are you unsure about?"*
      e) The teardrop is a symbol of sadness. *"What makes you sad?"*
      f) The banner announces your most important characteristic. *"What makes you uniquely you?"*

## Processing Questions:

1) What did you learn about yourself?
2) What did you learn about someone else?
3) What, if anything, surprised you in this activity?
4) We've made meaning for ourselves...what meaning can we make as a group?
5) How will the insight you've gained today influence your life outside of group?

## Special Considerations:

1) Group members with physical disabilities should be provided with appropriate materials and accommodations for a successful activity experience (e.g., verbal explication instead of illustration, or finger paint instead of colored pencils/markers in the case of limited manual dexterity).
2) In groups where impulse control or anger management behaviors are a primary focus, omit participant use of scissors.
3) In groups where suicidal ideation or self-injurious behavior is an issue, consider using pre-cut shapes.

## Adaptations:

This is an original activity, the adaptations for which are numerous. Cutouts could be omitted or added to meet the needs of a particular group or stage of group. For example, a "ribbon" shaped cutout could be added for a group focused on fostering self-esteem. Group members could be prompted to award themselves (or another group member) a "ribbon" to recognize growth-oriented behavior. A "thought bubble" or "call-out" could be added for groups focused on anger management. Members might be instructed to consider healthy ways of expressing thoughts and feelings. An "I'm #1" foam finger shape could be used in a parenting skills group at termination. Members might be encouraged to think of a time when they implemented a new technique with their child(ren). Additional shapes could include a "star" for shining moments, a "waste basket" (a trapezoid shape) for things to let go of, a "flame" for motivation, a "safe" or "vault" (a rectangle shape) for things that are sacred, and more.

## References:

Corey, G. (2012). *Theory and practice of group counseling* (8th ed.). Belmont, CA: Brooks/Cole.

Corey, G., Schneider Corey, M., Callanan, P., & Russell, J. M. (2004). *Group techniques* (3rd ed.) Belmont, CA: Brooks/Cole.

Hazler, R. J. (2007). Person-centered theory. In D. Capuzzi & D. R. Gross, *Counseling and psychotherapy: Theories and interventions* (4th ed.)(pp. 189-215). Upper Saddle River, NJ: Pearson Prentice Hall.

Meier, S. T., & Davis, S. R. (2011). *The elements of counseling* (7th ed.). Belmont, CA: Brooks/Cole.

Yalom, I. D., & Lescz, M. (2005). The *theory and practice of group psychotherapy* (5th ed.). New York: Basic Books.

## Author Notes:

*Aubrey Uresti* is a Doctoral Student at the University of California, Davis. She has had six years of group work experience, including designing and facilitating groups on grief and loss; healthy relationships; gender, race, and sexual identity development; and parenting skills.

## Correspondence:

Questions and comments related to this activity may be directed to:

Aubrey Uresti, M.A., PPS, LPCC
University of California, Davis
School of Education
One Shields Ave
Davis, CA 95616
auresti@ucdavis.edu

# THE SHAPE SORTER TEMPLATE

# TOTAL Your Anger

*By Richard Balkin*

## Populations:

Adolescents (12 -18) patients in an acute care psychiatric hospital

## Stage of Group Work:

Transition or Working Stage

## Type of Group:

Psychoeducational, Counseling, or Therapy

## Rationale:

This group activity was developed while working with adolescents placed in an anger management focus group as patients in an acute care psychiatric hospital. Many of the adolescents had histories of severe anger outbursts, poor anger control, aggression and violence, and family dysfunction. The purpose of the intervention is to provide a simple acronym emphasizing the steps to effective anger management and healthy communication.

## Goals:

Participants will:
1) use the TOTAL acronym to effectively manage anger;
2) utilize a self-initiated time-out process;
3) process issues that are difficult to resolve.

## Materials:

1) white board
2) markers

## Time Allotment:

75 to 90 minutes

## Directions:

Step:
1) The intervention begins with a focus on problems leading to anger outbursts. As a group leader, particularly with adolescents in crisis, beginning with an emphasis/re-emphasis of group norms/rules is appropriate. Such an introduction may be necessary for new group members joining the group in hospital settings, as turnover is often rapid. I recommend having a more seasoned group member review the group

rules, which I introduce as follows: *"we have some new group members todays, who would like to share the rules?"* Usually a group member volunteers and recites the following rules established at each group meeting:

- What comes in here stays in here.
- Be honest.
- Be willing to give feedback.
- Be willing to accept feedback.
- No talking about discharge planning.

The final rule is very important, as group members are encouraged to focus on issues as opposed to externalizing on issues more suited for individual sessions or frustration with being in-patient.

2) After review of the norms/ground rules, the leader may open the group up with a statement such as, *"Who wants to get us started today?"* If group members are resistant, a targeted query such as, *"Let's talk about specific issues related to anger."* In many cases, such as query encourages adolescent group members to vent or express their experience with anger issues. The group leader should focus on experiences in which the group member is magnifying the problem or over-reacting to a situation (Ellis, 1995). For example, *"I get so mad when my parents won't let me hang with my friends!"* Group leaders may wish to hone in on such comments through scaling questions. A typical exchange might go like this:

> Leader: *I can tell this conflict with your parents really gets you upset. On a scale of 1 to 10, with 1 being no problem at all and 10 being totally unmanageable, what would you rate this issue?*
> Group member: *Oh—definitely a 10!*

Other group members may also share their issues and provide extremely high ratings. Such over- magnification of issues is common among adolescents with anger management issues. At this point the leader may wish to engage the group in an example of an unmanageable situation. An example of one I use follows:

> *I had a 16-year old group member admitted through ER after a suicide attempt. During our initial session I asked      what was going on that she wanted to die. She said, "When my parents got divorced I went to go live with my Dad. I had no idea he was into drugs. We started getting high together and then he offered me crystal meth. I did not want it, so he started putting it into my food, and then he would rape me. This went on for over a year. So now I am addicted to drugs, raped by my Dad, and I want to die." I then tell the group, that's my idea of a 10.*

At this point group members generally disclose that their issues are probably not a 10. They identify the potential for their issues to be more manageable and are likely less on the 1 to 10 scale. Adolescent group members will likely volunteer with comments such as, "Oh...mine is a 4." Such disclosures provide a nice introduction into the TOTAL Your Anger strategy. For this next section, a board to write the steps is helpful.

3) T – O refers to Time-Out. Most adolescents and adults have only cursory understanding of the time-out process. Children and adolescents may have experienced the time-out process as a punitive measure, in which the child or adolescent is directed to take a time-out after some display of oppositional or disruptive behavior. The child or adolescent may be directed to go to a specified location to regroup. However, the fact that another person in reaction to a behavior directed the time-out may escalate the situation. For the purposes of this intervention, the time-out is neither punitive nor directed by another person. Rather, a time-out should be self-initiated and exercised in order to keep the situation safe, as opposed to escalating into a major disruption or explosive outburst (Weisinger, 1985). The group leader should re-emphasize that the purpose of the time-out is to keep the situation safe. Group members should voluntarily remove themselves from the situation and go to a safe place to de-escalate. Some processing of what a safe place entails should take place. A safe place for a time-out is not going out for a drive, going to a friend's house, using illicit drugs to de-escalate, and so forth.

4) T refers to Talk. After a time-out and group members identify a stronger sense of calmness, some processing of the situation that led to the anger should occur. This does not have to occur immediately following a time-out but should occur within a reasonable time frame. In other words, the episode should not be ignored and in the case of conflict between adolescents and parents, some processing may need to occur before a discussion of privileges or permissions are restored. Talking provides the opportunity for interpersonal and/or intrapersonal understanding, make amends or apologize, and/or resolve differences.

5) A – L refers to Accept Life. Many anger management strategies focus on the first two steps and fail to address that not all conflicts can be resolved to each party's satisfaction (Burt, Patel, Butler, & Gonzalez, 2013). At this point, group members may need to process *accepting life*, which is, recognizing that a resolution to an issue is not likely. Accepting life does not mean relinquishing all power or agreeing with an outcome. However, accepting life might include complying with requests that were not preferred. An example to process with adolescent group members follows:

*A typical argument between parents and adolescents often revolve around curfew. For example, let's say that you would like to hang out with your friends. You are going to go to someone's house, and you anticipate being there until 2 am. When you ask your parent(s), you are told "no" and that you are expected home by 10 pm. You disagree. You express frustration that other parents allow their kids to stay out. Your parent(s) remain un-phased. You get angry, perhaps even cuss at your parents. You feel your body tense, and at this point you recognize that you could easily lose control, so you take a time-out. You go to your room and slam the door. Your parent(s), however, allow you to remove yourself from the situation. After calming down, you revisit the situation with your parent(s). You try to negotiate for a midnight curfew. You even ask for 11 pm. Your parent(s) still refuse and insist your curfew is 10 pm. At this point, both you and your parent(s) are frustrated with each other. As an adolescent, you may recognize that the parent(s) technically holds the power in this situation and come to the conclusion that (a) you understand what your parent(s) is saying;(b) you disagree; and (c) you are going to do what you are told anyway. This is accepting life.*

When discussing this scenario or one like it brought up by a group member, the group leader might find that adolescents, in particular, are resistant to this phase and therefore process issues related to power and control. Group members often need coaching in de-escalating and accepting life. As a result, group members can memorize the following script. The script consists of three sentences, but the middle sentence includes an option.

    a.  "I understand what you are saying." This statement allows group members to express that they understand the request or the wishes/desires of the other person.

    b.  "I agree with you." **Or** "I disagree with you." This statement is a choice and allows group members to continue to have freedom and accurately express themselves.

    c.  "I'm going to do what you say." This is recognition of the power differential and accepting life. A parent may need to be coached to accept individual differences and differentiation, while also respecting the adolescent's willingness to comply.

## Processing Questions:

1. Where would you go to take a time-out? With this question, the group can provide feedback as to the effective and preventative nature of the location chosen for a time-out. Is the location likely to de-escalate the situation?

2. What are some signs that talking out a problem out is not working for you? With this question, group members may discuss triggers to anger outbursts.

3. Talk about the difference between understanding a person versus agreeing with that person. With this query, participants have the opportunity to identify that understanding the perspective of another person does not mean having to agree with that person.

4. To what extent could you use this strategy in dealing with issues of anger and conflict?

## Special Considerations/Cautions:

Parents/significant others need to understand the purpose and nature of a self-initiated time-out. Parents/significant others may feel the group member is being disrespectful by taking a self-initiated time out or may believe the time-out is evasive in addressing the issue at hand. Parents/significant others should be cautioned not to follow the group member when a time-out is self-initiated, as such an action defeats the purpose of curtailing potentially aggressive behavior.

With respect to accepting life, the individuals involved need to understand that there is a difference between compliance and agreement. For example, an adolescent may eventually succumb to a request but not agree with it. This independence should be respected, as opposed to trying to enforce agreement (e.g., see the aforementioned script).

Monitor carefully where group members indicate they would choose to take a time-out. Often, group members indicate that they would leave the house or go for a drive. Such options may be both inappropriate, due to escalating a dangerous situation (i.e., driving while angry) or viewed by the parent(s) as an attempt to escape the situation rather than work it out. Therefore, discuss appropriate boundaries, such as walking outside and staying within the property versus leaving.

## Adaptations:

As mentioned previously, this group intervention was developed for adolescents participating in an anger management focus group. Much of the information here could also be used in working with adults or families. Caution should be used in using this intervention with young children due to the lack of cognitive capacity to engage in the directives or scripted behaviors.

## References/Credits:

Burt, I., Patel, S. H., Butler, S. K., & Gonzalez, T. (2013). Integrating leadership skills into anger management groups to reduce aggressive behaviors: The LIT Model. *Journal of Mental Health Counseling, 35*, 124-141.

Ellis, A. (1995). *Better, deeper, and more enduring brief therapy: The rational emotive behavior therapy approach.* Bristol, PA: Bruner/Mazel.

Weisinger, H. D. (1985). *Dr. Hendrie Weisinger's anger workout book.* New York: William Morrow Publications.

## Author Notes:

*Richard S. Balkin*, Ph.D., LPC-S, NCC worked extensively in psychiatric hospital settings and continues to conduct research and consult with psychiatric hospital programs. His past experience includes incorporating group counseling/therapy with adolescents, adults, and geriatric group members, as well as family and multi-family groups.

## Correspondence:

Questions and comments related to this activity may be directed to:

Richard S. Balkin, Ph. D., LPC-S, NCC
College of Education, Department of Counseling and Educational Psychology
Texas A&M University-Corpus Christi,
6300 Ocean Drive, Unit 5834, ECDC 151, Texas A&M University-Corpus Christi,
Corpus Christi, TX 78412-5834
richard.balkin@tamucc.edu

# Shape Your Stress

By Amy Williams & Lilith Spry

## Population:
Adolescents/Older Adolescents seeking stress reduction

## Stage of Group:
Working

## Type of Group:
Counseling

## Rationale:
This activity, aligned theoretically with person-centered expressive art therapy (Rogers, Tudor, Tudor, & Keemar, 2011), allows individuals to connect with stress and relaxation experientially, to identify stressors and coping mechanisms for addressing stressors, and to exert control over stress by reshaping 'stress' into a calming three-dimensional shape. The act of shaping clay is, in and of itself, supportive of stress reduction, and exploration of stress levels before and after this activity afford participants with opportunities to gauge impact of this activity and others like it on stress levels.

## Goals:
Participants will:
1) identify stressors and coping mechanisms for addressing stress.
2) utilize art-based activity as a means for deconstructing stress.

## Materials:
1) Paper
2) Writing instruments
3) Clay or moldable dough
4) Paper towels
5) Paper plates
6) Water (for shaping clay)

## Time Allotment:
60 minutes; less time may be needed for smaller groups (4 or fewer people); additional time may be needed for large groups (greater than 10 people) and for clean-up.

# Directions:

Step:

1) Open group with introductions and Stress Check-In (Rating of current stress level on 1-10 scale).

2) Explain that stress can sometimes be difficult to verbalize, but it can impact us physically, mentally, and emotionally. This activity will give participants a chance to connect with stress, and with relaxation, through an art-based activity.

3) Explain that participants will use clay to create a three-dimensional model of their stress. Distribute clay, paper towels, and water and allow participants to work on shaping their stress into a 3-D model. Give ample time for creation, as participants may stop and revisit their sculpture during the process.

4) After all participants have created their shapes, distribute paper and writing instruments. Ask participants to list feelings or other words related to their stress on paper.

5) Invite willing participants to describe their sculpture-what it represents, why they chose the shape/image that was created, what feelings they have surrounding their stress.

6) Explain that coping mechanisms for managing stress can help to make stress less overwhelming. Have participants flip over their paper and list things that help them to feel more relaxed or things they do to help cope with stressors. Ask willing participants to share ideas and make connections between group members as appropriate.

7) Explain that one way of coping with stress is to re-shape it into something positive or manageable. Explain that participants will deconstruct and re-shape their stress shapes into a relaxing shape that can be used as a visual reminder of stress coping skills. Provide participants with time to re-shape their stress into a relaxing image/shape.

8) After all participants have created their shapes, allow willing participants to describe the relaxing shape they created and what about this shape helps them to feel relaxed.

9) After discussing this shape, discuss the process of shaping clay and whether the activity impacted stress levels. Complete Stress Check-In with participants following activity, and explore reasons for change in stress level if change is noted.

10) Help participants identify ways they can incorporate stress-reducing activities previously identified into their daily lives to support stress management.

11) Close by encouraging participants to track stress on a 1-10 scale throughout the week, both before and after engaging in stress-reducing activities. Participants

should be encouraged to keep their shapes as a reminder to engage in stress-management activities.

## Processing Questions:

1) How did it feel to shape your stress?
2) What were some of your relaxation words or activities and what about them helps you to relax?
3) How did it feel to reshape your stress into a relaxing shape?
4) How might you apply some aspect of this activity (e.g. physical outlet such as shaping clay) to managing stress in your daily life?

## Special Considerations:

This activity should be used with caution with stressors triggering strong emotions or crisis in a group member, as the group member may become overwhelmed or have difficulty containing emotions related to stressors.

## Adaptations:

Can be used with anger/calm instead of stress/relaxation; this is especially appropriate for adolescents who are working on anger management.

## References:

Rogers, N., Tudor, K., Tudor, L. E., & Keemar, K. (2011). *Person-centered expressive arts therapy: A theoretical encounter.* Person-Centered and Experiential Psychotherapies, 11, 31-47.

## Author Notes:

*Amy Williams* is a Current Student in the PhD in Counselor Education program at The College of William and Mary. She has two years of group work experience designing and facilitating art-based stress-reduction groups and facilitating substance abuse groups for adults, adolescents, and families.

*Lilith Spry* is a Counselor at Rivermont School in Lexington, VA, has two years of group work experience. She has designed and facilitated art-based stress-reduction groups and facilitated outpatient substance abuse and anger management groups.

## Correspondence:

Questions and comments related to this activity may be directed to:

Amy E. Williams, M.Ed., NCC
The College of William and Mary
P. O. Box 6396, Williamsburg, VA 23188
aewilliams@email.wm.edu

# What Others Can and Cannot See: The Public and Private Self

*By Melissa Halter*

## Population:

Adolescents and early adulthood and could be used with leadership programs, early adulthood transition or in recovery experiences (e.g. alcohol and other drugs, disordered eating, other addictive behaviors).

## Stage of Group:

Orientation Phase or the Termination Stage

During the Orientation Phase this activity encourages participants to take a risk with the group and share something they would like to better understand about themselves during the group process.

During the Termination Stage participants can reflect back on the group experience honoring what they were able to share about themselves during the group. Participants are honoring a piece of their "private self" that the group allowed them to share, due to the level of comfort created for self-disclosure.

## Type of Group:

This activity is primarily used in process related groups. However, it can be useful when working with task groups that will be facilitating the personal growth of others (i.e. team leaders involved in leadership develop experiences).

## Rationale:

Within social psychology the concept of public and private persona are discussed. Often one's public-self involves aspects of the self that individuals are more comfortable sharing with others; whereas, the private-self involves aspects of the self that may feel more vulnerable and individuals may believe society will place more judgment on the elements of one's private-self (Eisendrath, P. & Hall, 1991). This activity will allow individuals to explore how they view themselves, seek feedback from group members, enhance group members' understanding of themselves and others, and normalize feelings of various participants in the group. Basic elements of social psychology note that the way we perceive ourselves in relation to the rest of the world play an important role in our attitudes, beliefs, and behaviors (Hillman, 1996).

## Goals:

Participants will:
1) set a personal goal for the group experience (Orientation Phase) or identify an area of growth that occurred due to the group experience (Termination Stage).
2) gain awareness of one's public-self and personal-self and how one's individual persona impacts the sense of self and interactions with others.
3) improve in self-esteem through normalizing feelings and experiences and through feedback from other group members.

## Materials:

1) The group facilitator will need one bag that can easily be turned inside out. For example, a reusable bag that individuals often use when going to the grocery store is ideal.

## Time Allotment:

Time needed for this activity depends on the number of participants in the group. Each participant will need approximately 5 to 7minutes to share with the group. The group facilitator should plan for an additional 15 to 20 minutes to process the activity with the group.

## Directions:

Step:
1) Ideally, group members will be seated in a circle.

2) The facilitator will provide basic psycho-education about persona and tie the concept back to the group's purpose. Group leader could state the following: *"Often we feel comfortable sharing certain aspects of ourselves with the general public and there are certain aspects of ourselves that we may feel less comfortable sharing with others. Some make the distinction between the public-self and the personal-self. In an effort to grow and learn from each other each of us will have the opportunity to share a little bit about our public-self and our personal-self. I like to call this what people can see on the outside and what people might not know about because it is kept on the inside, more privately."*
   a) As the facilitator provides the basic psycho-education it is helpful for the facilitator to visually show the outside of the bag and then turn the bag inside-out to show the inside of the bag.

3) The facilitator will explain to the group that the bag will be passed around the circle and each group member will have the opportunity to share *"what is on the outside of the bag and what is on the inside of the bag"*; again the group facilitator should visually show the bag and turn the bag inside-out. The facilitator should note that each group member has 5 minutes to share with the larger group.

4) The facilitator should model the activity for the group or intentionally select a group member to model the activity appropriately.

5) After all group members have shared the facilitator should thank all participants for sharing in the activity.

6) The group facilitator should process the activity with the group.

## Processing Questions:

1) What did you observe during the sharing experience?
2) How did you feel when you shared and/or were listening to others sharing?
3) How did you determine what you shared and what you did not share with the group?
4) How was this process similar to sharing in other aspects of your life?
5) How will you use this information to better yourself or enhance the way our group works together?

## Special Considerations:

Group facilitators need to be sensitive to time, they may need to verbalize "challenge by choice" guidelines for the group, and they may need to be prepared to manage affect as the activity will illicit emotion. The emotional experience may be more intense for particular participants.

## Adaptations:

This activity can easily be adapted using an art element. For example, junior high students often engage successfully in this activity if they have two sides of a mask to write on or decorate. Engaging the group in an art project requires more time and supplies. Also, the facilitator will need to consider the developmental level of participants to determine if the adaptation noted for this activity can be successful with a younger population.

## References:

Eisendrath, P., & Hall, J. (1991) Jung's self psychology: A constructivist perspective New York: Guilford Press.

Hillman, J. (1996) The soul's code: In search of character and calling New York, NY: Warner Books.

## Author Notes:

*Melissa Halter* is a licensed Psychologist and she has been facilitating group experiences for over 20 years. Melissa began her group work in the field of human relations developing and facilitating programs for junior high school and high school students. More recently, Melissa has worked in higher education facilitating leadership development groups and therapeutic process groups.

## Correspondence:

Questions and comments related to this activity may be directed to:

Melissa Halter, Ph.D.
Director, Center for Health and Wellness Promotion
5998 Alcala Park – University Center 161
San Diego, CA 92110
melissahalter@sandiego.edu

# What's in Your Locker?

By Barb Wilson

## Population:
Adolescents

## Stage of Group:
Transition stage

## Type of Group:
Psychoeducational or Counseling

## Rationale:

School, friends, and feeling different are just a few concerns of adolescents (Oaklander, 1988). The use of visual arts helps facilitate the therapeutic process and helps symbolize feelings in a tangible way (Gladding, 2005). This creative arts activity was developed after working with middle school students and observing the theme lockers played. Lockers are a central focus in middle and high school. Students decorate lockers, share lockers, and have conversations while on locker breaks. Utilizing this theme, group members will understand self-image and esteem through the exploration of what is "inside" and what is "outside" of one's locker. This activity allows group members to conceptualize what image they may be presenting to others about themselves and understand which parts of themselves are kept private. As group members hear others' stories, a sense of universality may be attained, further increasing self-esteem and self-confidence.

This activity was recently used with a group of sixth grade boys and girls. The group was designed as a "Social Skills" group and members were referred by teachers, parents, and/or guardians. Through the use of this activity, one of the male group members gained the confidence to "come out" as gay to his friends and family. He began by processing the decision on the "inside" of his locker. Later, he spoke to his mother about the project and ultimately told her he was gay. His mother requested a meeting with me and her son so she could further understand her supportive role during this significant moment in their lives.

## Goals:
Participants will:
1) Understand the concept of self-identity.
2) Understand the right to privacy for self and others.
3) Increase self-awareness and identity development.
4) Practice cooperative behaviors with peers.

## Materials:
1) 8"x11" cardstock paper

138

2) Writing materials
3) Assorted decorating items (i.e. glue, stickers)

## Time Allotment:

30-45 minutes
The time needed for this activity can be affected by the developmental level of the group participants, the size of the group, and the work environment.

## Directions:

Step:

1) Welcome the group

2) Introduce the activity

3) Ask group members for a definition of "self-identity"

4) Discuss how others' impressions of us affect our self-identity

5) Distribute the paper and provide group members with access to the writing materials and decorating items

6) Ask group members to fold the cardstock paper lengthwise

7) Instruct the group members to start with the outside of their locker. Ask them to think about what others know about them, what others see, and what they are willing to allow others to know about themselves. Each group member decorates his/her locker with pictures, words, and/or symbols representing his/her "outside."

8) After group members have added several items to the outside of their lockers, ask them to open their lockers. Discuss what might be on our "inside," such as thoughts, talents, specific life events, and personal struggles. Allow members to add elements to their "inside."

9) After the lockers are completed, allow group members time to share their work. *This is completely voluntary.*

10) Allow group members to take their lockers with them. (See "Adaptations" below)

## Processing Questions:

1) What did you learn about "self-identity?"
2) What is something you learned about a group member?
3) What is something you learned about yourself?
4) What might move from your "inside" to your "outside" in the next 3 months, 6 months, 1 year? (i.e. share my talent with others)
5) What would you like to add to your "inside" or "outside" in the next 3 months, 6 months, 1 year? (i.e. big brother/sister)

## Special Considerations/Cautions:

Due to the sensitive nature of some potential items, the group leader may consider allowing group members to move to separate areas of the room for privacy while decorating their "lockers." Additionally, it is imperative to allow the group member to use words or pictures to represent his/her thoughts and not require one or the other.

## Adaptations:

The time required for this activity can be adjusted according to your work setting and/or the developmental level of the group members. The activity can be adapted to meet the needs of groups in private counseling settings in addition to school settings. Some groups which may benefit from this activity are social skills groups, self-esteem groups, and relationship building groups. This activity can also be split into two sessions, 20-30 minutes each. For further exploration, a follow-up session could include deeper discussion about specific items that may be causing stress or anxiety.

## References:

Erk, R. R., (2008). *Counseling treatment for children and adolescents with DSM-IV-TR disorders* (2nd ed.). Columbus, OH: Pearson Merrill Prentice Hall.

Gladding, S. T., (2005). *Counseling as an art* (3rd ed.). Columbus, OH: Pearson Merrill Prentice Hall.

Oaklander, V., (1988). *Windows to our children*. Highland, NY: The Gestalt Journal Press.

Yalom, I. D., & Leszcz, M., (2005). *The theory and practice of group psychotherapy* (5th ed.). NY: Basic Books.

## Author Notes:

*Barb Wilson* is a School Counselor with the Hall County School System in Georgia. She has over ten years of group experience, including working with suicidal and homicidal children and adolescents, students at the elementary, middle, and high school levels, advising undergraduate and graduate students, and working with international students at the college level. She also has experience as a school counseling internship supervisor.

## Correspondence:

Questions and comments related to this activity may be directed to:
Barb Wilson, Ph.D., LPC, NCC
Hall County Schools
5470 McEver Road
Oakwood, GA 30566
drwilson@yahoo.com

# Wheel of Misfortune

*By Katrina Cook*

## Population:

The activity is most appropriate for adolescents who abuse substances.

## Stage of Group:

Orientation stage or termination stage.

## Type of Group:

This activity would be most appropriate for a counseling process group.

## Rationale:

Often adolescents who use substances have a difficult time identifying the negative consequences they have experienced as a direct or indirect result of their substance abuse (Vernon, 2009).

## Goals:

Participants will:
1)  discover how their substance abuse negatively impacts them.
2)  identify self-defeating behaviors that keep them stuck in the cycle of substance abuse.

## Materials:

1)  A large dice
2)  A white board
3)  Dry erase markers
4)  Dry erase board eraser
5)  An optional material is the "Wheel of Fortune" theme song (Griffin, 1983, track 1) to play as the game begins.

## Time Allotment:

In general, plan for the activity to last 45 minutes to an hour. The game continues until every participant "dies" out of the game, or decides to not roll the dice anymore. Typically, I have found that participants keep playing until everyone "dies." Since the roll of the dice is random the number of the participants does not necessarily impact how much time is needed. Similarly, I have not experienced that participant demographics impact the time of the game. However, it is important that the participants are able to complete the game within a single group session.

## *Directions:*

Before the game:

1) Draw a large circle on the white board and draw lines across it to make pie slices that can be written in. Make 16 pie slices.

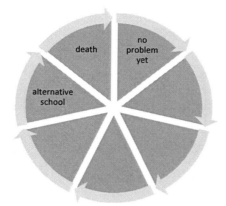

2) In one of the pie slices, write "No problem yet" and in another pie slice write "Death".

3) Ask the group members to list negative consequences they or someone they care about may have experienced related to their drug use. The consequences can relate to any area of their lives: Academic, Legal, Financial, Family, Relationships, Personal Integrity, Health, etc.

4) As the group member call consequences out, write one in each of the pie slices.

5) Continue until all the pie slices have a consequence written in them.

Playing the game:

Step:

1) Optional: Play the theme music to Wheel of Fortune and invite all participants to come see what wonderful prizes they will win.

2) Toss the dice to one of the participants and ask him or her to roll the dice.

3) Starting at the "No problem yet" pie slice, count in clockwise fashion the number of pie slices to correspond to the number rolled on the dice (i.e. if the dice lands on 6, count to the 6th pie slice). Whatever consequence is listed in the pie slice the group member lands on is what happens to him or her in the game.

4) The next group member rolls the dice. Begin counting from the pie slice the previous group member landed on to the next slice. Whatever consequence is listed in that pie slice happens to the group member who landed on it.

5) As a group member lands on a consequence (except the "death" slice), ask him or her to describe a time when they may have experienced that particular consequence.

142

6) If a group member lands on the "No problem, yet" slice, remind him or her of all the other pie slices they have already landed on, and point out that this might be denial.

7) When a group member lands on the "death" slice, he or she is out of the game, but the other group members continue rolling the dice without him or her.

8) Eventually, all group members will land on the "death" slice marking the end of the game. Occasionally, a group member will decide to no longer play the game, but this rarely happens. Other times a client will hesitate before rolling the dice, saying "Do I still go?" Respond "It's your turn."

9) The following discussion questions can be used following the game:
   a) Why did you play this game?
      i. Answers most often given include "You told us to", "I was curious", "It looked like fun", or "Everyone else was playing". *Remind the group members that nobody made them play the game and the reasons they are giving are the same reasons people often give for using substances.*

   b) Why did you continue playing once you saw what the end result would be?
      i. *Remind the participants that they could have stopped anytime they wanted, but they chose to continue on this path until everybody landed on the "death" slice.*
      ii. A general guideline for games is to stop playing while it is still fun. However, the goal is for this game to become tedious. Sometimes there is only one participant left in the game, rolling the dice over and over again, but always missing the "death" slice. Often, the last group member will turn the dice to a number that will land him or her on the "death" slice to end the game.
      iii. If that happens ask that group member:
          1. *What other options did you have for getting out of this game besides landing on the "death" slice?*

   c) What patterns developed for you in the game? (.i.e., one group member may often land on the "jail" slice while another group member may often land on the "drop out of school" slice.

   d) How do you think that mirrors what actually happens with substance abuse?
      Not everyone who abuses substances will experience all the possible consequences that come with that behavior, but all people who abuse substances will experience some of those consequences.

## Processing Questions:

1) What was this experience like for you?
2) What feelings surfaced during this activity?
3) What surprised you the most about this experience?

## Special Considerations:

3) Leaders and co-leaders of this activity do not roll the dice and play the game with the participants. Instead, the leader guides the game by passing the dice to the next player and keeping track of where the players are on the Wheel of Misfortune.
4) Sometimes group members want to focus on the positive consequences of substance abuse, not the negative consequences. I remind them that they are well aware of what they like about abusing substances, but the purpose of the group is to explore the negative consequences of their substance abuse.
5) Allow participants to call out the consequences to fill the pie instead of calling on particular participants or putting any of the students on the spot. It is not necessary that every participant contribute a specific consequence.

## Adaptations

The activity as described here is used in an Intervention group for those adolescents who have already been identified as using substances. To adapt this to a prevention activity for group members who might not have tried substances yet, ask them to list consequences that they have heard about or learned about, not consequences they themselves have experienced.

## References:

Griffin, M. (1983). Wheel of fortune. On *Classic TV game show themes* [CD]. Studio City, CA: Game Show Network.

Vernon, A. (2009). *Counseling children and adolescents.* (4th ed.). Denver, CO: Love Publishing Company.

## Author Notes:

*Katrina Cook* is an Assistant Professor of Counselor Education at Texas A&M University – San Antonio. She has had twenty-nine years of group work experience, including facilitating groups with children and adolescents.

## Correspondence:

Questions and comments related to this activity may be directed to:

Dr. Katrina Cook, Ph.D., LPC-S, LMFT-S, CSC
Texas A&M University San Antonio
One University Way
San Antonio, Texas, 78224
Katrina.cook@tamusa.tamus.edu

# A Body of Water with Water Colors

*By Emi Lenes & Jacqueline M. Swank*

## Population:

Adolescents ages 12-18 who are addressing healthy coping skills and/or increased self-awareness.

## Stage of Group:

Working

## Type of Group:

Counseling

## Rationale:

This group can provide an opportunity for members to express themselves in a safe environment where they can experience witnessing and be witnessed by others. The activity invites an increased self-awareness and acceptance of one's present situation. Gladding and Newsome (2003) emphasized that art stimulates emotions and can facilitate a deeper understanding of oneself in a larger context. Participating in this activity empowers group members to later use this activity on their own, or with others, as a coping skill.

## Goals:

Participants will:
1) gain clarity as group members learn and grow through shared self-expression.
2) experience relaxation through community engagement in an expressive arts technique.
3) acquire knowledge about painting as a coping skill.

## Materials:

1) Paint
2) Paper
3) Paintbrushes
4) Cups to hold water
5) Paper towels
6) Relaxing music for background ambiance

## Time Allotment:

Ideally, for a group of 7-10 members, a 2-hour group could have the following structure:
1) 1: 10 minutes to welcome the group and settle into the space, and introduce the activity
2) 2: 30 minutes of painting

3) 3: 70 minutes of processing the paintings
4) 4: 10 minutes of a closure activity

Alternatively, if only 1 hour was available for this group, the following structure may be utilized:

1) 1: 5 minutes to welcome the group and settle into the space, and introduce the activity.
2) 2: 20 minutes of painting
3) 3: 30 minutes of processing the paintings
4) 4: 5 minutes of a closure activity

## Directions:

Step:

1) Start off the group by the group leader welcoming the group members, and then <u>slowly</u> reading the script below. Throughout the script, the symbol, ... , is utilized as an indication to pause for a moment before reading on:

   *"Whenever you feel comfortable, please close your eyes, or choose an unmoving spot in the room with which to focus a soft gaze... Take a couple deep breaths... Check in with your heartbeat rhythm right now... What are you aware of around the room?... What are you aware of within yourself right now?.... Take another breath or two, and breathe into any areas that may feel tight. See if you can bring some nourishing airflow into those areas... Where in your body feels loose and relaxed? ... As you take a few more deep breaths, please invite your inner critic to be open and kind to yourself and others today, with a gentle curiosity about what is about to happen... when you feel ready to engage your imagination, ... Please allow an image of a body of water to emerge in your mind's eye... Invite a vision of any body of water that represents your inner state in this moment...It could be an ocean, river, waterfall, hurricane, a lake, etc. See if you can envision yourself somewhere in this scene... Where are you in the picture?... What is the water like? ... Once you have a vision of a body of water, and where you fit into this scene, you can open your eyes."*

2) With relaxing music in the background, the group leader invites members to quietly paint any body of water that connects them with their inner experience in the moment. *"Engage your inner kindergarten child, who is an artist, and doesn't care what the painting looks like."* Members are requested to depict themselves in the painting somewhere. They can draw themselves as a stick figure, or as any metaphoric image (animal, plant, object, etc.). If some members finish early, encourage them to add finer details to the painting.

3) Once the bodies of water are painted, the group leader invites members to share whatever they would like to about their paintings, one at a time. No one is required to share if they do not want to. Once each member has finished describing their own piece, before moving on, the group leader asks this person if she/ he is open to process questions (examples in section below), and/or respectful group comments on the painting. After answering the process questions, if the member is open to others'

reflections, the intentional framework that group members can use is: "if this were my painting, _____ would mean _____."

   a. An important rule for the group is that the members take responsibility for their own interpretations. Whatever is said about someone else's art, may reveal an insight about the person saying it, but this may or may not have anything to do with the person who made the painting.

   b. Another important rule for the group is that everyone treats their own artwork, and all other members' artwork, with respect.

4) Closing activity – Have a check in around the circle one final time, with everyone sharing what they will remember from this experience. This may include the title of her/ his painting or the title of someone else's painting, or anything about the process or content of the group experience.

## Processing Questions:

1) What was/is this experience like for you?
2) If you were to imagine that this painting was a metaphor for something or someone significant in your life, what do you see?
3) If you could change something in the painting in some way, what would you change, and how?
4) If something inside the painting could speak to you somehow, and give you a message to take with you, what would that message be?
5) What is the title of this painting?

## Special Considerations:

1) Having a heightened multicultural awareness and sensitivity to respecting the diversity of group members is of utmost importance. As with most creative techniques, this experiential activity can invite participants to delve into a deep aspect of themselves. The level of emotional activation that can arise is a special consideration and caution. Group leaders facilitating this activity should feel adequately trained in group processing of highly charged emotional topics, and have multicultural competence.
2) Please make sure there is enough time for each step of the group. Ample space is needed for participants to get settled into the space, experience the relaxation of painting, process their paintings, and have closure for the group.
3) Emphasizing the invitation for group members' inner critic to be open and kind to self and others is important because comfort with painting varies considerably on an individual basis. Some members may be distracted by a perceived lack of skill, or a block with feeling a lack of self-efficacy to transmit onto paper the vision they may have in their mind. Also, some members may find it difficult to use their imagination because they are so accustomed to left brain, analytical conceptualizations. Encouraging curiosity and childlike artwork is helpful with this area.

## Adaptations:

Another population particularly suited for this activity is graduate counseling students who are learning creative techniques to use with their group members. This activity also could be used for adult populations in various settings who are working on coping skills or increased self-awareness. The participants who may benefit the most from this group activity have intact deductive reasoning skills and a willingness to make abstractions from images. This activity can be adapted to any of the natural elements (fire, earth, air, water, etc.) Additionally, the group leader can facilitate the activity using various types of paint, colored pencils, crayons, craypas, etc.

## References/Credits:

Gladding, S. T., & Newsome, D. W. (2003). Art in counseling. In C. Malchiodi (Ed.), *The handbook of art therapy* (pp. 243–253). New York: Guilford.

\*Thank you to the Lenes, Schlitt and Cortez family, my sisters, and friends who have deeply encouraged the infinite possibilities of creative and spiritual techniques for enhancing mental health; Mary Rockwood Lane, Ana Puig, Jacqueline Swank & Kathie Southwick for training on being a counselor/group facilitator who is both professional and authentic; Sara Nash & Pat Korb for teaching radical respect, and the technique: "if this were my piece, ___ would mean __."

## Author Notes:

*Emi Lenes* is a Doctoral Student at the University of Florida. She has seven years of experience with psychoeducational and process groups in graduate level classrooms, an alternative school for at-risk adolescent females, and at an in-patient child/adolescent psychiatric hospital.

*Jacqueline M. Swank* is an Assistant Professor of Counselor Educator at the University of Florida. She has 12 years of group work experience working with children and adolescents and their families in outpatient, day treatment, inpatient, and residential settings and with counseling students in the classroom environment.

## Correspondence:

Questions and comments related to this activity may be directed to:

Emi A. Lenes, NCC, LMHC, LMFT
University of Florida
College of Education, SHDOSE, Counselor Education Program
1204 Norman, PO Box 117046
Gainesville FL, 32611
Emi.Lenes@ufl.edu

# Breath & Being in the Present Moment

*By Jeffry L. Moe, Madeline Clark-Kesler,*
*& Amanda Brookshear*

## Populations:

Inpatient or outpatient groups, composed of adults or adolescents with anxiety and/or stress-management concerns; See adaptations below for other recommended populations.

## Stage of Group:

While conceived as most appropriate for the orientation stage/sessions, with modifications this could work in the transition, working, or termination phases as well.

## Type of Group:

Psycho-educational and Counseling Groups

## Rationale:

The purpose of this activity is to introduce the concept of mindfulness to group members, to teach a basic mindfulness practice that members can learn to use in different situations, and support group work in the present moment through the practice of mindful awareness. Mindfulness techniques used in group work have been shown to reduce group member stress reactions (Bergen-Cico, Possemato, & Cheon, 2013) and to increase empathy (Chiesa & Serretti, 2009; Murphy, 2006). Mindfulness-based methods can enhance self-awareness, encourage self-acceptance over self-criticism, and may also decrease social apprehension (Hayes & Smith, 2005; Rasumseen & Pidgeon, 2011). Activity questions encourage group members to explore mindfulness in relation to themselves, other group members, and their life experiences. Process questions can help group members connect this activity to personal thoughts, feelings, and barriers to mindfulness. Group members will leave the group with a specific tool to reduce stress and to increase empathy and self-compassion based upon an increase in group member present-centeredness.

## Goals:

Participants will:
1) Connect with breath and breathing as a means of anxiety and stress reduction.
2) Use breathing techniques to increase group member mindfulness in terms of self and others.
3) Use mindfulness techniques as a basis for group discussion, bonding, and universality.

## Materials:

1) Paper
2) Writing utensils

## Time:

Allow 10-20 minutes to distribute materials, conduct, and process this activity. More time may be necessary for groups of more than 8 members.

## Directions:

Step:

1) Distribute paper and pencils to group members.

2) Group leader will introduce the concept of mindfulness using the following text:

*The concept and practice of mindfulness is based on becoming intentionally aware and committed to the present moment (Hanh, 2005). When we are mindful, we are more in tune with our thoughts and feelings and allowing them to be just that: what we are thinking or feeling at the time. Mindfulness also involves experiencing our internal and external worlds more richly and fully in the here and now. Instead of eating an apple and wishing we had a banana, being mindful would help us pay more attention to the richness of the apple's flavor, the texture of its skin, and the joy of biting into something so full of nourishment and nutrition.*

3) Group leader will begin the mindfulness exercise by saying:

*Sit comfortably with your feet flat on the floor, and begin to focus on your breathing. Say out-loud or to yourself as you inhale and then exhale: "Breathing in, I am breathing in. Breathing out, I am breathing out."*

4) Group leader will have group members Repeat 3 or more times by saying:

*Repeat 3 or more times and if you find your mind drifting, that is OK! Tune back into your breathing, and keep saying to yourself "Breathing in, I am breathing in. Breathing out, I am breathing out" until you feel more relaxed and awake. Continuing to breathe mindfully.*

5) Group leader will then direct the group members to pick up their pencils and paper and compose short responses to the following prompts:

*In our group, I am most grateful for...*
*In our group, I am most looking forward to...*
*In our group, I know I will contribute...*

6) Facilitate members' sharing of their experiences during the breathing exercises, and their responses to the prompts, either using a round or popcorn-style. Transition into process questions.

## Processing Questions:

1) How was this activity for you?
2) As you experienced this activity, what thoughts, feelings, and sensations did you become more aware of?
3) What surprised you about your experience of this activity?
4) How did this activity change your perception of the group?
5) Where could you practice mindful breathing in your daily life?

## Special Considerations/Cautions:

This activity can cause painful thoughts, feelings, and memories to come into awareness for some individuals (Hayes & Smith, 2005) and may require additional processing time within or outside of group. Group members can be directed to imagine themselves comforting their own upset feelings and thoughts as though they were soothing an upset child (Hanh, 2005), breathing mindfully until a state of calm acceptance is achieved.

## Adaptations:

The breathing portion of this activity could be conducted at the beginning of every group session, reminding members about the importance of noticing their many thoughts, feelings, and sensations as they emerge and fade in their awareness. This activity can be expanded to include a mindfulness journal that group members utilize outside of group to record mindfulness practices. Group members in the working phase can be encouraged to share how mindful breathing improved their coping with anxiety or stress in the context of their daily lives as part of their check-in. Role-play activities centered on reducing anxiety in awkward moments can incorporate a mindful breathing component. If the topic of group is depression or other mood disorders, asking the group members to silently or verbally identify their somatic feelings prior to and at the conclusion of the activity may also be helpful. This group technique can be used with children and adolescents by incorporating more frequent encouragements to use mindful breathing throughout the group work encounter.

## References:

Bergen-Cico, D., Possemato, K., & Cheon, S. (2013). Examining the efficacy of brief mindfulness-based stress reduction (Brief MBSR) program on psychological health. *Journal of American College Health.* 61(6), 348-360.

Chiesa, A. & Seretti, A. (2009). Mindfulness-based stress reduction for stress management in healthy people: A review & meta-analysis. *The Journal of Alternative and Complementary Medicine.* 15(5), 593-600. doi:10.1089/acm.2008.0495

Hanh, Thich Nat. (2005). *Being Peace.* Berkley, CA: Parallax Press.

Hayes, S., & Smith, S. (2005). *Get Out of Your Mind and Into Your Life.* Oakland, CA: New Harbinger Publications, Inc.

Murphy, M.C. (2006). Taming the anxious mind: An 8-week mindfulness meditation group at a university counseling center. *Journal of College Student Psychotherapy.* 21(2), 5-13. doi:10.1300//J035v21n02_03

Rasumseen, M.K. & Pidgeon, A.M. (2011). The direct and indirect benefits of dispositional mindfulness on self-esteem and social anxiety. *Anxiety, Stress & Coping.* (24)2, 227-233. doi: 10.1080/10615806.2010.515681

# Author Section:

*Jeffry Moe* has experience using mindfulness-based counseling techniques with individuals and groups. His group experience and interests includes court-ordered and voluntary group members, applied cognitive-behavioral and solution-oriented methods, groups with sexually and gender diverse people including self-identifying lesbians, gay males, bisexual, and questioning people, and training groups for graduate counseling students.

*Madeline Clark-Kesler's*, MSEd, NCC group experience includes facilitating groups in community mental health and in the college setting. Madeline has facilitated anger management groups, a mood disorders groups, wellness groups, mindfulness groups for children, process groups for undergraduate & graduate students, and deployment support groups for military partners and military children.

*Amanda Brookshear*, LPC, LMFT has led groups in school, college and mental health setting. The groups she has facilitated range in topics and populations. Some of the groups she has enjoyed facilitating are children's social and emotional skills groups, parenting groups, adolescent anger management groups, sex offender groups and adult addiction groups.

# Correspondence:

Questions and comments related to this activity may be directed to:

Jeffry L. Moe, PhD, LPC-S, NCC, CCMHC
Assistant Professor of Counseling
Old Dominion University
110 Education Building
Norfolk, VA 23529
jmoe@odu.edu

# Color the Music

*By Kathie T. Erwin*

## Population:
Older Adolescents/Adults

## Stage of Group:
Transition or Working

## Type of Group:
Counseling

## Rationale:

This group activity focuses on connecting with feelings and changes in feelings by using music, color and artistic expression as prompts. The blend of music, color, and art combine to by-pass the critical editor in cognition to reach what may be blocked or inappropriate affective responses. Using these sensory elements to "color the music," group members have a visual representation of changing moods that may be less obvious when discussed in a cognitive oriented exercise.

Gabrielsson and Lindstrom's (2003) study of SEM (strong experiences related to music) demonstrated the therapeutic connection of music to feelings and emotional responses. When used within a group, music is "a non-threatening way to build rapport" (Erwin, 2013) and motivates individuals toward social interaction (Murrock & Higgins, 2009) both of which are desirable for advancing the stages in group work.
Music and art are used in the group process as means through which members identify ways to distinguish between their positive and negative responses to feelings. Slobada's (1991) study of emotional responses to music found that various musical styles give a "cathartic outlet sometimes offered through stories or drama, but without their specific semantic content" (p. 120). In this group design, the presenting issues are circumvented when the focus is on feelings and responses prompted by music which becomes a metaphor for identifying alternative behavioral responses.

## Goals:

Participants will:
1) connect with music as metaphor for feelings.
2) identify changes in feelings and responses as music changes.
3) recognize how external changes influence feelings and responses.

# Materials:

1) Audio source: Mp3 player with speaker or CD player with speaker
2) Timed recording of instrumental music with several tempos and intensity. Mix the music in unpredictable order such as this example: Clair De Lune, The Way We Were, 1812 Overture, Let It Be, Hawaii 50 Theme, Somewhere Over the Rainbow, Chariots of Fire. Choose music mix based on age range of group members.
3) Poster board for each group member
4) Colored markers
5) Chairs and table (or lap board) on which to do art work

# Time Allotment:

With a group of 8-10 plan for:

10 minutes to introduce group activity
15 minutes to color to the music
35 minutes to display work and process

# Directions:

Step:

1) Group Leader begins by explaining: "*Music is a powerful way to connect with feelings. For some listeners, classical music or a ballad is soothing while other listeners are drawn to the strong beat of a march. Today we are going to color the music as we listen. You do not have be to artistic, just feel the music and let that feeling travel down to your hands as you color what you feel. This is a personal expression, so we will remain silent to allow everyone to fully enjoy and music.*"

2) Distribute poster board and markers to each group member.

3) Group Leader introduces the art activity by saying: "*these colored markers are your instruments. Choose any color or combination of colors. You can create a design or be totally free form, the art is your personal expression of feelings. When the music changes, decide how your coloring will respond to that change. Are there any questions? Remember, we will remain silent to enjoy the music as you create. (pause) If everyone is ready, I will start the music.*" (start music)

4) During the activity, the Group Leader steps back from the table and does not view works. The Group Leaders asks for questions to be addressed before beginning to avoid interrupting the concentration of the members. When the music ends, the Group Leader steps back to the table and says: "*let's take our chairs from the table and form a circle. Please bring your art work into our circle.*" When members are settled, the Group Leader continues with the processing phase.

## Processing Questions:

1) When you look at your picture, what words describe the feelings that you present in this picture?
2) Did any of these feelings surprise you? In what way?
3) The music went from fast to slow, soft to loud and classical to rock. These changes are shown in colors and designs of the pictures. If music was replaced by words and attitudes that changed in intensity without warning, how might that influence your feelings? Do you respond differently to words that are soft compared to harsh or slow compared to rapid?
4) If you cannot change the tempo or intensity of the 'music' around you, what are some ways you can manage your responses?
5) What thoughts do you take away from this experience that you can apply in your life this week?

## Special Considerations:

1) The coloring activity requires moderate digital dexterity. Larger markers can be useful for older adults or those who have difficulty holding smaller markers.
2) This activity is not well suited for persons with limited vision or hearing loss. Eliminate distracting sounds in the group room such as phones, PA system announcements or background "elevator music" so the group can focus on the music with the activity.

## Adaptations:

By choosing age appropriate, familiar music, this group could be conducted with middle school age children to process loss, grief or separation (as with foster children or loss of parent). Process questions need to be altered for the level and therapeutic concerns of the children's ages. A school counselor who is trained in group work could use this approach to working with a small group of students who are having problems adjusting to middle school.

## References:

Erwin, K. T. (2013). *Group techniques for aging adults*, (2nd ed.). New York: Routledge.

Gabrielsson, A., & Lindstrom, W. S. (2003). Strong experiences related to music: A descriptive system. *Musicae Scietiae, 7*(2), 157-217.
doi: http://0-dx.doi.org.library.regent.edu/10.1037/a0030781.supp

Murrock, C. J. & Higgins, P. A. (2009). The theory of music, mood and movement to improve health outcomes. *Journal of Advancement in Nursing, 65*, 2249-2257. PMID 20568327

Sloboda, J. A. (1991). Music structure and emotional response: some empirical findings. *Psychology of Music, 19*, 110-120. Retrieved from http://www.brainmusic.org/MBB91%20Webpage/Sloboda_1991.pdf

## Author Notes:

*Kathie T. Erwin* is an Assistant Professor at Regent University and has 20 years of group experience with adoptive families, mood disorders and elder groups including teaching group work in Nord Mag Intensive at University of Iceland in Reykjavik, Iceland.

## Correspondence:

Questions and comments related to this activity may be directed to:

Dr. Kathie T. Erwin, LMHC, NCC, NCGC
Assistant Professor, School of Psychology & Counseling
Regent University
1000 Regent University Drive, Virginia Beach, VA. 23464
kerwin@regent.edu

# Communication and Interpretation: It's More Complicated than You Think!

By Kevin Tate

## Population:

Adolescents and adults who have the capacity for meaningful, empathic communication with a variety of clinical issues. See special considerations for populations that may not benefit from this activity and adaptations section for younger children.

## Stage of Group:

This activity would be most relevant for the orientation (setting group norms) or transition (engaging in complex interpersonal learning) stages of a group.

## Type of Group:

This activity would be most appropriate for psychoeducational or counseling groups.

## Rationale:

This activity is intended to help group members understand the complexity and nuances of how ideas are communicated and interpreted by others. The process of deliberate communication has been found to lead to higher levels of empathy (Andreoni & Rao, 2011). Empathy, in turn, can be considered an intricate part of mental wellness (Myers, Sweeney & Witmer, 2000) as well as central to meaningful cross-cultural relationships (Chung & Bemak, 2002; Freire, 1970).

Specifically, this activity is intended to help group members build empathy for those having a difficult time understanding others, as well as for those who are having a hard time communicating their thoughts and feelings to others. Such empathy is crucial for group work given the vast differences among group members in terms of cultural and contextual backgrounds. Finally, this activity will help group members to develop strategies and skills for more meaningful and effective communication in the group setting.

## Goals:

Participants will:
1) build empathy for those who experience difficulties in communicating with others, and for those who have difficulty understanding what others are trying to communicate.
2) develop skills and strategies for effective communication of ideas.
3) develop skills for listening to and interpreting the thoughts and feelings of others.

# Materials:

1) 2-3 sheets of blank paper for each group member
2) Pen or pencil for each group member
3) Simple, black-and-white, cartoon-like images (should be simple line drawings with no shading needed to effectively recreate with a pen or pencil)

# Time Allotment:

For a 1-1.5 hour adult or older adolescent group, this activity could take up to 45 minutes, depending on the amount of processing done throughout the activity.

# Directions:

Note: This activity occurs in two different stages that include steps and questions to facilitate discussion.

<u>Stage 1: One person communicating an idea to the whole group</u>

Step:

1) One person should be positioned in such a manner that they are separated from other group members such that they can look at an image without others being able to see      the image.

2) Other group members should then be given a piece of blank paper and a pen/pencil.

3) The person who has been separated from other group members is then given a simple cartoon-like drawing, and instructed to not let others see this image. *For example, a simple line drawing of a house, animal, or person could be used.*

4) This person is then instructed to describe the drawing so that others in the group can draw the picture on their piece of paper.

   a) *The only rule is that the person describing the image can only use language – no hand or body motions can be used to describe the image.*

5) The group leader can utilize questions following this stage to further process the experience for the group members that were drawing and for the person who was describing. Below are some possible questions:

   a) For the people who were drawing
      i.  What was this like?
      ii.  What made the process easy? What made it more difficult?
      iii.  After seeing the image, what advice would you give the person who described the image
      iv. Did you all communicate with each other to figure this out? Why or why not?

b) For the person who was describing
  i. What was easy and difficult about this process?
  ii. How did you feel when you were trying to communicate this image?
  iii. What would you do differently if given the chance to do it again?

## Stage 2: The whole group communicating an idea to one person

Step:

1) A different person should be positioned in such a manner that they are separated from other group members such that they can look at a blank piece of paper without others being       able to see it.

2) Other group members should each be provided with an identical copy of a simple cartoon-like drawing, and instructed to not let the singled-out person see this image. For example, as before a *different* simple line drawing of a house, animal, or person could be used.

3) These group members are then instructed to describe the drawing so that the singled-out person separated from the group can draw it

   a) *Again, the only rule is that the people describing the image can only use language – no hand or body motions can be used to describe the image.*

4) The group leader can utilize questions following this stage to further process the experience for the group members that were drawing and for the person who was describing. Below are some possible questions:

   a. For the person who was drawing
     i. What was this like?
     ii. What made the process easy? What made it more difficult?
     iii. After seeing the image, what advice would you give the people who described the image
   b. For the people who were describing
     i. What was this like?
     ii. What made the process easy? What made it more difficult?
     iii. Did you all communicate with each other to figure this out? Why or why not?

## Processing Questions:

1) What did we learn about the process of communication and understanding others?
2) How does this relate to your experience outside of this group? Can you think of examples when you experienced something similar?
3) How might this help us as we work together in future groups?

## Special Considerations:

The developmental level of group members will have a significant impact on the images that you choose, as well as the level of abstraction used when processing the follow-up questions for each stage. While this activity may be relevant for several presenting concerns, it may be more applicable to issues that are rooted in effective communication in regard to relationships with family, friends, peers, and/or co-workers. Although this activity could be used with a large range of individuals, it may not be appropriate for some populations. For example, those with symptomology similar to borderline personality disorder, those that may be somewhere on the autism spectrum, or individuals who might be considered sociopaths would likely not benefit from this activity.

## Adaptations:

This activity could be used for children ages 5 and above, with increasing levels of abstract processing possible with increasing age. Some important modifications should be made to match the developmental level of individuals in the group. For example, a 30-45 minute child or younger adolescent group could either be used as a brief intro activity (~10-15 minutes) to move the group into working mode, or could be structured as an activity to be used for the entire group period. Additionally, with very young group members, concrete aspects of the drawing and description process should be of focus, while older group members may be able to abstract to ideas such as cultural and personality differences in communication styles. This activity may also be adapted according to a specific group topic. For example, groups focusing on body image issues might be best served to use images of the human form in this activity.

## References:

Andreoni, J., Rao, J. M., (2011). The power of asking: How communication affects selfishness, empathy, and altruism. *Journal of Public Economics, 95,* 513-520.

Chung, R. C-Y., Bemak, F. (2002). The relationship of culture and empathy in cross-cultural counseling. *Journal of Counseling and Development, 80,* 154-159

Freire, P. (1970). *Pedagogy of the oppressed.* New York: Continuum.

Myers, J. E., Sweeney, T. J., Witmer, J. M. (2000). The wheel of wellness counseling for wellness: A holistic model for treatment planning. *Journal of Counseling and Development, 78,* 251-266.

*\*This exercise was adapted from an exercise the author learned during his time working at the University of Florida Career Resource Center*

## Author Notes:

*Kevin A. Tate* is an Assistant Professor in the Counselor Education and Counseling Psychology Department at Marquette University. His professional experiences include developing and co-facilitating a counseling group for individuals participating in a homeless transitional housing program for the Alachua County Crisis Center, facilitating group supervision for counselors-in-training, designing and co-facilitating career counseling groups for first generation, low-income college students, and teaching the group counseling course at Marquette University.

## Correspondence:

Questions and comments related to this activity may be directed to:

Dr. Kevin A. Tate PhD, LPC, NCC, MCC
Marquette University
PO Box 1881
Milwaukee, WI 53201
kevin.a.tate@gmail.com

# Do You Agree or Disagree?

By Jennifer Capps

## Population:
Older Adolescents/Adults

## Stage of Group:
Orientation Stage

## Type of Group:
Psychoeducational/Counseling

## Rationale:

This activity gives group members opportunities to become acquainted with one another, create group norms and buy-in, to the group and its purpose. Establishing group norms and cohesion are essential in moving groups toward achieving their goals and identifying ways to resolve conflict (Yalom & Leszcz, 2005). Engaging in this activity also requires group members to physically move around the room and actively participate which promotes group member engagement.

## Goals:
Participants will:
1) get acquainted with one another.
2) establish group norms.
3) create a common sense of purpose.

## Materials:
1) Two pieces of paper
2) Tape
3) Marker

## Time Allotment:

15-45 minutes
The amount of time required to complete this activity depends on the number of questions the group leader poses to the group.

## Directions:

Step:

1) Prior to the arrival of group members, place two sign at opposite sides of the room. One sign should read "Agree" and the other should read "Disagree."

2) When group members arrive, instruct them to sit or stand in the middle of the room.

3) Tell the group members that there is a sign on one side of the room that says "Agree" and a sign on the opposite end of the room that says "Disagree."

4) Instruct the group members that they will hear statements that they will have an opinion about concerning a particular issue (therapy, alcohol, gangs, etc.). They may choose to "Agree" or "Disagree" with any statement read.

5) After each statement is read, ask group members to move to whichever side of the room most closely corresponds with their belief about the statement. Group members are able to remain in the middle of the room if that best reflects their point of view.

6) Once all of the group members have physically moved to the area that best represents their point of view, the group leader suggests that a few volunteers share their rationale. This is an opportunity to create a conversation around their answers and provide some gentle psychoeducation (when appropriate).

7) Examples of statements:
   o Drinking alcohol reduces my stress.
   o Joining a gang is cool.
   o Finding a good counselor is easy.
   o It is difficult to avoid peer pressure.

## Processing Questions:

1) How comfortable were you expressing your opinion/beliefs?
2) What commonalities did you observe in the group?
3) What differences did you note in the group?
4) How did familiarity with group members impact your responses?
5) What pressure did you feel to come up with the "right" answer? Why?

## Special Considerations:

There is the potential for group members to experience judgment by other participants or by an inexperienced group leader. It is important to clarify for group members the specific intent of this exercise and caution group members when they express their viewpoint to use I-statements.

People with mobility issues may require some adaptations by the group leader to participate in this activity.

## Adaptations:

This activity can be used at the beginning of groups to establish norms and help members become acquainted with each other. Additionally, this activity can be used during the working phase of groups to take the pulse of the group when introducing new or controversially concepts.

This activity can be modified for people who are physically unable to participate by moving around by offering a paper and pen to the participant where they can denote their level of agreement or disagreement to the statements. Additionally, the group leader can ask the member (on selected questions) if they have would like to verbally express his or her perspective.

## References:

AlcoholEdu® for High School Media Competition (2009-2010). Retrieved September 5, 2013: http://www.outsidetheclassroom.com/Upload/WordDocuments/ HSMediaComp_Activity.pdf

Heathfield, S. M. Take a stand group ice breaker: Use various issues to encourage participants to take a stand. Retrieved September 5, 2013: http:// humanresources.about.com/od/icebreakers/a/take-a-stand-group-ice-breaker.htm

Yalom, I. D., & Leszcz, M. (2005). *The theory and practice of group psychotherapy* (5th Ed.). New York: Basic Books.

## Author Notes:

*Jennifer Capps* is an Assistant Professor in the Criminal Justice and Criminology Department at Metropolitan State University of Denver. She has 15 years of experience running groups, including designing and facilitating groups for adolescents and adults in schools, juvenile prisons, community mental health centers and health departments.

## Correspondence:

Questions and comments related to this activity may be directed to:

Jennifer Capps, PhD, LPC, NCC
Metropolitan State University of Denver
Campus Box 10
P.O. Box 173364
Denver, CO 80217
jcapps5@msudenver.edu

# Emerging From Shame

*By Nicki Nance*

## Population

People in recovery from addictions and codependents in recovery.

## Stage of Group:

Working

## Type of Group:

Psychoeducation, guided imagery

## Rationale:

Shame is often an underpinning of addiction, codependence, low self-esteem, post-traumatic stress disorder, and depression (Bradshaw, 1988). It is beneficial for group members to recognize how shame can shade their cognitions and emotions, and undermine treatment progress. The first therapeutic encounters with shame can be overwhelming. This activity provides psychoeducation, experiential healing, and support in diminishing the effects of shame (Bradshaw, 1990).

## Goals:

Participants will:
1) identify the original sources of shame.
2) understand the role of shame in sustaining problems.
3) conceptualize shame on a continuum.
4) develop resources for diminishing and coping with shame.

## Materials:

1) Whiteboard and Markers

## Time Allotment:

Allow 90 minutes for a group of 5 to 8. Larger groups may require more time for processing questions

## Directions:

1) Define shame, differentiating it from guilt, and relating it to early childhood messages and family secrets (addiction, abuse, neglect, infidelity)

2) Ask group members to identify shaming messages they received as a child and any dark secrets they kept.

3) Introduce the self-concept continuum with shame on one end and high self-esteem on the other end.

4) Draw the continuum line on the whiteboard, briefly defining the markers of shame, low self-esteem, lack of self-awareness, self-acceptance, and high self-esteem. Write each below the line. Emphasize the concept of a continuum.

5) Passing a marker from one participant to the next, instruct each group member to sign their first name at the place on the continuum that best represents their current state.

6) Once each group member has signed, the white/black board might look like this:

7) When all have finished writing their names and returned to their seats, discuss the following statement: *"Shame is installed by others, operated by you."* During this discussion, ask the group members to assist each other in identifying one thing they can do to move them one step closer to self-esteem on the continuum. Once again, be sure to emphasize the continuum, stressing that shame is often released a little at a time. At the end of the discussion, state that to move forward it is necessary to uninstall the shame.

8) Lead the group through the following guided imagery:
   a. *Remember a time in the past that causes you to feel ashamed. Imagine where you were when you first felt shameful. Take a moment to visualize this. How old are you? What are you wearing? What are you doing? How are you feeling?*
   b. *Now imagine that your bedroom door opens. Your shameful self sees you enter as you are today, hopeful, motivated, and recovering. Imagine you, as you are today. Tell your shameful self, "You did nothing to invite this feeling. It's okay to leave it behind and make room for yourself to like yourself and to heal.*
   c. *Imagine how light you feel as the heavy blanket of shame is lifted away. As the shame becomes lighter, focus on feeling free of the burden of shame that you have been carrying. Repeat the following: "It's okay to leave it behind me, and make room for myself to like myself." When you feel lighter, join yourself, as you are today, hopeful, motivated, and recovering. Now, walk away from that room and come join us in this room. If your head is lowered, raise it. If your eyes are closed, open them, and come back to the here and now.*

## Processing Questions:

1) Is there anything you wish to share about the experience you just had?
2) Where do you deserve to be on the continuum?
3) What is one thing you can do to move you closer to high self-esteem?
4) How can you help each other in your journey to better self-esteem?
5) Are you willing to return shame to its original owner and move forward without it?

## Special Considerations:

This activity may induce intense memories for people with post-traumatic stress disorder. Prior to guided imagery, assure the group that they may stop at any time and wait for the others to complete the exercise. It is not uncommon for participants to become tearful while being guided through the imagery and the facilitator should not disrupt the imagery to address this. Participants whose memories have become too intense to process within the imagery may appear flush or out of breath. If this is observed in any participant, you can keep the exercise intact and support the struggling person by saying, *"You are safe and in control of this important moment and you may open your eyes and return to the group at any time."* If a group member should open their eyes suddenly, an affirming nod is generally enough to stabilize them. In either case, incorporate balanced breathing into the exercise before processing the experience. Offer individual processing time after the group to support any participant whose discomfort is not resolved by the end of processing.

## Adaptations:

If childhood shame is being addressed specifically, incorporate the phrases "as a child" and "in your childhood" in the imagery script.

## References:

Bradshaw, J. (1988). *Healing the shame that binds you.* Deerfield Beach, FL: Health Communications.

Bradshaw, J. (1990). *Homecoming: Reclaiming and championing your inner child.* Deerfield Beach, FL: Health Communications.

## Author Notes:

*Nicki Nance* is a Professor of Counseling at Webster University. She has conducted therapy groups in substance abuse facilities, psychiatric, settings and correctional programs since 1970.

## Correspondence:

Questions and comments related to this activity may be directed to:
Nicki Nance, Ph.D., LMHC, NCC
Webster University
4414 SW College Rd., Suite 942
Ocala, FL 34474
nnance@webster.edu

# Externalizing Your Ism's

*By Mariaimee Gonzalez*

## Populations:

Adults and adolescents (over the age of 13). Populations who have been systemically denied social resources, rights, and opportunities. Example include, but are not limited to, Native or Aboriginal groups, persons with disabilities, older adult populations and teenage populations, immigrants, refugees, racial and ethnic minorities, gender minorities, persons with mental health issues and physical health issues, persons who are homeless or low SES, persons with criminal convictions, religious minorities, and LGBTIQQA.

## Stage of Group:

Working Stage

## Type of Group:

Psychoeducational, Counseling, Therapy

## Rationale:

Narrative therapy focuses on the life stories of group members as the central focus of group counseling. Story telling allows members to share how social constructs have played a part in the creation of one's life story. Leaders help group members to identify what they want in their own lives and to use their knowledge, diversity and strength to achieve their goals and construct a preferred narrative (White & Epston, 1990). Narrative approaches use language to externalize problems (White, 2007); group members are encouraged to name and characterize a problematic form of oppression, then take the problem from an intrapersonal perspective to a relational perspective by using the narrative technique of externalizing. Externalization allows the group member to recognize that they are separate from their problems.

Cultural forms of oppression, specifically oppressive *ism's* such as sexism, racism, ageism, heterosexism are influential determinants in many group members' lives; a narrative approach allows each group member to focus on an specific oppression as the externalized problem, deconstruct the oppression, and reconstruct the narrative to help each group member develop a more satisfying self-worth. This activity allows the group member, with the support of the group, to share their story of how a specific oppression has impacted their constructed meaning of self and others and empower the group member to be their own agent of change (White, 2007, White & Epston, 1990).

# Goals:

Participants will:
1) externalize and deconstruct a specific form of oppression they have experienced.
2) collaborate with other group members to confront their identified forms of oppression and promote universality and group cohesion.
3) examine the power relationships in our culture, especially against marginalized populations, and how these relationships cause mental health issues.

# Materials:

No Materials Needed.

# Time Allotment:

Allow 10-15 minutes per group member to externalize an oppressive construct. Allow at least 5-10 minutes to debrief.

# Directions:

Step:
1) Have group members sit in a circle and identify a member to go first; members will then volunteer one at a time.

2) Encourage the group member to choose a social label or social construct that has been oppressive to him or her to be explored in the activity. The group member is asked to pick only one oppressive *ism* that she/he feels has impacted his/her life in a negative way. For example, *"As a woman of color, you may have experienced some forms of sexism or racism that you would like to explore."*

3) Ask the group member to take on the persona of the oppression. For example, *"So Jane, I want you to take on the persona of sexism. When we ask you a question, answer the question as if you were Sexism and ways you have impacted Jane."* Jane is then to take on the persona of sexism and refer to herself (Jane) in the third person.

4) At this time, group members are encouraged to ask questions to Sexism about its impact on Jane. For example, the leader could start the conversation by asking *"So Sexism, when did Jane first notice you in her life?"* Jane is to respond to questions through the persona of Sexism; she might respond, *"Jane noticed me when she turned 13 and people started treating her differently."*

5) This continues until allotted time is complete. After the completion of each group member, have the group member reflect on the experience and how these scripts have impacted their life story.

## Processing Questions:

1) What did you learn about yourself and your life story?
2) What part of this process was most impactful? In what way?
3) How did it feel to hear your group members ask your *ism* questions on your behalf?
4) Which question stood out the most?
5) How will you reconstruct your life story to benefit you outside of this group?

## Special Considerations:

Cultural constructs often intersect, as a result, externalizing just one oppression at a time may be challenging. Help the group member narrow down the most problematic oppression for the activity. If time allows, group member may externalize another oppressive construct, but only one oppression can be externalized at a time.

## Adaptations:

This activity may be too abstract for group members. Facilitator may need to make the activity more concrete, such as asking the group member to role play with their persona. *"Ok, Jane, let's try something different, Joe will be your persona and you are to ask him questions."* This still allows for Jane to externalize her problem and develop a sense of personal agency.

## References/Credits

White, M. (2007). *Maps of narrative practice.* New York: W. W. Norton & Company.

White, M., & Epston, D. (1990). *Narrative means to therapeutic ends.* New York: W. W. Norton & Company.

## Author Notes:

*Mariaimee Gonzalez* is currently a Visiting Assistant Professor at University of San Diego. She has seven years of group experience, including six years of teaching and supervising counseling students' facilitating or co-facilitating group counseling. Her professional goals are to advocate through education, mental health, and community service the importance of identifying and breaking down the systemic barriers to equality. As a result, she has implemented cultural narratives into all her group work. She has facilitated groups with men, women, and children from different cultural backgrounds with life stories of oppression, trauma, anger, substance abuse, grief, reliance, hope, change and much more.

## Correspondence:

Questions and comments related to this activity may be directed to:
Mariaimee' Gonzalez, PhD, LPC
Visiting Assistant Professor
University of San Diego
6615 Canyon Rim Row Unit 155
San Diego, CA 92111
Mymae78@hotmail.com

# Finding Balance through Humor

*By Lacey Ricks & Elizabeth Hancock*

## Population:

This activity is designed for use with the graduate student population, but may be modified to be use with other populations (see adaptation section).

## Stage of Group:

Termination

## Type of Group:

Counseling

This activity is designed to be used within counseling or therapy groups. The group facilitator may choose to use this activity in a psychoeducational session while incorporating educational materials on stress management or reduction.

## Rationale:

Students on college campuses experience a variety of stressful situations (Maina, Burrell, & Hampton, 2011); graduate school may extenuate this amount of stress on students. Some factors contributing to graduate student stress include balancing school, work, finances, graduate assistantships, jobs, and career planning (Oswalt & Riddock, 2007). Studies have shown stress to be at the center of a graduate student's experience (Offstein, Larson, McNeill, & Mwale, 2004). Additionally, graduate students "are particularly vulnerable to pressures related to conducting research and teaching, publishing, and finding employment" (Hyun, Quinn, Madon & Lustig, 2006). Hyun et al., completed a study in 2006 in which they identified a significant need for mental health services for graduate students, specifying that half of the respondents reported "experiencing a stress-related problem that significantly affected their emotional well-being and/or academic performance" (Hyun et al., 2006).

In response to the reported mental health needs of graduate students, counselors working with this population may develop groups such as counseling, therapy, psychoeducational or support groups to address the mental health needs of graduate students. Such groups may incorporate the use of humor, or other creative techniques. The use of humor in a group setting may provide the participants with some degree of control over their responses and participation, allowing participants to express happiness, amusement, nervousness, stress and many other emotions (Goodrich, Hancock, Ricks, & Evans, 2012; Weisenberg, Tepper & Schwarzwald, 1995). The activity "Finding Balance through Humor" utilizes humor in the form of comic strips as a unique technique for facilitating discussion within the group.

# Goals:

Participants will:
1) understand the importance of balancing the obligations of school and private life.
2) identify personal support systems.
3) identify resources for managing school and personal commitments.

# Materials:

1) Markers/color pencils
2) Pens
3) Paper
4) Premade comic strip templates (optional used to accelerate the activity)
5) Projector (optional to display premade comic strips)

# Time Allotment:

The estimated time requirement for this activity is approximately one hour for a group of six; however, the length of time required to complete this activity may vary depending on the size of the group.

# Directions:

Step:
1) Prior to beginning the group activity, the group leader should identify or create two to three premade comic strips that illustrate stressful school life balance scenarios to the group. These comic strips will be used later in the group process to illustrate to the group how to create their personal comic strips.

2) To begin the group process, the group leader should ask group participants to answer the group starter questions. These questions are designed to help the group to begin discussing challenges that they face in graduate school balancing their school and personal lives. To start the activity, group leaders may begin the discussion by saying, *"Today we are going to discuss the challenges encountered in graduate school."* Discussion can then begin with the following questions.
   a. How do you define success and failure in general?
   b. What achievements must you accomplish in order for you to consider yourself successful?
   c. How does your education fit into your definition of success?
   d. What other factors fit into your definition of success?
   e. What would it be like for you not to reach your definition of success?

3) Next, the group leader should show the group members the premade comic strips illustrating stressful school life balance scenarios to the group.

4) Once the group leader has reviewed the comic strips with the group members, the group leader should hand out pieces of paper or the premade comic strip templates to the group and instruct them to design their own comic strip depicting a stressful

situation they have encountered while trying to balance their personal and school lives (remind the group members that not all comic strips need be funny).

5) Before beginning the design of their personal comic strips, group members should be informed that they will be asked to share their personal comic strips with the group.

6) After all group members are finished designing their personal comic strip, they should take turns presenting their comic strip to the group.

7) After each member of the group has presented their personal comic strip, the group leader should use the group closing questions listed in the processing questions section to process the activity with the group.

## Processing Questions:
1) What was it like for you sharing these experiences with the group?
2) How do you balance your drive for success with your personal self-care?
3) What impact does this "balancing act" have on you?
4) What are some new resources/ideas for balancing your personal and school life?
5) What roles/commitments can you eliminate in your life to help reduce your constraints?
6) What will you do differently today, this week, this month as a result of what we learned in this group?

## Special Considerations:
1) Group members should be reminded before beginning the group process to be respectful of other group member's feelings and experiences.
2) Group members should be reminded of the importance of confidentiality within the group process. Group leaders should also monitor the group discussion to encourage all group members to engage in the group process.
3) Modification should be made for students who have visual, reading/writing, or motor disabilities. These modifications can include the use of an aid to assist the students or modification of the assignment.

## Adaptations:
This group process can be modified for any age group K-12 students, college students, graduate students, or adapted for work life balance for adults in all areas.

# References:

Goodrich, T., Hancock, E., Ricks, L., Evans, A., & Honderich, E. M. (2012). *Forward: Creative resource manual.* Virginia Association for Counselor Education and Supervision (VACES).

Hyun, J., Quinn, B., Madon, T., & Lustig, S. (2006). Graduate student mental health: Needs assessment and utilization of counseling services. *Journal of College Student Development, 47*(3), 247-266. doi:10.1353/csd.2006.0030

Offstein, E., Larson, M., McNeill, A., & Mwale, H. (2004). Are we doing enough for today's graduate student? *The International Journal of Educational Management, 18*(7), 396-407. doi:10.1108/09513540410563103

Oswalt, S. B., & Riddock, C. C. (2007). What to do about being overwhelmed: Graduate students, stress and university services. *College Student Affairs Journal, 27*(1), 24-44.

Weisenberg, M., Tepper, I., Schwarzwald, J. (1995). Humor as a cognitive technique for increasing pain tolerance. *Pain, 63*(2), 207-212. doi:10.1016/0304-3959(95)00046-U

# Author Notes:

*Lacey Ricks* is a Doctoral Candidate in Counselor Education and Supervision at Auburn University. She has five years of experience working as a school counselor. She has individually facilitated and co-facilitated groups with at-risks students, students in transition, and students with special needs.

*Elizabeth Hancock* is a Doctoral Candidate in Counselor Education and Supervision at Auburn University. Elizabeth's experience in group work began while working with adolescents in a residential treatment facility for adjudicated youth. Here, she conducted multiple weekly group sessions including counseling and psychoeducational groups. Elizabeth continued to expand her experience in group work while working with students in a university counseling center.

# Correspondence:

Questions and comments related to this activity may be directed to:

Lacey Ricks, Doctoral Candidate
Auburn University
2084 Haley Center
Auburn, AL 36849
Lar0019@tigermail.auburn.edu

# Guy Rules: How We Are Expected to "Be a Man."

*By Chris Burden*

## Population:

Masculine gendered men. See adaptations for adolescence.

## Stage of Group:

Orientation

## Type of Group:

Counseling or psychotherapeutic group. See adaptations for a psycho-educational strategy

## Rationale:

The Guy Rules are designed to aid a men's counseling group in identifying hegemonic masculinity and any associated gender based cultural norms experienced by group members. Often, men who identify with traditional expressions of masculine gender experience psychosocial strain. This task invites group member to share their observations of culturally prescribed gender norms. As a result, the group begins reflect upon gender role strain. Somewhat paradoxically, as group members share their understanding of "Guy Rules" (gender based behaviors), the group begins to identify common experiences and shared meaning which inform the group process. Lastly, the task allows men to engage in a manner consistent with their socialization by "thinking" about the social experience of gender performance. This thinking task is an appropriate precedent to more in-depth explorations of individual gender role conflicts (O'Neil, 2006) and fears about emotional expression.

## Goals:

Participants will:
1) examine the concept of male gender code (hegemonic masculinity).
2) provide a foundational frame for the men's group, which will enable members to critically analyze messages associated with the performance demands associated with gender.
3) develop an emotionally safe therapeutic task designed to engage men around exploring gender socialization.
4) aid the group formation by encouraging initial group dialogue.

# Materials:

1) Butcher paper
2) Pen/ pencil/ or markers
3) Tape if rules will be displayed
4) A computer with Internet access to enable viewing of YouTube videos

# Time Allotment:

The activity can take as long as 45 minutes. The processing of the rules expressed by the members can occur after each group member's sharing. The facilitator should use the activity to help model how content will be processed in the group.

# Directions:

Step:

1) The group will be seated in chairs in a circle

2) The facilitator will introduce the task by providing some education regarding male gender socialization. The facilitator will discuss how socially constructed norms exist in the culture. An example of social construction gender expectation can be described or viewed via YouTube.

   a) The facilitator can highlight how the colors associated with infant clothing (pink colored clothing is "female" and blue colored clothing is "male") represents a socially constructed expectation.

   b) The group can view YouTube videos of gender role performance (various beer/alcohol advertisements which are replete with gendered expectations and cultural prescriptions).

3) Facilitators then invite group member to share what gender expectations they observe. Facilitators can ask participants what messages about:

   a) "How to be a man" did you see in the video?

   b) What "rules" about being a man do you see in our community?

   c) What "rules" about being a man do you follow?

4) Group member reflections are written on butcher paper.

5) As the "Guy Rules" are generated, by the group, a facilitator can write the rules on a piece of butcher paper. The "Guy Rules" can be placed on the walls of the consultation room as a reminder of the group's shared experience of gender socialization.

6) Facilitators affirm group members' reflections and help to illuminate common themes (restricted emotionality, intimacy, and affective expression).

    a) For example, facilitators can reflect common themes such as "men should not cry/display tears").

    b) Facilitators can use affirmations such as "I appreciate your observation" or "thank you for being willing to share your thoughts with the group." These affirmations are designed to reinforce group dialogue.

## Processing Questions:

1) What was reflecting on your experience of gender like for you?
2) What did you hear that surprised or challenged you?
3) Can you identify a feeling word or reaction in the wake of listing the "Guy Rules?"
4) Based on our discussion today did a topic or theme emerge that you would like the group to explore?

## Special Considerations:

This activity can often elicit some resistance amongst group members given the nature of the task and the early stage of the group. Facilitators should be mindful to affirm members who risk more vulnerable self-disclosures and provide praise and encouragement when appropriate (particularly when engaging adolescent and young adult men).

## Adaptations:

Since hegemonic masculinity informs so much of how many men perform and process in groups, this intervention is integral to all stages of men's counseling groups. For example, male group members can share their experience of navigating and challenging gender based norms throughout the group. However, if time constraints exist, the group can be given a list of "Guy Rules" to discuss and process. Group members can select the cultural norms most salient to their experience. This adaptation can also be effective with an adolescent age group who may be less conscious of gender roles. Additionally, the content of YouTube videos can be adapted if the activity is implemented with an adolescent population. Finally, this activity can have a psycho-educational strategy that targets greater awareness of cultural prescriptions and how such norms impact social behaviors and choices.

# References:

Englar-Carlson, M., & Stevens, M. (2006). *In the room with men: A casebook of therapeutic change.* Washington, D.C.: American Psychological Association.

Rabinowitz, F., & Cochran, S. (2002). *Deepening psychotherapy with men.* Washington, D.C.: American Psychological Association.

# Author Notes:

Chris Burden is a licensed Clinical Psychologist and has been Director of University of San Diego's Disability Services since 2012. Currently, Chris works in the field of Student Affairs and has an expertise in male student development. Chris has facilitated "Guy Talk," a weekly campus discussion group for men since 2009.

# Correspondence:

Questions and comments related to this activity may be directed to:

Christopher Burden, Psy.D.
Director, Disability Services
University of San Diego – Serra Hall 300
5998 Alcala Park
San Diego, CA 92110
cburden@sandiego.edu

# I Love You: Self-Healing from Within

*By Angela Colistra*

## Population:

Adolescents and Adults with Substance-Use Disorder

## Stages of Group:

Working Stage and can be repeated in the Termination Stage

## Type of Group:

Counseling/Therapy

## Rationale:

Learning self-love is one of the first steps to healing from within. This was acknowledged early on by Freud (1924), "A strong ego is protection against disease, but in the last resort we must begin to love in order that we may not fall ill, and we must fall ill if, in consequence of frustration, we cannot love" (p. 42). The domain of love is thought of as one of the most essential feelings of the human condition (Neto, 2003). Natterson (2003) stated that "as the actualization of love progresses during therapy so does actualization of self (p. 509). Therefore, it is important for group leaders to evaluate the meaning of love when working with group members, which requires appropriate measures, clinical methods, or both (Myers & Shurts, 2002). This group activity is a clinical method to assess the meaning of love from the group members' internal point of view. Whether a group member is dealing with trauma, depression, anxiety, or self-hatred, this exercise invite group discussions about what is getting in the way of self-love. Once group members can identify their feelings, thoughts, and behaviors that are roadblocks to self-love, they can begin to welcome love into their lives.

## Goals:

Participants will:
1) To identify and process self-love road blocks.
2) To raise awareness about personal responsibility in one's healing process.
3) To open the heart so group members can begin to love themselves by identifying thoughts, feelings, and actions that prevent self-love.

## Materials:

1) Tissues
2) Calm Space
3) A quote or passage focused on love

# Time Allotment:

Recommended Group: 60 minutes
Adapted Group: Two, 60 minute groups

# Directions:

Step:

1) Check in with the group. Read a quote or passage about love.

Group Leader: *"It is good to see each one of you in group today. I would like to start off with sharing this quote by Sam Keen: "You come to love not by finding the perfect person, but by seeing an imperfect person perfectly." I want you to think about the following question: How can you apply this quote to yourself and how you love yourself?"*

2) Inform the group members that the focus of the group is on self-love.

Group Leader: *"The focus of today's group will be on self-love."*

3) Ask permission from each group member to be open to this simple yet revealing exercise to begin their journey towards self-love. Request from group members who do not feel ready to embark on this journey that they observe and assist the other group members throughout their process. This will require that they remain quiet and act as an observer.

Group Leader: *"I ask that each of you be open to this exercise focused on self-love. If you do not feel ready for this journey, please observe the process and assist other members throughout their process. If you are acting as an observer I ask that you please remain quiet and respectful of other group members during the mindfulness exercise. Can everyone give permission to move forward with this exercise as a group?"*

4) Once permission is granted, inform group members that there will be a mindfulness exercise followed by group processing of the exercise. Please note the following: if a group member(s) decides he cannot move forward with the exercise and he cannot be an observer please excuse him from the group.

Group Leader: *"Now that we all agree to this experience lets continue. We will move forward with a mindfulness exercise followed by group process."*

5) Direct group members to sit comfortably. The group leader should model this position. Once grounded instruct group members to close their eyes and begin concentrating on their breath. At that moment the group leader can turn down the lights.

Group Leader: *"Please find a comfortable sitting position with your back straight on the chair, feet grounded on the floor, and hands rested on your legs with palms facing upwards towards the sky. I invite you to shut your eyes and begin concentrating on your breath as you take a deep inhale and exhale. Continue to focus on your breath and make each breath longer and deeper as you inhale and exhale. Feel your body relaxing with each breath."* (Group leader turns down lights or dims the room)

6) Once the group is relaxed and calm, the group leader instructs the members to begin silently repeating the simple mantra, "I Love You".  To begin, the group leader calmly repeats this mantra out loud by saying "I Love You" and then he or she can calmly inform the group to continue repeating this mantra to themselves or out loud for the next couple of minutes.

Group Leader: *"Now that we are feeling relaxed, I invite you to repeat this simple mantra "I Love You". Please continue to repeat this mantra out loud or to yourself for the next couple of minutes. I love you, I love you, I love you"*

7) After 3-5 minutes have passed. Inform group members to come back into their bodies by moving their fingers and toes and when ready to open their eyes.

Group Leader: *"I invite you to stop repeating the mantra and come back into your bodies. With your eyes still closed begin moving your toes and fingers. Take a few deep breaths and when you're ready please open your eyes and come back into the group."*

8) Once the group is focused on the group circle you can discuss the exercise using the following discussion questions:
    a. What internal dialogue was stimulated from the "I Love You" meditation?
    b. Do you love you? What would it take to begin loving yourself?
    c. How does your own self-love dictate the love you receive from others?

9) Process the activity with below processing questions.

## Processing Questions
1) What was the experience like for you personally?
2) What thoughts arose during the exercise?
3) What feelings arose during the exercise?
4) As a result of this group experience, what will you leave here with today?
5) How will participating in this group impact what you do differently today, this week, or this month?

## Special Considerations/Cautions

This group activity can be very healing and very emotional for most group members. It is not uncommon for group members to cry as a result of this experience and have difficulty processing these emotions in that initial group. Group leaders may consider allotting two group periods for this group process. Group members that have recently experienced trauma may have individual counseling needs following this group experience.

## Adaptations:

This group can be adapted as a 2 group series. Initially, the group leader could start with process questions 5 and 6. Once those questions are discussed the group leader can do the "I love you" exercise and process questions 1-4 with group members. Lastly, the group can revisit questions 5 and 6 and identify if new awareness's were made as a result of the "I Love You" exercise and discuss questions 7 and 8. This group can be adapted to work with other populations such as in patient or outpatient adults managing a mental health disorder or grief. It can also be utilized for inpatient or outpatient adults managing mental health disorders and who are from oppressed populations such as racial and ethnic diversity, sexual minorities, and/or low socioeconomic status.

## References:

Freud, S. (1924). On narcissism. In J. Rivier & J. Strachy (Eds.), *Collected papers of Sigmund Freud.* New York: International Psychoanalytic Press.

Myers, J., & Shurts, M. (2002). Measuring positive emotionality: A review of instruments assessing love. *Measurement and Evaluation in Counseling and Development, 34,* 238-254.

Natterson, J., M. (2003). Love in psychotherapy. *Psychoanalytic Psychology, 20(3),* 509 521. doi: 10.1037/0736-9735.20.3.509

Neto, F. (2005). The satisfaction with love life scale. *Measurement and Evaluation in Counseling and Development, 38,* 2-13.

## Author Notes

*Angela Colistra* is an Assistant Professor of Counselor Education and Counseling Coordinator at Webster University Greenville Metropolitan Campus. She has 13 years of group work experience and she has been providing professional trainings focused on the positive power of Group Therapy since 2009. She has group experience with adults managing substance use disorders and co-occurring disorders, developmental and cognitive delays, adolescent girls, and master's level counseling students.

## Correspondence:

Questions or comments related to this activity may be directed to:

Dr. Angela L. Colistra, Ph.D., LPC, LCAS, CCS
Webster University
Counseling Coordinator and Counselor Educator
124 Verdae Blvd. Suite 400, Greenville, SC 29607
angelacolistra04@webster.edu

# Major and Career Family Tree

*By Lindsey Fields & Delini Fernando*

## Population:

Undergraduate college students taking a first-year seminar or career exploration course

## Stage of Group:

Working

## Type of Group:

Task/Work or Psychoeducational

## Rationale:

Few college students have an opportunity to learn and explore the world of work (Brown & Lent, 2013). Additionally, few are aware of what their family members studied in college, what work and careers they chose, and what the reasons may have been for those choices. Some students find it difficult to decide on a major, or explore what kind of work they may want to do, or what career they want to follow after graduation as evidenced by the need for a designation of "undecided" or "exploring major" rather than a traditional declared major. A shared college context allows a safe place for these first-year students to engage in self and family career exploration and shared experience, while supporting each other's career and work aspirations, and work values.

## Goals:

Participants will:
1) explore the world of work
2) learn about their family's world of work through interviewing.
3) identify themes or trends of work and careers in their own family.
4) gain perspectives on work satisfaction and things to consider as they explore their own career desires.

## Materials:

1) A worksheet explaining the assignment (attached)
2) Pen or pencil OR computer (unless sharing out loud is enough for the group)

## Time allotment:

The time required will vary depending on how many people the student chose to interview and how long each interview session takes.

## Directions:

Step:

1) Ask participants to complete the Major and Career Family Tree Interview (attached) according to the given instructions.

2) After interviews are completed group will meet to discuss and process the activity.

## Processing Questions:

1) What similarities do you see between family members or any differences based on gender or age?
2) Are your family members in established careers or do you see their work as a job that pays the bills?
3) What are similarities in career fields? (ex. Service, hospitality, medical, education)
4) How did each family member's level of education or training contribute to the type of work the currently do?
5) What advice, if any, did family members give through this interview that you'd like to share with the group?
6) What barriers came up in the interview as reasons family could not change jobs or contribute to dissatisfaction with their jobs/careers?
7) What did you learn from any family members who are not working or experienced a gap in their work history? (retired or experienced job insecurity)
8) What new insights did participants gain about their family and the world of work as a result of the assignment?

## Special Considerations:

Consider the timeliness of introducing this activity and the distance some family may live from the group member and this homework activity may take more than a week to reach willing family members for participation.

## Adaptations:

This activity can be adapted for use in High Schools or Learning communities in Residence Halls where students live together sharing a common theme/major/interest. This can also be used in groups where participants are considering a career change.

## References/Credits:

Brown, S. D. (Ed.) and Lent, R. W. (Eds.) (2013). *Career development and counseling: Putting theory and research to work.* Hoboken, NJ: John Wiley & Sons, Inc.

The Academic Counselor team in the Office for Exploring Majors at the University of North Texas.

## Author Notes:

*Lindsey Fields* is an Academic Counselor at the University of North Texas. She has had six years of experience in teaching First-Year Seminar and Career Exploration coursework with undergraduate students. Her group work experience additionally includes training First-Year Seminar instructors and Peer Mentors on activities around group dynamics, personality and interest assessments, and college adjustment issues in social, academic, and emotional contexts; leads college student groups in residence halls.

*Delini Fernando* is an Associate Faculty member at the University of North Texas. She has group work experience with numerous populations, supervises group facilitators, teaches masters and doctoral level group counseling courses at University of North Texas; has specialized training and experience in group work and family counseling.

## Correspondence:

Questions and comments regarding this activity may be directed to:

Lindsey Fields, M.S. and M.Ed., LPC
Academic Counselor, University of North Texas
1155 Union Circle #311277
Denton, TX, 76203-5017
Lindsey.Fields@unt.edu

# Musical Timeline over the Lifespan

*By Lynn L. Brandsma & Gregory K.P. Smith*

## Population:

This activity is appropriate for adolescents or adults seeking treatment for various issues in an inpatient or residential setting or partial hospitalization program. This activity could also be used with the elderly in a nursing care facility.

## Stage of Group:

Transition

## Type of Group:

Counseling or Therapy

## Rationale:

The purpose of this group exercise is for group members to discuss significant events, and any related feelings, of their lives through memories of the music that was important to them during those specific times. Music can often be a less threatening way of sharing personal information with group members making it an ideal medium to use during the transition stage of a group. Music may often even transcend verbal communication in its ability to elicit emotion (Gfeller, 2005).

## Goals:

Participants will:
1) express thoughts and emotions through music and lyrics.
2) understand others' experiences on a level that is different than typical verbal communication.
3) understand the role music may have played in our own and others' lives.

## Materials:

1) Paper
2) Pencil
3) Ideally recordings and a listening device such as a computer or iPod would be helpful to play some of the songs for the group.

## Time Allotment:

90 minutes (approximately). The time frame could vary due to the size of the group. Ideal group size would be 8-10 participants.

## Directions:

Step:

1) The group leader asks each member to divide a piece of paper into either five (adolescents and young adults) or ten (middle age and older adults) year increments beginning at age 5, or younger if preferred.

2) The group leader asks each member to list 5-10 (this number can vary) songs under each five or ten year age group. The songs chosen should hold special or significant meaning.

3) Each member takes turns sharing their musical timeline and why/how the songs listed are significant.

4) Each group member picks one or two important songs to play for the group. The length of the song played will be determined by the number of participants. The fewer the participants, the more time can be allotted to play songs. If the group has a large number of participants, the leader should ask the member to share a sample of the song most important to him/her.

5) There should be sufficient time left at the end to compare and contrast the role music played in the lives of the members.

## Processing Questions:

1) Which of the developmental stages did you find the easiest to choose songs?
2) Which of the developmental stages did you find the most difficult to choose songs?
3) Do you associate certain music with pleasant memories?
4) Do you associate certain music with unpleasant memories?
5) What were the similarities and differences between music choices of the members?

## Special Considerations:

Music can be a very powerful medium for eliciting feelings and this may sometimes take people by surprise. The group leader should be aware that if strong feelings should arise for a member, he/she may need additional time after the group to allow for appropriate closure.

## Adaptations:

It is possible to adapt to a different purpose or population by eliminating the discussion of the significance of each musical piece and use the exercise as more of an ice breaker by just having members play snippets of favorite music for each other.

# References:

Gfeller, K.E. (2005). Music as communication in R.E. Unkefer & M.H. Thaut (Eds.), *Music therapy in the treatment of adults with mental disorders: Theoretical bases and clinical interventions.* Gilsum, NH: Barcelona Publishers.

# Author Notes:

*Lynn L. Brandsma* is an Associate Professor of Psychology at Chestnut Hill College. Dr. Brandsma has taught Group Process and Leadership at both the undergraduate and graduate levels for 18 years. She has extensive experience facilitating counseling and therapy groups for adolescents and adults with eating and weight related issues. She is also a Board Certified Music Therapist and has led numerous music therapy groups with various populations.

*Gregory K.P. Smith* is a Professor of Recreation, Health and Physical Education in Hospitality and Recreation Management Department at Cheyney University of Pennsylvania. Dr. Smith has extensive experience in facilitating task/work groups in his current role as advisor to the Muslim Student Association, as past advisor to numerous student clubs, and as President of the Faculty Union, APSCUF (Association of Pennsylvania State College & University Faculties) at Cheyney University of Pennsylvania from 2003-2007.

# Correspondence:

Questions and comments related to this activity may be directed to:

Lynn L. Brandsma, Ph.D., LPC, MT-BC
Chestnut Hill College
Department of Psychology
9601 Germantown Avenue
Philadelphia, PA 19118
brandsmal@chc.edu

## Major and Career Family Tree Interview Instructions

You are to interview family members to find out information related to their major and career development. Interviews must be conducted either in person, by phone, or via video chat not via email. Choose your closest family members, whoever these individuals may be. This might include your parents, grandparents, aunts and uncles, cousins, siblings, or even close family friends who were like family to you growing up. All families are different, so your tree may include *anyone you consider family*. You will however not want to include yourself or family members younger than yourself. Please include five individuals in your family tree. Make sure there is a balance between male and female family members. Please include the following information about your family members:

1. What was their major and/or academic background or training?
2. What is their job title, and what activities do they do on a regular day of work?
3. What do they like about their job? Or what do they wish they were doing more of?
4. What do they wish was different about their job? Or what do they wish to do less of?
5. How did they start doing this job/choose this job?
6. What other careers/jobs have they had in their life?
7. Why did they stop doing each of those?
8. Do they work multiple jobs? If so, why?
9. What makes a job *interesting to them*?
10. What about a job leads one to be *happy*?
11. What is a misconception that others may have about your job or profession?
12. How long do they intend to continue this particular job? Or continue in the same line or work?
13. If they could <u>not</u> do the profession/job they currently are doing, what would they choose to do instead?

*Be thorough* in gathering information and get lots of information, as one or two word answers and/or short sentence answers will make it more difficult for you to discuss trends in your family and the careers you are hearing about. Do not feel limited to only the questions on this page, I encourage you to ask what questions come to your mind during the interview. Answer all questions for all members – one page per family member.

# Navigating the Sojourn: A Group Activity for International Students

*By Natalya Lindo & Delini Fernando*

## Population:
International students enrolled in a college or university in their host countries

## Stage of Group:
Orientation

## Type of Group:
Counseling

## Rationale:

Few international students have the opportunity to process the experience of leaving their home country and studying abroad (Chavajay, 2013). In their host country, these students face many challenges related to prejudice, language barriers, and low social self-efficacy (Chapdelaine & Alexitch, 2004; Rienties, Beausaert, Grohnert, Niemantsverdriet & Kommers, 2012). They share a common experience as a result of leaving their home country. This shared experience allows for the safety to engage in self exploration and mutual support without the added pressure of having to explain their culture, traditions, values, and beliefs.

## Goals:

Participants will:
1) discuss common experiences related to leaving their home country and learning to acclimate to their host country.
2) increase in their awareness of other international students' experiences thereby reducing some of the isolation they may feel while dealing with acculturative stress.

## Materials:

1) Blank 4" by 6" cards/white paper
2) Markers
3) Double sided tape
4) Sketch/white paper (large sheets)
5) Small white board

## Time Allotment:

Allow for 30 to 45 minutes. If there are more than 6-8 group members, allow for 50 minutes to 1 hour.

## Directions:

Step

1) Place two large sheets of paper on opposing room walls

2) Label one sheet 'Challenges' or 'Fears' and label the other sheet 'Hopes,' 'Dreams' or 'Desires.' (You also may choose a combination of these labels).

3) Using the 4" by 6" cards, ask participants to write words or phrases that describe their concerns related to a) leaving their home country, and b) adapting to their host country (one word/phrase per card). Some examples might be "leaving family behind" or "language barriers."

4) Encourage participants to write as many words/phrases as possible.

5) Ask participants to tape their completed cards to the large sheet labeled 'Challenges/Fears.'

6) Ask participants to take a few moments to look at all the words/phrases generated by the group.

7) Ask participants to identify concerns or struggles that appear to be common among group members. List these on the white board.

8) Repeat **steps 3 to 7**, instead asking participants to note their hopes and desires related to a) leaving their home country, and b) adapting to their host country. Some examples might be "a new adventure" or "education."

9) Follow up with process questions and a reminder that participants are not alone in their journey.

10) End with a motivational poem or saying

## Processing Questions:

1) Would anyone like to share what this experience was like?
2) OR What were your initial reactions to the activity?
3) What was it like to identify challenges or fears related to leaving home and adapting to a new country?
4) What was it like to identify hopes or desires related to leaving home and adapting to a new country?
5) Were you surprised that others had the same kinds of experiences?
6) How does it feel to know that you share these experiences with others in this group?
7) What (if anything) did you learn about yourselves as a result of the activity?
8) What did you learn from (or about) each other?
9) How will you use what you have learned here today in your life outside of this group?

## Adaptations:

This activity can be adapted for use with immigrant populations (middle school age to adult). Immigrant populations face similar challenges to international students in terms of acculturative stress, prejudice, language barriers, homesickness etc.

## References:

Chapdelaine, R. F., & Alexitch, L. R. (2004). Social skills difficulty: Model of culture shock for international graduate students. *Journal of College Student Development, 45,* 167-184.

Chavajay, P. (2013). Perceived social support among international students at a U.S. university. *Psychological Reports: Sociocultural Issues in Psychology, 112*(2), 667-677.

Rienties, B., Beausaert, S., Grohnert, T, Niemantsverdriet, S., & Kommers, P. (2012). Understanding academic performance of international students: The role of ethnicity, academic and social integration. *Higher Education, 63*(6), 685-700.

## Author Notes:

*Natalya A. Lindo* is an Assistant Professor of counseling at the University of North Texas. She has ten years of group work experience including training counselors to work with parents, children and families in a group setting.

*Delini Fernando* is an Associate Professor of counseling at the University of North Texas. She has eighteen years of group work experience including family counseling. She regularly teaches the group counseling course at UNT.

## Correspondence:

Questions and comments related to this activity may be directed to:
Natalya A. Lindo, PhD
University of North Texas
1155 Union Circle #310829,
Denton, TX, 76203-5017
Natalya.Lindo@unt.edu

# Perfect Day in a Dream Job

*By Lindsey Fields & Delini Fernando*

## Population:

Undergraduate College students taking a first-year seminar or career exploration course

## Stage of Group:

Working

## Type of Group:

Task

## Rationale:

A well-informed work or career choice decision needs to take into consideration one's values regarding work (Sinetar, 1995). Few college students have opportunities to think about what is important to them when joining the world of work or choosing and following a career as evidenced by author's experience in working with undergraduate college students. Although some may have knowledge of their parents' or family work values, they may have difficulty in identifying their own values. A checklist of work and/or career values could help them consider what they hope to become rather than a direct assessment of who they are currently. A guided visualization activity and subsequent journaling allows students to project the perfect day without influence of a pre-determined list of imposed values. Working through a detailed written journal to identify the values that were expressed through the visualization activity, followed by a rationale for each value can heighten the students' awareness of their top values as they visualize the perfect day.

## Goals:

Participants will:
1) learn ways to identify work-related values through journaling.
2) gain self-awareness through an opportunity to dream big and imagine the perfect day.
3) identify themes and values.

## Materials:

1) The attached worksheet
2) Pens or pencils

# Time Allotment:

This activity should take 20 - 30 minutes to complete the visualization exercise and the values checklist. Processing will take longer depending on the size of the group and their willingness to elaborate and share.

# Directions:

Step:

1) Prior to passing out the worksheet, begin by having group members close their eyes and imagine the perfect day. Walk them through a visualization exercise using this prompt:

   *"Close your eyes and imagine the perfect day. As you wake up to start your day, what time is it? Where do you wake up and who is around you? What do you wear as you are getting ready for work? Who do you say goodbye to as you depart for work? How do you travel to work and what stops, if any, do you make along the way? When you arrive at work, who greets you? Throughout your day what do you do that provides you a sense of accomplishment? Are your tasks the same each day or do they vary by the day or by the hour? What time did you arrive at work and leave from work? Who do you interact with while you are at work? Do you work alone or with a group of people? What does your work space look like? As you go home at the end of the day, where are you traveling to? How long is your commute to where you live? What do you do when you arrive at your home? How do you know it has been the perfect day?"*

2) Have group members take a few minutes to journal the details of their visualization activity. Group leaders may want to record the visualization prompts on a marker board or at the top of a journaling worksheet.

3) Request that members make observations about the values that they see within their perfect day using the values checklist.

4) Have members check off what they value as they read back through their visualization journal.

# Processing Questions:

1) Would anyone like to share what this experience was like? OR What were your initial reactions to the activity?
2) What was it like to identify your values related to your ideal work day?
3) Were you surprised by the values you identified as being common to multiple members of the group?
4) When you reviewed the list of values provided to you, what values were you surprised you did not express as an important part of your perfect day?
5) What values do you have that were not expressed on the checklist you were provided?
6) How does it feel to know that you share these experiences with others in this group?

## Special Considerations:

The writing abilities may vary based on education and experience. The questions in the visualization activity may need to be adapted based on group member's educational background or previous work environments and/or experiences. The writing and reading portions of this activity will vary by time based on each participant's level of education and abilities.

## Adaptations:

This activity can be adapted for use with high school students and adapted for adults going through a career transition of changing jobs or career fields, or entering retirement. The processing questions may need to be adapted to suit the particular target group.

## Reference:

Sinetar, M. (1995). *To build the life you want, create the work you love: The spiritual dimension of entrepreneuring.* St. Martin's Press: New York, NY.

## Author Notes:

*Lindsey Fields* is an Academic Counselor at the University of North Texas. She has had six years of experience in teaching First-Year Seminar and Career Exploration coursework with undergraduate students. Her group work experience additionally includes training First-Year Seminar instructors and Peer Mentors on activities around group dynamics, personality and interest assessments, and college adjustment issues in social, academic, and emotional contexts; leads college student groups in residence halls.

*Delini Fernando* is an Associate Faculty member at the University of North Texas. She has group work experience with numerous populations, supervises group facilitators, teaches masters and doctoral level group counseling courses at University of North Texas; has specialized training and experience in group work and family counseling.

## Correspondence:

Questions and comments related to this activity may be directed to:

Lindsey Fields, M.S. and M.Ed., LPC
Academic Counselor, University of North Texas
1155 Union Circle #311277
Denton, TX, 76203-5017
Lindsey.Fields@unt.edu

# Values Checklist

____ **Help Society:** Do something to contribute to the betterment of the world I live in.

____ **Help Others:** Be involved in helping people in a direct way, either individually or in small groups.

____ **Public Contact:** Have a lot of day-to-day contact with people.

____ **Work with Others:** Have close working relationships with a group; work as a team toward common goals.

____ **Affiliation:** Be recognized as a member of a particular organization.

____ **Friendships:** Develop close personal relationships with people as a result of my work activities.

____ **Competition:** Engage in activities which pit my abilities against others where there are clear win-and-lose outcomes.

____ **Make Decisions:** Have the power to decide courses of action, policies, etc.

____ **Work Under Pressure:** Work in situations where time pressure is prevalent and/or the quality of my work is judged critically by supervisors, customers, or others.

____ **Power and Authority:** Control the work activities or (partially) the destinies of other people.

____ **Influence People:** Be in a position to change attitudes or opinions of other people.

____ **Work Alone:** Do projects by myself, without any significant amount of contact with others.

____ **Knowledge:** Engage myself in the pursuit of knowledge, truth, and understanding.

____ **Artistic Creativity:** Engage in creative work in any of several art forms.

____ **Creativity (General):** Create new ideas, programs, organizational structures or anything else not following a format previously developed by others.

____ **Aesthetics:** Be involved in studying or appreciating the beauty of things, ideas, etc.

____ **Supervision:** Have a job in which I am directly responsible for the work done by others.

____ **Change and Variety:** Have work responsibilities which frequently change in their content and setting.

____ **Precision Work:** Work in situations where there is very little tolerance for error.

____ **Stability:** Have a work routine and job duties that are largely predictable and not likely to change over a long period of time.

____ **Security:** Be assured of keeping my job and a reasonable financial reward.

____ **Fast Pace:** Work in circumstances where there is a high pace of activity, work must be done rapidly.

____ **Recognition:** Be recognized for the quality of my work in some visible or public way.

____ **Excitement:** Experience a high degree of (or frequent) excitement in the course of my work.

____ **Adventure:** Have work duties which involve frequent risk taking.

____ **Profit, Gain:** Have a strong likelihood of accumulating large amounts of money or other material gain.

____ **Independence:** Be able to determine the nature of my work without significant direction from others; not have to do what others tell me to do.

____ **Moral Fulfillment:** Feel that my work is contributing significantly to a set of moral standards which I feel are very important.

____ **Location:** Find a place to live (town, geographic area) which is conducive to my life style and affords me the opportunity to do the things I enjoy most.

____ **Community:** Live in a town or city where I can get involved in community affairs.

____ **Physical Challenge:** Have a job that makes physical demands which I would find rewarding.

____ <u>**Time Freedom:**</u> Have work responsibilities which I can work at according to my own time schedule; not having     specific working hours.

____ <u>**Intellectual Status:**</u> Be regarded as a person of high intellectual prowess or as one who is an acknowledged  "expert" in a given field.

____ <u>**Family Friendly:**</u> Work with others who value my desire for a flexible work schedule to allow me to spend time with my family.

____ <u>**Professional Development:**</u> Be provided opportunities to travel and attend conferences and events related to my work.

____ <u>**Education:**</u> Work where my education is valued and my work is directly related to the degree I intend to pursue

# Rock Ice Breaker

*By Katrina Cook & Jackie Redding*

## Population:
Older Adolescents/Adults

## Stage of Group:
Orientation

## Type of Group:
Counseling

## Rationale:

Ed Jacobs (1980), known for promoting the use of props in counseling sessions, describes a mutual sharing process in which participants share their thoughts, experiences, fears and hopes during the initial sessions of a group counseling process. The rock ice breaker activity provides an opportunity to use a prop to facilitate a mutual sharing process among group members. Group members may introduce themselves to each other while also reflecting on how they perceive themselves. By comparing themselves to the selected item, they can choose what they would like the other group members to know about them beyond the surface introductions. To hasten the processing, the counselor can share an initial story. For example: *"I have seen some people choose this rock that is heart shaped because it may remind them of something that hurt their heart. Also, this rock has a crack in the center. Some people have shared that divorce or loss can make them feel like they have a crack on their heart."*

## Goals:

Participants will:
1) introduce themselves to each other genuinely.
2) begin a reflective process of discovering how they view themselves.
3) begin a mutual sharing process.

## Materials:

1) A collection of small items such as rocks, sea shells, sea glass, and other trinkets. Each of the items needs to vary from the others in terms of color, texture, size, and shape. Have more items available than there are group participants so every group member has a choice when making a selection.
2) A bowl or container for these items that allows the participants to view the collection of objects they are choosing.

## Time Allotment:

In general, this activity usually takes 30-45 minutes. Although this is intended as an initial ice breaker activity, and not necessarily the entire group session, depending on the size of the group and the extent of the following discussion, be prepared to use an entire group session to process the activity if needed.

## Directions:

Step:

1) Introduce the activity by saying *"As we begin our group together, we are going to take some time and do an activity that will help us get to know each other better."*

2) Pass the bowl containing all the objects in it around the group and ask each group member to select one of the items. At this time, do not give the members any other instructions so that they don't consciously select items, but rather spontaneously select an item that appeals to them at the moment.

3) After everyone has selected an item, ask each of the group members to answer the following questions.
   - What drew you to this particular item?
   - How are you like the item you selected?
   - What about the item reminds you of a particular challenge you have faced?

## Processing Questions:

1) What was this activity like for you?
2) What was it like for you to share something about yourself with the rest of the group?
3) What are some things you learned about other group members that you did not know before?

## Special Considerations:

1) Group members who might not be ready to share this kind-of personal information this early in the group process have the option to pass.
2) For group members that prefer expressing themselves through writing, allow the option of writing their responses in journals and then give them the option of deciding whether or not to share what they have written with the rest of the group.

# Adaptations:

1) Depending on the group dynamics, the group leader might decide to use this activity later in the group process after some cohesiveness has been developed.
2) This activity can also be used with counseling practicum students to help facilitate self-reflection on their professional identity development.
3) This activity can be used with young children, however they may have difficulty with the abstract nature of comparing themselves to a rock. Instead, use toy animal figures and have them describe how they are like the particular animal they selected. Avoid providing items that represent well-known figures such as superheroes and Disney princesses, as this may inhibit the child's ability to realistically compare him or herself to the selected item.
4) It would also be appropriate to use with members dealing with issues related to self-esteem.

# References:

This is an original group activity from Jackie Redding in Northside Independent School District in San Antonio, Texas.

Craig, G. J., & Dunn, W. L. (2010). *Understanding human development* (2nd ed.). Saddle River, NJ: Pearson Education.

Masson, R. L., & Jacobs, E. (1980). Group leadership: Practical points for beginners. *Personnel and Guidance Journal, 62*(5), p. 52-55.

# Author Notes:

*Katrina Cook* is an Assistant Professor of Counselor Education at Texas A&M University – San Antonio. She has had twenty-nine years of group work experience, including facilitating groups with children and adolescents.

*Jackie Redding* is a Safe School Initiatives Program Prevention Counselor at Northside Independent School District. She has 20 years of group work experience with elementary, middle, and high school level students.

# Correspondence:

Questions and comments related to this activity may be directed to:

Katrina Cook Ph.D., LPC-S, LMFT-S, CSC
Texas A&M University – San Antonio
Assistant Professor
One University Way
San Antonio, Texas, 78224
Katrina.cook@tamusa.tamus.edu

# The News Is About YOU!

*By Jacqueline S. Hodes*

## Populations:

This activity would be appropriate for college students entering a paraprofessional role. Students training to be orientation leaders, resident assistants, peer educators, peer mentors, etc. would benefit from this activity. Graduate students studying higher education counseling or higher education/student affairs administration would benefit from this exercise as well. This activity would also be appropriate for other populations such as a people changing careers, moving into retirement, and changing life roles.

## Stage of Group:

Orientation

## Type of Group:

Task or Psychoeducational

## Rationale:

College students often take on new roles as helpers or paraprofessionals on their campuses. Many of the paraprofessional roles are ones that interface with traditional age first year students. This activity will assist these new student leaders in remembering their own transition from high school to college and becoming aware of what students really worry about during that critical first semester (Shanley & Johnston, 2008). This same activity can be used with graduate students who plan to have careers in higher education. Reflecting on their own growth can be the first step in understanding the students they will serve.

## Goals:

Participants will:
1)  understand their own growth from high school to college <u>or</u> from college to graduate school.
2)  increase their ability to empathize with traditional first year college students.
3)  appreciate how the college experience contributes to the growth and development of students.

## Materials:

1)  Newsprint or construction paper
2)  Markers
3)  Masking Tape (if you choose to display the final product)

# Time:

Depending on the number of participants, approximately 30-45 minutes.

# Directions:

Step:

1) Give each group member a piece of newsprint and a few markers.
2) Ask each member to reflect on their first year of college.
   - What did they learn about themselves in that year?
   - What experiences did they have that they might not have imagined?
   - How do they think they have changed in the year?
3) Have each member create a headline that would appear in their hometown newspaper for a story written about them and their first year in college. It is helpful for the group leader to provide examples, which might include:
   - *Small town boy makes good*
   - *Shy girl becomes a student leader*
   - *Student athlete excels academically*
   - *It is helpful to the group if the facilitator gives examples*
4) Instruct the members to write on the newsprint the name of the paper and the headline.
5) When everyone is done, ask each member to share their headline and the story behind the headline.
6) The group should be prepared to ask follow up questions of each member so that the story is clear and understandable to the rest of the group.

# Processing Questions:

1) What did you learn about your own growth in the first year of college?
2) What did you learn about other students' growth and experiences in the first year of college?
3) As you reflect on your experiences and growth, what messages might be important to communicate to new students as they transition to college?
4) How might you communicate those messages?
5) What would you like your headline to read next year at this time?

# Special Considerations/Cautions:

One assumes that if a student is moving on to a paraprofessional leadership role that they had a good experience during their first year. There may be some students who struggled during their first year and reflecting back on the year might be difficult. Students may get in touch with a difficult high school experience as they reflect on where they began their journey. Students often have trouble remembering their hometown newspaper. They can make up a name or use a more recognized national publication.

## Adaptations:

1) This exercise can be used effectively with graduate students. Have the graduate students reflect on their college experience and ask them to use their college newspaper name.

2) This exercise can be used effectively with people who are transitioning careers, moving into retirement, and changing life roles. Have the participant reflect on their current role and what a newspaper headline might read about their experience and transition.

3) This exercise can also be used with high school students in a similar manner as graduate students. Have the high school students reflect on their high school experience and ask them to use their high school newspaper or yearbook name.

4) Instead of using newsprint, the facilitator can use a template of a newspaper on an 8.5 X 11 paper.

5) This technique of reflecting on one's story of growth and development can be used with other topical and more specific issues such as: What would the newspaper say about your understanding of diversity since coming to college?

## References/Credits:

Shanley, M.K. and Johnston, J. (2008). Eight things first-year students fear about college. *Journal of College Admissions, 201,* 3-7.

I participated in a similar activity as a part of *Project Flourish* training in 1987. The training was facilitated by Dr. Vivian Nix-Early. The training was designed for faculty and staff who were teaching the now defunct *University 101* (first year student seminar). I adapted the exercise and used it in many different venues with many adaptations to fit the audience.

## Author Section:

*Jacqueline S. Hodes* spent twenty-six years as a Student Affairs administrator, working in a variety of areas such as Wellness Education, LGBTQA Services, Orientation and New Student Programs, Judicial Affairs, Assessment of Student Learning, Fundraising and Development, Paraprofessional Training and Development. Over those years she designed and implemented countless group trainings and psychoeducational groups. Currently, she is a full-time, tenure-track professor in the Department of Counselor Education.

## Correspondence:

Questions and comments regarding this activity should be directed to:

Jacqueline S. Hodes, Ed.D.
Higher Education Coordinator
Department of Counselor Education
West Chester University
1160 McDermott Drive, Suite 102
West Chester, PA 19383
jhodes@wcupa.edu

# The Safe Zone

*By Rochelle Ritzi*

## Population:

Older Adolescents/Adults

The Safe Zone can be used to help group members who have difficultly setting or identifying healthy boundaries. This activity is most effective when used with teens or older. Although younger children can participate in this activity, a firm understanding of what it means to feel safe (emotionally and physically) would be most effective. Read adaptation section for other possible modifications.

## Stage of Group:

Working

## Type of Group:

Counseling and therapy

## Rationale:

Learning what feels safe is an important goal for group members to protect and take care of themselves (Corey, 2012). Every group member, depending on age, gender, personality, family of origin, and other outside influences, has different safety needs. What feels safe to a 20-year-old male who was raised in an environment with two supportive parents is most likely different than what feels safe to an 8-year-old female with a history of sexual abuse who lived in foster care. Recognizing, understanding, and articulating safety needs are important first steps for individuals to build self-confidence and feel in control of their lives (Sommers-Flanagan, 2007). Not only is it important for group members to understand their own safety needs, understanding that others may have different safety needs and learning to respect those needs can foster compassion, empathy, communication, and other skills needed to accept others and feel accepted in a social or family setting (Corey, 2012).

## Goals:

Participants will:
1) understand and increase self-acceptance through communicating personal safety needs.
2) gain empathy and understand the safety needs others.

## Materials:

1) One to three packs of white index cards, depending on # of group members.
2) Boxes of markers.

204

## Time Allotment:

20 to 30 minutes. Allow more time for larger groups.

## Directions:

This activity is most effective when given the least amount of instruction.
Step:

1) Place a stack of cards near each group member and instruct them to write their name on one card and place it in front of them.

2) Tell them to use the other cards to *"surround themselves with a safe environment."* They can use as few or as many cards as necessary to create their environment.

3) If members ask for specific instructions, the leader can share that *"some people use pictures, names or other words, colors, symbols, etc."* Be careful not to lead them in any other way because how they intuitively create their safe environment will be important insight to understanding the group members.

4) Be aware of any excitement or anxiety that arises within the individuals throughout the activity and note which of their cards led to those emotions.

5) Discuss these observations when processing through the activity.

## Processing Questions:

1) What feelings do you have as you look at the environment you created?
2) What do you find more safety in (people, places, or things)?
3) Discuss differences in how other people perceive safety. (Groups members can look at the other cards.)
4) Now that you have had a chance to explore your safe environment, discuss any surprises.
5) What changes, if any, would you like to make? Instruct them to use any new insights learned to modify their environment at this time.

## Special Considerations:

Depending on the type of group (such as sexual abuse or trauma), some members may have difficulty creating their safe zone and additional and/or educational support could be provided or referred.

## Adaptations:

The Safe Zone is a wonderful tool to empower group members to protect and take care of themselves. Members, especially those who have experienced a traumatic event such as a major storm or abuse, can explore and practice implementing what they need to say and do to feel safe. The Safe Zone can be used to assess family dynamics as well. Each family member may have different safety needs; therefore, the acceptance, rejection, or minimization of others' needs may prove valuable insight. This activity can be used in the beginning stages of counseling to identify where group members are mentally and emotionally. Strategies can then be made to help members feel more in control of their lives. The Safe Zone can also be used throughout the counseling process and in the terminating phase to review safety needs and strategies learned in therapy. If group members use drawings on their cards, their drawings can also be used to gain insight. For example, a member might draw his or her family but leave out a sibling. This omission could be explored further.

This activity can be modified to help individuals, groups, or families identify, understand, and communicate appropriate boundaries. Similar to understanding and articulating safety needs, having boundaries is another way for individuals to protect and take care of themselves. It is important for individuals to be able to explain to others when they are treating them inappropriately. Before individuals can articulate their boundaries, they need to know that they have a right to protect and defend themselves. The same procedures can be followed, except appropriate boundaries can be written on the cards instead of safety needs. There will probably be some overlap between safety needs and boundaries.

## References:

Corey, G. (2012). *Theory and practice of group counseling* (8th ed.). Belmont, CA: Brooks/Cole.

Sommers-Flanagan, J. (2007). The development and evolution of person-centered expressive art therapy: A conversation with Natalie Rogers. *Journal of Counseling & Development, 85,* 120-125.

## Author Notes:

*Rochelle Ritzi* is a third year Doctoral Student in the Counseling Program at the University of North Texas and a licensed Professional Counselor and registered Play Therapist at Therapy on the Square, a private practice. She has had six years of group work experience, including designing and facilitating groups for children and adults in private practice, domestic violence shelters, grief support group, and in school settings.

## Correspondence:

Questions and comments related to this activity may be directed to:

Rochelle Ritzi, MS, LPC, RPT
University of North Texas
Therapy on the Square
114 E. Louisiana St., Suite 201
McKinney, TX 75070
Rochelle@tots.pro

# View From My Window

*By Kimberly N. Frazier*

## Population:
Adolescents, College Students or Adults

## Stage of Group:
Orientation

## Type of Group:
Psychoeducational/Task

## Rationale:
Group members must be reminded of the agreed upon group rules. The group leader(s) must also remind the group members to be respectful of what is being shared and the leader(s). It is imperative that group members and counselors are aware of the individual differences that each person brings to the counseling experience (Lee, 2013). This exercise is designed to allow group members to become aware of individual differences among group members. Group members can gain a better perspective of what has shaped each of the member's worldview while gaining insight into how that might impact the group process. This also ensures that the group will be cognizant of these individual differences when moving through each of the stages of the group and while analyzing the various aspects of the group process.

## Goals:
Participants will:
1) Gain insight into the worldview each of the members bring to the group process
2) Gain insight into how individual differences can impact the subsequent stages of the group process

## Materials:
1) Sheets of colored paper for each group member
2) Colored pencils or markers (remember to have size appropriate for young children if applicable)

## Time Allotment:
10-15 minutes (depending on group size)

## Directions:

Step

1) Have each group member select a sheet of colored paper and a colored pencil and fold the colored sheet of paper into four sections.

2) Members should write a response to the following prompts in the sections:

> Section 1) Write one tradition that they continue that they learned from a family member.

> Section 2) Write special talent that they have.

> Section 3) Write two things they hope to gain from this group as individuals.

> Section 4) Write one thing they hope to accomplish together as a group.

3) After each member has completed answering each of the questions/sections, the group leader should ask each member to share and discuss their answers with the group.

4) After each member has had an opportunity to share, the group leader should ask the group members to discuss similarities and differences among the answers of the group members.

5) After discussing the similarities and differences as a group, process the activity with group members using the following questions.

## Processing Questions:

1) What is one thing that you learned about one group member through this exercise?
2) What is one thing that you learned about yourself through this exercise?
3) What similarities among group members did you notice that might impact the group?
4) What differences among group members did you notice that might impact the group?
5) What is one specific way in which similarities and differences in the group might help you accomplish your individual goals?

## Special Considerations:

I have been using this exercise in my classes for over 10 years to help set the tone of what each member of the class would like to get out of the course and what they hope to learn about themselves. I also use this as a tool for each class member to learn something about each person in the class. I also use this activity with psychoeducational groups to help group members get a better idea who they are working with in the group as well as to set the tone for the working group and to remind members to respect each other and to allow them to be cognizant that everyone brings something to the process and each thing is impacted by the worldview of each of the members.

## Adaptations:

When using this activity for children: Have each child select a sheet of colored paper and a colored pencil/marker. Be sure that the colored pencil or markers are size appropriate for the children that will be in the group. Using the colored pencil/markers have each child trace one of their hands on the colored sheet of paper they selected. In the traced fingers have each child write the answers to the following questions:

1) favorite TV show
2) Number of siblings you have
3) one activity that you do with a person in your family
4) your favorite holiday
5) one thing you hope to learn in the group.

## References:

Lee, C. C. (Eds.). (2013). *Multicultural issues in counseling: New approaches to diversity*. American Counseling Association: Alexandria, VA.

## Author Notes:

*Kimberly Frazier* is a Professor in the department Counseling and Educational Psychology at Texas A&M University-Corpus Christi. She holds licensure as a licensed Professional Counselor (LPC), licensed Marriage and Family Therapist (LMFT); and is certified as a Nationally Certified Counselor (NCC). Dr. Frazier research interests include using cultured centered counseling with pediatric populations and families, the use of culturally based counseling strategies with children and families experiencing trauma and crisis.

## Correspondence:

Questions and comments related to this activity may be directed to:

Kimberly N. Frazier, Ph.D., LPC, LMFT, NCC
Texas A&M University-Corpus Christi
Counseling and Educational Psychology
College of Education, ECDC 148
6300 Ocean Drive, Unit 5834
Corpus Christi, TX 78412
Email: kimberly.frazier@tamucc.edu

# Who am I? Diversity Exploration for Student Leaders

*By Matthew R. Shupp & Jayleen Galarza*

## Population:

The population most appropriate for this activity would be undergraduate students engaged in some type of leadership role on campus. This includes, but is not limited to, Student Government Executive Boards, Student Activity Steering Committees, Club Executive Board Members, Orientation Leaders, Campus Tour Guides, and Resident Assistants.

## Stage of Group:

Working

## Type of Group:

Task/Work: While the spirit of this activity is geared toward a Task/Work group, it is Psychoeducational in theory due to the topics discussed.

## Rationale:

As the student population at institutions of higher education become more and more diverse, it is important for students, particularly student leaders, to explore important issues around the topic of diversity. This includes gaining greater empathy for others' worldview as well as establishing a strong sense of self. Using Baxter Magolda's (2008) Theory of Self-Authorship (specifically *Phase 3: Becoming the Author of One's Life*) and Barrera and Corso's (2003) Model of Skilled Dialogue in Responding to Cultural Diversity as a framework, this exercise prompts students to ponder the questions *Who am I?* and *How do I know?*.

Baxter Magolda (2002b) emphasized the need for students and educators to work collaboratively to develop student self-authorship, which Baxter Magolda (2008) defined as "the internal capacity to define one's beliefs, identity, and social relations" (p. 269). Barrera and Corso's model presents the idea that skilled dialogue is needed in developing cultural competency. Skilled dialog has 3 key components: respect, reciprocity, and responsiveness. In order to fully integrate and "sustain" these components, individuals need two essential skill sets: anchored understanding of diversity and third space. Anchored understanding of diversity is a skill that "generates compassionate knowledge that evolves from active and intentional, face-to-face engagement with those from whom one differs" (Cooper & Lesser, 2011, p. 79). Third space is defined as "When people anchor their understanding of differences, both experientially and cognitively, they move from an 'either-or' frame to a mindset that is able to hold two different perspectives simultaneously" (Cooper & Lesser, 2011, p. 80). Utilizing intensive self-reflection, this group activity allows students the opportunity to gain self-authorship and cultural competence while "demonstrating respect for each other and actively sharing ideas and viewpoints" (Evans et al., 2010, p. 191).

## Goals:

Participants will:
1) engage in self-disclosure around personal experiences with diverse identities.
2) experience a safe space to dialogue around the topic of diversity.
3) develop a stronger sense of self while gaining cultural competence.

## Materials:

1) List of group norms (to be displayed in room for reference)
2) Large sheets of newsprint (white)
3) Scotch tape
4) Markers
5) Wall space to tape newsprint onto

## Time Allotment:

90 minutes; however, for an exceptionally large group, an additional 30 minutes may be needed for processing purposes.

## Directions:

Step:
1) Before the group activity, create headings on separate sheets of newsprint that represent diverse groups/identities within the United States. These headings can include the following: lesbian, gay, bisexual, transgender (LGBT), African Americans, Latina(o) Americans, Asian Americans, Indigenous Cultures (Native American, others), Irish Americans, Italian Americans, German Americans, Multicultural or Biracial, individuals with physical disabilities, Military veterans, and individuals with mental health problems.

2) Before participants arrive, place the newsprint sheets around the room.

3) Once participants have arrived, review group norms.

4) Then, explain the goals of the activity: to encourage self-disclosure around personal experiences with diverse identities; provide a safe space for students to dialogue around the topic of diversity; and allow students the opportunity to develop a stronger sense of self while gaining cultural competence. (Time: 5 mins)

5) Explain to students that in order to fully tackle the topic of diversity, it is essential that they explore their own cultural assumptions and worldviews. Therefore, they are going to be encouraged to share their personal experiences of diverse cultures/identities with others. They will be asked to listen to the experiences of other students and share any reactions they may have. (Time: 5 mins)

6) Following the introduction to the activity, draw participants' attention to the newsprint sheets around the room.

7) Read aloud the identities/groups represented on each sheet.

8) Ask students to walk over to the sheet that reflects an aspect of their own identity/experience. Invite students to create additional identities/groups not listed that better reflect their experience.

9) After students have clustered around the newsprint of their choice, ask them to talk as a group about what that particular identity means to them. They can remain in the room or find a space outside of the room that may be more comfortable. Ask students to write down the various meanings of the identities on their sheet(s). Encourage students to reflect on and provide concrete examples related to their experiences. These can include strengths and challenges. Allow students 20 minutes to engage in small group dialogue. Be sure to monitor small groups in order to answer any individual questions they may have. (Time: 20 mins)

10) After 20 minutes, ask small groups to return to the main room and convene as a large group. Ask students to sit with their small group.

11) Ask each group to stand up, introduce themselves and their identity/group, and share key points from their discussion.

12) Following each small group presentation, ask students in the larger group to share any reflections they may have. Allow time for each small group to respond to questions, comments, or general reactions. (Time: 30 mins)

13) Once all the small groups have presented and shared their personal experiences of diversity, process the experience as large group. Emphasize that cultural competency is a lifelong process that requires individuals to continuously reflect on their personal assumptions, beliefs, and biases about culture and diverse experiences. (Time: 30 mins)

## Processing Questions:
1) What was your overall experience with sharing your personal experiences of diversity?
2) Through this experience, what personal assumptions, beliefs, or biases did you notice?
3) How will you address these cultural blind spots in the future?
4) What is something new that you learned about your understanding of who you are?
5) How can you utilize this experience in your work as student leaders?

## Special Considerations:

Drawing from the literature on developing safe space in classroom environments (Holly & Steiner, 2005), it is essential for group facilitators focusing on sensitive topics to develop an environment in which students feel comfortable sharing ideas and engaging in meaningful discussions and/or disagreements. The ultimate goal of developing safe space is encouraging mutual respect. Therefore, due to the nature of the topic(s) discussed and the amount of self-disclosure shared, it is important to spend a considerable amount of time setting up shared norms that must be abided by throughout the duration of the activity. These can include: honesty, respect for differing points of view, respectfully challenging others' blind spots, maintaining confidentiality, assuming no harm, and step up/step back. *Assuming no harm* speaks to encouraging dialogue around difficult topics without assumptions that others are trying to offend or harm them with their comments. Essentially, we are all curious learners. *Step Up/Step Back* addresses the topic that all participants' thoughts and comments are valued. The idea allows for those participants that are more talkative to talk a "step back" and allow the participants that are more quite an opportunity to "step up" and be heard.

## Adaptations:

This group activity is designed for 20-25 group participants; however, it may be adapted for a smaller number of group participants. With fewer participants, group facilitators do not have to designate diverse group/identities ahead of time. Following the introduction of activity, group facilitators can ask students to shout out examples of diverse groups/identities. One facilitator can write down group responses as the headings on individual newsprint sheets. Time may also be altered to provide the most appropriate amount of dialogue given the number of participants present.

## References:

Barrera, I., & Corso, R.M. (2003). *Skilled dialogue: Strategies for responding to cultural diversity in early childhood.* Baltimore, MD: Paul H. Brookes Publishing Co.

Baxter Magolda, M. B. (2002b). Helping students make their own way to adulthood: Good company for the journey. *About Campus, 6*(6), 2-9.

Baxter Magolda, M. B. (2008). Three elements of self-authorship. *Journal of College Student Development, 49,* 269-284.

Cooper, M. G., & Lesser, J. G. (2011). *Clinical social work practice: An integrated approach* (4th ed.). Boston: Pearson Education.

Evans, N. J., Forney, D. S., Guido, F. M., Patton, L. D. & Renn, K. A. (2010). *Student development in college: Theory, research, and practice* (2$^{nd}$ ed.). San Francisco, CA: Jossey-Bass.

Holley, L., & Steiner, S. (2005). Safe spaces in the classroom. *Journal of Social Work Education, 41*(1), 49-64.

## Author Notes:

*Matthew R. Shupp* is an Assistant Professor in the Department of Counseling and College Student Personnel at Shippensburg University of Pennsylvania. Dr. Shupp has over 12 years of experience working with student leaders in a variety of college settings.

*Jayleen Galarza* is an Assistant Professor in the Department of Social Work & Gerontology at Shippensburg University of Pennsylvania. Dr. Galarza specializes in sexuality issues in social work practice, and she has extensive experience in clinical work with individuals, groups, and families, specifically with adolescents and young adults.

## Correspondence:

Questions and comments related to this activity may be directed to:

Matthew R. Shupp, Ed.D., NCC, DCC
Assistant Professor, Department of Counseling and College Student Personnel
Shippensburg University of Pennsylvania
Shippen Hall 111
Shippensburg, PA 17257
mrshupp@ship.edu

# Working Toward Me

*By Lisa Aasheim & Kathryn van Asselt*

## Population:

This activity is intended primarily for females in late adolescence through any stage of adulthood, most notably those who are experiencing transition, role stress, or identity confusion. This group is appropriate for an inpatient or outpatient setting and is intended for closed groups with consistent membership for the duration of the group. In this chapter, the example group will be a closed group of 8 young women ages 22 through 29 in an outpatient setting.

## Stage of Group:

This is a series of planned activities to begin in the orientation stage and progresses until termination.

## Type of Group:

Counseling

## Rationale:

This is a series of activities intended to assist group members in considering their own potential in a manner that bypasses real or perceived internal and external limitations. Exposure to the goal-setting processes of other group members will help group members understand that feeling "stuck" and unsuccessful in achieving one's goals is a common experience and can be overcome, and the group members can assist each other in "resetting" the limiting messages and self-talk. Studies have demonstrated that women have a tendency to endorse and pay more attention to beliefs that focus on dependency and a need for approval (Calvete & Cardenoso, 2005). This group setting allows participants to focus on appropriate levels and demonstrations of dependency and approval-seeking but in a moderated, pro-social capacity.

Many group members report to counseling at a time in their lives when they feel "stuck" or unable to progress toward the quality of life they wish to have. Craven, Marsh, and Burnett (2003) referred to the *self-concept enhancement conundrum* as a challenge faced by helpers who are tasked with helping others continually develop and enhance self-concept through the life span. These authors emphasized the importance of self-concept as a direct influence on one's desired outcomes. To help group members reach their goals, self-concept must be addressed and solidified. Many find this process difficult to do on their own and thus utilize tools such as self-help books, counselors, and other guides. In this case, this group activity allows members to engage in supportive and collaborative exploration in which the peers serve as reflecting agents and providers of necessary feedback and support.

# Goals:

Participants will:
1) develop a specific, thoughtful vision of one's future functioning in 3 specific life domains selected by the group participant (e.g., academic, career, social, psychological, physical, emotional, financial).
2) create 5 action steps toward the achievement of each of the three domain goals.
3) implement 1-2 action steps prior to the end of group.

# Materials:

1) Writing utensils (markers, colored pencils, and pens)
2) large paper or poster board (one per participant and 2 spare)
3) magazines/photos, glue sticks (one per member)
4) string (recommend a ball of yarn or string)
5) index cards (approx. 10/member)
6) stapler

# Time Allotment:

Each group session should be at least 60 minutes, preferably 75. Groups with adolescents or adults with more difficulty attending to tasks may be shortened to 45-50 minutes if necessary.

# Directions:

This activity takes place over several group meetings. Group leaders will adjust the steps based on the group composition, and the authors provide an example of how this activity might be divided up in an 8 session group.

**Group Session One**
**Step:**
1) During the orientation phase of group, introduce the group to the activity. Explain the intention which is to help group members become the "me" they wish to become. Explain that the main product of the group is a "goals board" that will be completed over the course of the group. The goals board can be completed in any way the group member sees fit, but the board need to be large enough to include great amounts of writing (poster board size is optimal). Ask group members to start dreaming of who they want to be, and prepare to get specific with those goals.

2) Have group members select their goal domains. Give them suggestions (career, financial, academic, romantic, familial, physical, etc...) and ask them to select the three domains that feel the most important to them. Limit them ONLY to three domains.

3) Have group members select each domain and write 2-3 descriptors of "success" in each domain. Give them a prompt such as "I know I will have achieved my (career) goals when I _____, _____, and _____."

4) Have group members discuss their process and ideas. Use processing questions such as "as you considered your goals, what are some of the self-statements you made automatically that made you doubt your ability to achieve your goals?" and "How do you define 'success'?"

**Group Session Two**
**Step:**

5) Once group members have written these down (either in the prior group or as homework prior to group two), they are to review these goals with the group. Before the sharing begins, group members are assigned to provide supportive feedback to one another on the following two items: first, group members will ensure the goals are achievable and realistic. Second, group members are to consider what qualities they notice about one another that may help one reach his/her goals. The group leader provides these instructions to the group, then asks the group who would like to share first. The group leader then guides the sharing by prompting that participant to share their goals by reading what they wrote. The leader instructs other participants to listen without judgment until the sharing is complete. Once the sharing is complete, the leader reminds the members to evaluate the goals in terms of how realistic and achievable they are. The person who shared initiates the process by providing an explanation of what makes her believe the goal is achievable and realistic. The group members are then asked to help find any potential barriers in the rationale, and are asked to approach with supportive curiosity. The leader models this through a prompt such as, *"Have you considered what will happen to your goal of becoming branch manager if a manager position doesn't open up?"* The leader sets a tone of non-judgmental, supportive curiosity and reminds the group that everyone is responsible for helping the sharer create achievable and reasonable goals.

6) If any group member provides feedback that a goal is not realistic, the group can work together to help the member find an achievable goal.

**Group Session Three**
**Step:**

7) Once everyone has shared, group members work independently to create picture boards that express their goals graphically. Group members will include their goals on the boards.

8) Group members work independently to create 3-5 action steps to work toward each goal. Each step is written on an index card and should go in sequence from step 1 (the first step toward the goal) to a final step that involves reaching the goal.

9) Action steps are discussed with the group. Group members provide feedback about additional steps or other ways of approaching the goals. The leader encourages group members to use phrases such as *"have you considered doing (this) in addition to what you have planned?"*

10) Action steps are revised, then attached to the posters using string or ribbon. The cards should be assembled so that the final step is closest to the poster board.

Group members are instructed to cut the cards off as they accomplish each step, then attach the removed cards to the back of the poster board so that, at the end, they can see the steps they used to accomplish their goal(s).

**Group Session Four**
**Step:**

11) Each group member is now instructed to take at least 1 action step prior to subsequent groups. In this group, members discuss which action step they will start with and how they will overcome obstacles, real or perceived. The group leader will help members consider their prior success in achieving action toward goals, and will help group members identify potential barriers. Group members will commit to an action step prior to the close of group and will discuss their action plans as it relates to their goal boards.

12) The leader instructs group members to take their action steps as homework, and group members will return to the next group to report their progress, collect feedback and encouragement, and elicit assistance from other group members when motivation wanes. Use processing questions such as, "What can the group provide you with to help you stay motivated? How might you stay motivated on your own when doubt or unwillingness creeps in?"

**Group Session Five/Six/Seven:**
**Step:**

13) Group members return to the group to report their progress, collect feedback and encouragement, and elicit assistance from other group members when motivation wanes. Each group member will present their board to the group each week and will discuss the action steps taken and any barriers or challenges that came up. Group members will encourage each other in continuing to take action and make progress toward goals.

**Group Session Eight:**
**Step:**

14) At the conclusion of group, each member celebrates the steps taken and the movement towards the goal. Each member describes how life has changed, even slightly, and describes the reasons to continue the momentum.

## *Special Considerations:*

The steps of this activity process will be condensed or expanded based on the population and setting. When the group is more time-limited, group leaders should consider having certain tasks become homework that the group members return with. For instance, writing the goals can become homework and step 11 can be reduced to a one or two-time occurrence.

## *Adaptations:*

This group can be adapted for use in an academic setting with students working toward specific academic goals. The group can be used for specific types of goal-setting activities, such as fitness or weight loss, sports performance, or productivity goals.

## *References:*

Calvete, E., & Cardenoso, O. (2005). Gender differences in cognitive vulnerability to depression and behavior problems in adolescents. *Journal of Abnormal Child Psychology*, 33(2), 179-192.

Craven, R. G., Marsh, H. W., & Burnett, P. (2003). Cracking the self-concept enhancement conundrum. *International Advances in Self Research*, 1, 91-126.

## *Author Notes:*

*Lisa Aasheim* is an Associate Professor at Portland State University in Portland, Oregon. She is the Director of the Community Counseling Clinic and the Coordinator of the School Counseling Program. She has 14 years of group experience in community mental health, schools, and training settings.

*Kathryn van Asselt* is an Assistant Professor at Portland State University in Portland, Oregon, and is the current President of the Western Association of Counselor Educators and Supervisors. She is a specialist in school counseling and group work and has over a decade of experience working with groups in various settings including schools and community mental health.

## *Correspondence:*

Questions and comments related to this activity may be directed to:

Dr. Lisa Aasheim, Ph.D.
Portland State University
SPED/COUN, PO Box 751
Portland, OR 97207
aasheim@pdx.edu

# A Dead-End Street

*By Stefi Threadgill & Brandy Schumann*

## Population:

Inpatient and outpatient adults dealing with addiction

## Stage of Group:

Orientation, transition, or working

## Type of Group:

Counseling

## Rationale:

A strong, integrated sense of self generates positive self-esteem and self-regulation (Oaklander, 2007). An inaccurate perception of self creates disintegration and polarity, which negatively shape an individual's self-concept and how one experiences him or herself and his or her world. The ability to make contact is essential to promoting a strong sense of self. This activity encourages a person to fully experience, or to be present, and increases awareness of one's thoughts, feelings, and senses.

The well-known poem, "Autobiography in Five Short Chapters" by Portia Nelson (1993), was originally printed in *There's a Hole in My Sidewalk*. In this poem, the author utilizes a pothole metaphor to describe the process of change through an increase in awareness. The pothole, experienced as a hurdle to the traveler's path, decreases in influence as the traveler gains experience and insight.

If introduced in session, the "street" in this poem provides a visual representation of a person's subjective experience. The potholes can symbolize difficult challenges the group member has withdrawn from his or her awareness. Fantasy provides a safe, non-threatening way to re-experience, reconnect, and increase awareness of the challenges (Oaklander, 2007). Parts of self that are denied or restricted result in unexpressed emotions that create an incomplete gestalt, or fragmented sense of self. Increased self-awareness promotes authenticity and accuracy, which creates an opportunity for change (Oaklander, 2007). This activity can increase awareness that personhood is holistic and is not defined only by experience. It also promotes the awareness that that perception of self occurs in the context of the environment.

By participating in this activity, individuals gain awareness of how others experience them. This can lead to a more accurate self-concept and empower one to focus on more authentic qualities.

Through the I/Thou relationship of the group and the here-and-now immediacy of the experience, the individual is able to gain awareness and self-acceptance through the process of the activity. This promotes re-integration of a holistic and authentic self (Oaklander, 2007). Additionally, a group setting provides social support, normalization, and increased opportunity to understand that perception is subjective (Berg, Landreth, & Fall, 2013).

## Goals:

Participants will:
1) increase self-awareness.
2) increase an accurate and authentic sense of self.
3) experience a strong, integrated sense of self.
4) increase awareness that personhood is holistic and not solely defined by an experience.
5) increase understanding that sense of self occurs in the context of the environment.
6) experience social support and normalization of concerns.
7) experience stimulation of the senses and increase mindfulness.

## Materials:

1) Crayons, markers, or colored pencils
2) Paper
3) "Autobiography in Five Short Chapters" by Portia Nelson, which can be obtained online or through e-book at http://books.simonandschuster.com/Theres-a-Hole-in-My-Sidewalk/Portia-Nelson/9781451686357
4) Caution tape (optional)

## Time Allotment:

90-minute group therapy session.

## Directions:

Step:
1) Read the poem, "Autobiography in Five Short Chapters" by Portia Nelson (1993) aloud to the group.

2) Begin the activity with a visualization instructing group members, *"Close your eyes. Imagine you are walking down a street. This is your street. This is the street you navigate when _____* (insert the addictive behavior).

3) Ask group members to open their eyes, saying, *"Now open your eyes and draw your street. Include potholes on your street that you fall into, things that make you feel (insert feeling word) or want to (insert addictive behavior)."* Feeling words and addictive behaviors should be selected by the group leader and are dependent on the population and goal of the group session.

4) Ask members to engage in the experience by saying, *"What do you see, hear, smell, and feel?"*

5) Ask members to identify their potholes. These are triggers to their addictive behavior. This can be facilitated by a prompt for the drawing or talking aloud during group processing.

6) Ask members to name the street in the drawing they have created.

## Processing Questions:
1) What self-awareness did you gain from this activity?
2) Describe where you are: chapter I, II, III, IV, or V.
3) What is your next chapter?
4) Optional homework: Do three things in a different way than usual.

## Special Considerations:
1) More prompts may be necessary for child and adolescent populations.
2) Adaptations may be necessary for group members with hearing, visual, or motor difficulties.

## Adaptations:
1) Other populations for which this activity can be utilized are: individuals with disorders, grief, anxiety, anger management, and depression. The potholes would include the triggers where members become stuck.
2) This activity can be done individually in a group setting or as a group, with members drawing a neighborhood on butcher paper. Each group member draws his or her street and the group connects their streets to create a neighborhood or community.
3) The product of this activity can be used as a treatment plan to track progress of what chapter group members identify as potholes over time.

## References:

Berg, R. C., Landreth, G. L., & Fall, K. A. (2013). *Group counseling: Concepts and procedures.* (5th ed.). New York, NY: Routledge.

Nelson, P. (2012). *There's a hole in my sidewalk.* New York, NY: Simon & Schuster.

Oaklander, V. (2007). *Hidden treasure: A map to the child's inner self.* London, UK: Karnac.

## Author Notes:

*Stefi Threadgill* has received training specialized in group therapy through Southern Methodist University and currently provides group therapy to pre-adolescents to improve social skills and increase self-esteem.

*Brandy Schumann* has a decade's worth of experience delivering group therapy services to children, preadolescents, adolescents, adults and parents. In addition to teaching about group therapy as a Clinical Assistant Professor at Southern Methodist University, she also services the public from her private practice, Therapy on the Square in McKinney, TX, providing groups to address self-esteem, divorce support, social skills and parenting needs.

## Correspondence:

Questions and comments related to this activity may be directed to:

Stefi Threadgill, Student
SMU Counseling Program
Southern Methodist University in Plano
5228 Tennyson Parkway, Bldg 3
Plano, TX 75024-3547
sthreadgill@smu.edu

# An Abundance of Riches: What are the Strengths of My Special Needs Child?

*By Aimee Brickner*

## Population:

Parent(s) with at least one child that would put them in the category of "special needs" which can include any deficits such as autism, learning disabilities, and conduct disorder.

## Stage of Group:

Working

## Type of Group:

Psychoeducational

## Rationale:

Much of the information in the popular media about the emotions of parents whose children are diagnosed with a cognitive deficit (e.g., PDD, ID, ASD) focuses on their negative feelings such as sadness, anger, and frustration. However, the media and society tend to ignore the joy and happiness that parents with a special needs child also experience (Hillman, 2006). This activity is designed to invite persons to talk about their child's strengths and how those strengths can be viewed in the context of their diagnosis.

## Goals:

Participants will:
1) explore the positive qualities of their special needs child.
2) understand how these strengths exist within the context of a diagnosis that may often have negative stereotypes.
3) focus on the strengths of their child rather than the deficits.

## Materials:

1) At least a dozen photographs of their child
2) A variety of magazines
3) Markers
4) Glue
5) Scissors

## Time Allotment:

1 hour to work on the collage, 1 hour to process the activity

## Directions:

Step:

1) This activity will begin with a brief guided imagery exercise in which parents will be invited to close their eyes and picture one of their favorite moments with their child. For example, *"Close your eyes and focus on your breathing. Take a deep breath in...and slowly exhale. Breathe in and exhale for four counts. Breathe in for one...two...three...four. Exhale for one...two...three...four (do this several times). Think about your special needs child. Focus on their face—see their eyes, their smile. Now think about a special moment you have had with your child. Remember the sounds, the smells, the feelings you had in that moment (be quiet and let the group focus). When you are ready, open your eyes and we will start working on the collages."* This part of the activity should take approximately 5 minutes.

2) After this exercise, parents will be invited to reflect on strengths their children possess and to write down at least 5 strengths.

3) They will then be encouraged to use pictures that they have brought from home or from magazines and create an 8x11 collage that they can frame and give to their child as a reminder of their many positive attributes.

## Processing Questions:

1) What is it like to focus on your child's strengths instead of their deficits?
2) Given your child's diagnosis, how can these strengths be utilized in their therapy/schooling/peer interactions?
3) What was it like to hear other parents talk about the strengths of their special needs child?
4) What was it like to talk about your child's strengths with others?

## Special Considerations:

Parents may become very emotional when realizing how infrequently they focus on their child's strengths. Also, some parents may struggle to come up with 5 strengths for their child and that may cause distress. The therapist should allow the parents to express their feelings and then talk about the parents can find ways to focus on their child's strengths in the future.

## Adaptations:

This activity can also be used with high functioning adolescents who have been identified as "special needs" as a way to encourage them to recognize their own strengths.

## References:

Hillman, J. (2006). Supporting and treating families with children on the autism spectrum: The unique role of the generalist psychologist. *Psychotherapy: Theory, Research, Practice, Training, 43*(3), 349-358.

## Author Notes:

*Aimee Brickner* is a Doctoral Student at James Madison University and a Resident in Counseling at Compass Youth and Family Services. At Compass she is the Clinical Behavior Support Specialist where she provides supervision and training to clinicians working with group members who have an autism spectrum diagnosis and also regularly meets with the families of group members on the spectrum.

## Correspondence:

Questions and comments related to this activity may be directed to:

Aimee Brickner
James Madison University
MSC 2106
Harrisonburg, VA 22807
bricknar@jmu.edu

# Blue Goodbye

*By Barb Wilson*

## Population:
Adults

## Stage of Group:
Termination

## Type of Group:
Counseling

## Rationale:

Termination is an important event when working with small groups but is often overlooked (Yalom & Leszcz, 2005). Bibliotherapy is a creative arts technique which can be employed by the counselor or therapist during the termination phase. The use of bibliotherapy can provide group members opportunities to gain alternative feelings, perspectives, and actions (Gladding, 2005). Bibliotherapy also facilitates a greater understanding of the world (Gladding, 2005). This activity utilizes bibliotherapy to end a series of group sessions. Through the use of a story about moving on but leaving a piece of you behind, group members are able to conceptualize the process they have experienced together.

I have utilized this activity with a group of adults as they transitioned to a new work setting. We read the story together and each group member received a small blue bead. Years later group members not only talked about how that process helped, but two group members also read the book to people in their lives during transitional stages.

## Goals:

Participants will:
1) gain a sense of closure with grief and the group itself.
2) increase group cohesion.

## Materials:

1) Book, "One Small Blue Bead" by Byrd Baylor (please see references for publication information)
2) Blue beads
3) Thread for making a necklace or keychain (optional activity)

## Time Allotment:

30 minutes

# Directions:

Step:

1) Welcome the group. Say, *"Good morning/afternoon/evening, everyone. Thank you for joining us again today. As we discussed last time, this is our last meeting together for this group. But, just because we may stop meeting formally, our growth and learning will continue."*

2) Introduce the activity. Say, *"I am reading a story to you today. This story is about hope, dreams, and belief in oneself. As you listen to this story, reflect upon your time here in the group. Think about what you have learned about yourself. Think about what you have learned from others. Think about where you were in the beginning of our time together and where you have come. Where are you headed? Think about what you have learned from others that you may carry with you after today."*

3) Discuss "closure" and what that means for the group. Allow group members to process this idea of ending the group sessions. Say, *"As we said at the beginning of our session today, this is our last formal meeting. There are times in our lives when we must say goodbye to people, places, and things. There is sorrow and growth in these moments. Despite sadness, the experience of closing one part of our lives and moving on to a next can be very healthy. We carry lessons learned with us as we move forward. Let's read the story and think about our closure here and moving forward."*

4) Read the story to the group.

5) Ask the group members to discuss their reactions to the story. Encourage group members to think about what elements of themselves they may have left in others.

6) Distribute the blue beads, one per person. Explain that the bead can be used however the owner feels appropriate. Some may make jewelry, some may make a key chain, and others may decide to put the bead in a special place.

7) Allow the group members to share final thoughts and move to the processing questions

# Processing Questions:

1) How do you feel about the group coming to an end?
2) What is something you left behind with the other group members (like the bead in the book)?
3) What is something you gained from someone else in the group?
4) What was your experience in this group?
5) What might be different in your life because of this group?

## Special Considerations:

1) Some people are visual learners; be sure to show the pictures.
2) The activity may need adaptation for group members with vision or hearing limitations.
3) The group leader must obtain a copy of the book prior to conducting this activity.
4) If conducting this activity with younger children, please be aware that beads could be a choking hazard. Monitor group members for safety.

## Adaptations:

This lesson can be used with children and adolescents as well. Processing questions would be adjusted accordingly. The book itself can also become a "take away" for the group members, rather than only receiving a bead. However, this can become costly. Additionally, the book may be better received by group members if read by one or more of the group members themselves. Adjust the activity according to the group dynamics.

## References:

Byalor, B. (1965). *One Small Blue Bead.* New York: Simon and Schuster Children's Publishing Division.

Erk, R. R. (2008). *Counseling treatment for children and adolescents with DSM-IV-TR disorders* (2nd ed.). Columbus, OH: Pearson Merrill Prentice Hall.

Gladding, S. T.(2005). *Counseling as an art* (3rd ed.). Columbus, OH: Pearson Merrill Prentice Hall.

Oaklander, V. (1988). *Windows to our children.* Highland, New York: The Gestalt Journal Press.

Yalom, I. D. ,& Leszcz, M., (2005). *The theory and practice of group psychotherapy* (5th ed.). New York: Basic Books.

## Author Notes:

*Barb Wilson* is a School Counselor with the Hall County School System in Georgia. She has over ten years of group experience, including working with suicidal and homicidal children and adolescents, students at the elementary, middle, and high school levels, advising undergraduate and graduate students, and working with international students at the college level. She also has experience as a school counseling internship supervisor.

## Correspondence:

Questions and comments related to this activity may be directed to:

Dr. Barb Wilson, Ph.D., LPC, NCC
Hall County Schools
5470 McEver Road
Oakwood, GA 30566
drwilson@yahoo.com

# Collages of Past Traumas, Present Surviving, and Future Thriving

*By Jamie Hoffmann*

## Population:

This activity is appropriate for adult women who have experienced trauma.

## Stage of Group:

Working

## Type of Group:

Counseling

## Rationale:

Trauma impacts the right hemisphere of the brain, which stores sensory memories related to the trauma but not in a linear order (Steele & Malchiodi, 2012). Consequently, group activities that rely on talking alone may be unable to tap into the implicit trauma memories stored in the right hemisphere. Participating in sensory-based activities that encourage artistic expression can activate the creative part of the brain, which is then more likely to be able to access the trauma memories stored in the right hemisphere (Cozolino, 2002). This activity can help group members create symbolic representations of their past traumas, their challenges, their strengths and hopes for the future.

## Goals:

Participants will:
>    1) give expression to implicit memories of past traumas.
>    2) examine their current emotional state.
>    3) envision their future as trauma survivors.

## Materials:

>    1) Notebook (preferably 8"x12") - per group member
>    2) Scissors - per group member
>    3) Stick of glue - per group member
>    4) Variety of magazines
>    5) Decorative materials as desired

## Time Allotment:

60 minutes is recommended for groups of 5 or smaller. 90 minutes is recommended for groups with 6 or more members. 90 minutes would also be more appropriate for a smaller group if you wish to have more time for sharing and processing.

## Directions:

Step:

1) Briefly discuss the impact of trauma on the brain and the purpose of using artistic expression in the process of healing from trauma (5 minutes). For example:

> "Survivors of trauma often have difficulty when prompted to retell what has happened to them with words. The story may seem scattered or to have gaps in it. The way that trauma is stored in the brain makes it difficult to recall those memories with words, because traumatic memories are stored in a part of the brain that is associated with the senses such as taste, smell, and sight. Through the expressive arts, some people are able to more easily convey their traumatic experience and emotions related to that experience than when they rely on words alone. This activity is designed to help you explore your inner world and give voice to your experiences in a new way."

2) Distribute a spiral notebook, pair of scissors, and glue to each group member.

3) Place magazines in a central location that group members can easily access.

4) Ask that group members sift through the magazines and cut out pictures and words from the magazines that represent three categories:

How trauma has impacted them in the past;

How their trauma impacts them now;

How they envision themselves in the future as they continue their journey of recovery as trauma survivors.

5) Ask the group members to paste the pictures in the spiral notebook, under the three separate categories.

6) Encourage group members to personalize their collages in whatever way is meaningful to them with the other materials available (i.e. glitter, paint, stickers, etc.).

7) Allow 30 minutes for group members to complete their collages.

8) Afterwards, invite group members to share their collages with the group.

9) Ask discussion questions (15 minutes):

> What physical and emotional responses did you notice as you worked on the collages?

> What part of your collages did you identify with the most?

> Did anything surprise you while working on this activity?

10) At the conclusion of the session, allow group members to take their collages home and encourage them to continue building their collages or create new collages as part of their recovery journey (10 minutes).

11) Steps 8-10 could be completed during a following session if more time is needed.

## Processing Questions:

1) What did you discover about your trauma and about your own strengths?
2) What stood out to you from the collages of others?
3) What is your next step on your journey to thriving?

## Special Considerations:

1) This activity could inspire some deep emotional discoveries for group members. Some group members may wish to keep some of these private for the present. Members need to be given the options of sharing with the entire group, one-on-one with the group leader, or not at all. It is recommended that the leader discuss possible triggers with the group before beginning the activity and how they could respond if this occurs.
2) If the activity is conducted with a group that includes a disabled individual who is unable to cut and paste materials for their collages, but is able to talk, the group leader may cut and paste materials following the verbal instructions of the individual. The group leader could also give the group member the option to participate through verbal processing.

## Adaptations:

If the group is large, or time more limited, the group leader can opt to remove Step 9 or Step 10. The time of the group can be extended when there are more members or if the group leader would like to provide more time for the activity. The group leader may want to play soothing music during the activity. Additionally, the activity could be implemented with men as well as adolescent boys and girls who have experienced trauma.

## References:

Chew, J. (1998). *Women survivors of childhood sexual abuse: Healing through group work.* Binghamton, NY: The Haworth Press.

Cozolino, L. (2002). *The neuroscience of psychotherapy.* New York: Norton.

Steele, W., & Malchiodi, C. (2012). *Trauma-informed practices with children and adolescents.* New York: Routledge.

## Author Notes:

*Jamie Hoffmann* is Clinician in the Counseling Center at Shenandoah University. She initiated and developed the first support group at Shenandoah University for survivors of sexual assault. She has continued to facilitate this group for the last two years. Ms. Hoffman is a Doctoral Student in the Counseling and Supervision program at James Madison University.

## Correspondence:

Questions and comments related to this activity may be directed to:

Jamie Hoffmann
Shenandoah University
1460 University Drive, Winchester, VA 22601
jhoffman2@su.edu

# Cups of Priorities

*By Quinn M. Pearson*

## Population:

Adults in outpatient settings with mental health disorders or phase-of-life challenges; see below for adaptions with psychoeducational groups

## Stage of Group:

Working

## Type of Group:

Counseling, therapy

## Rationale:

This activity is grounded in the existential concepts of creating meaning and being aware of and responsible for choices. Existential therapy centers around such anxiety producing questions as "why are we here, who am I, and how should I live my life" (Gehart, 2013, p.153). Because this approach lacks defined techniques, much of what the counselor does in this therapeutic process is provide encouragement to group members in this scary exploration (Gehart, 2013). Given the abstract and challenging nature of this existential exploration, Mannion (2011) suggested using creative activities as a vehicle and source of connection for group members who are exploring these difficult questions.

## Goals:

Participants will:
1) Recognize limits regarding personal time, energy, and other resources
2) Increase awareness of personal values and goals
3) Reorganize priorities based on insights

## Materials:

1) Paper, pencil or pen
2) Permanent markers of various colors
3) One larger plastic cup (9 ounces), filled with water, per group member
4) Five to eight smaller plastic cups (3.5 ounces) per group member

## Time Allotment:

45 minutes is the approximate time needed to complete this activity. For groups containing more than 8-10 group members, allow for 15 additional minutes.

## Directions:

Step:

1) Keep empty cups and cups filled with water out of view until they are needed.

2) Provide paper and pens or pencils to group members.

3) Ask group members to list five to seven priorities on a piece of paper and write brief notes related to each. *"Think of the most important priorities in your life—four to seven—and write down each one, leaving space to add notes for each. After you have written down all of your priorities, make some personal notes about each one."*

4) Give each group member the smaller plastic cups, one for each of their priorities, and one permanent marker. Instruct group members to label each cup with a priority. *"Using the permanent marker, label each cup to represent one of your priorities. Use a word or symbol that represents your priority."*

5) Ask group members to fill each "priority" cup with an amount of water that represents the amount of time and energy they are currently dedicating to that priority. Then, they will use a permanent marker to mark the level of water in each cup. *"Reflect on each priority and the current amount of time and energy you are devoting to that priority. Pour the amount of water in each cup that represents the amount of time and energy you are devoting to each. When you are finished, draw a line on the cup that shows the level of water you have poured in each cup."*

6) Process the activity with Part One questions indicated below.

7) Ask group members to fill the cups according to the amount of time and energy they would like to devote to each priority. Give the group members a permanent marker of a different color or ask them to switch markers with another group member. Then they will mark the level of water in each cup using the second marker. *"Reflect on the importance of each priority and pour a level of water into each cup that represents the amount of time and energy that you want to devote to each priority. Using a different colored marker, draw a line on the cup that shows the level of water you have poured in each cup."*

8) Process the activity with Part Two questions indicated below.

## Processing Questions:

For Part One:

1) As you notice the level of water in each cup, particularly cups with lots of water and those with little water, how satisfied are you with the level of water in each cup?
2) What do you notice about the number of cups?
3) If a cup has little to no water in it, whose values are reflected in this priority? Your values? Someone else's values?

For Part Two:
1) How would you explain any discrepancies between your current dedication to each priority and your desired level?
2) What changes, if any, do you need to make?
3) What will you do more of or less of this week that will move you closer to your desired levels on one or two of your priorities?

## Special Considerations:

1) Group leaders need to be aware of reading and writing abilities of group members. When these limitations exist, group leaders may want to emphasize using symbols rather than words to represent each priority and omit asking group members to write notes about each priority in steps three and four above.

## Adaptations:

1) Sand, rice, or another dry item may be used instead of water.
2) If conducting a psychoeducational group with adolescents on time management, stress management, or study skills, the labels for each cup could be more defined according to specific life roles (e.g., student, basketball player, dancer, etc.) or subjects in school (e.g., English, Spanish, math, history, etc.).
3) If conducting psychoeducational groups with adults on stress management, each cup could be defined according to a life role (e.g., parent, caretaker, worker, etc.).

## References:

Gehart, G. (2013). *Theory and treatment planning in counseling and psychotherapy*. Belmont, CA: Brooks/Cole.

Mannion, M. P. (2011). Existential theory. In S. Degges-White & N. L. Davis (Eds.), *Integrating the expressive arts into counseling practice* (pp. 87-106). New York: Springer Publishing.

## Author Notes:

*Quinn M. Pearson* is a Professor of Counselor Education at the University of North Alabama. She has taught group counseling courses for the last18 years and has facilitated counseling, therapy, and psychoeducational groups in various settings, including university, inpatient, outpatient, and intensive outpatient settings.

## Correspondence:

Questions and comments related to this activity may be directed to:

Quinn M. Pearson, Ph.D., LPC
University of North Alabama
UNA Box 5154
Florence, AL 35632
qmpearson@una.edu

# Evaluating the Group Experience: A Check-In Exercise for a Substance Abuse Group

*By Melissa M. McConaha, Amanda M. Evans, Kelly J. Veal, Elliot E. Isom, Serey B. Bright, Juliana Groves Radomski & Sam Booker*

## Population:

For this specific intervention a substance abuse group was identified. Of particular interest is the lack of consistently applied evidence based techniques with group member's experiencing substance abuse issues (Sorenson & Midkiff, 2002). The activity continues a necessary effort to provide valid approaches within substance abuse counseling.

## Stage of Group Work:

This intervention was developed to be used during the working stage. The working stage was identified specifically because this is the stage that relies heavily on member participation, introspection and promotes member "ownership" of the group (Gladding, 2003 p. 155). By checking-in with the group, the facilitator can identify what is working with members, what is not working with members and can develop a plan to address the group's needs.

## Type of Group Work:

This activity would be most appropriate for counseling or psychotherapy group as these types of groups attend to process, norming, and achieving personal goals (Gazda, Ginter, & Horne, 2001 p. 14). Ideally, this group intervention would be offered in a substance abuse counseling group that is closed and member participation is voluntary.

## Rationale:

It is well documented in the literature that a significant contributor toward negative change on the part of group member outcome is a lack of or poor therapeutic relationship. (e.g., Lambert & Shimokawa, 2011 ; Ahn & Wampold, 2001; Safran, Muran, Samstang, & Winston, 2005). Responding to the research and recommendations for counselors, intervention combines all the elements of client-centered techniques that are paramount to a successful therapeutic relationship (Norcross & Hill, 2004). These relationship elements include: establishing a therapeutic alliance, having empathy for group members, establishing cohesion in group therapy and having an agreement on therapist-patient treatment goals and collaboration (Norcross & Hill, 2004; Norcross, 2012). The activity highlights the importance of the empirically supported therapeutic relationship within a group setting; which is critical for a working group to be successful. Using an activity such as this can effectively increase cohesion and safety, as well as, facilitate a deeper group process.

# *Goals:*

Participants will:
1) Individually provide verbal or written feedback over the course of the group session based upon perceptions of the current treatment direction, group dynamics, and counselor relationship. Members will discuss ways that these areas can be enhanced.
2) Evaluate individual needs and group needs pertaining to the current group format, and verbalize feedback to address those needs with potential suggestions to modify the current group approach. This is addressed by group members stating one thing about the group treatment that is most helpful and one thing that is least helpful.
3) Process their current progress in the group by verbalizing their progress toward long term goals, and assess two areas of group work they would like to adjust to better fit their treatment goals.

# *Materials:*

Practitioners will need pens/pencils and paper to provide the option for written feedback to counselor's questions, and provide a means for group members to give anonymous feedback about the group.

# *Time Allotment:*

The Evaluating the Group Experience: A Check-In Exercise for a Substance Abuse Group can be facilitated over a 50 to 90 minute group. However, an extension into the next session may be needed if time doesn't permit dialogue for addressing the therapist/client relationship, as it is central to this activity.

# *Directions:*

Step:

1) Provide instructions for the activity. Group leader would state:

   *"Today I'd like to do a check-in with everyone. It is important for all of us to know how each member are doing and how we are doing as a whole. Today's session will be devoted to seeing where we are, what's going well, and what we could do to make this time together more beneficial. I know it can feel uncomfortable to speak openly about concerns or provide feedback; so I ask that you be as honest as you can. It can be very powerful to voice your needs, especially when considering how crucial honesty, openness, and feedback are to your new life in recovery. I've also provided a way that you can submit anonymously after the session if you don't feel comfortable sharing out loud."*

2) Review group guidelines/norms if established. If not, begin creating them before the dialogue and review at the end of the session, adding information gained from this exercise.

3) Facilitate dialogue that evaluates the following topics:

a)  The group goals.
  i.    *What do you wish to gain from our time together?*
  ii.   *How does everyone feel about our effort to accomplish your goals?*

b)  The group process.
  i.    *What is going well with the group? (most helpful)*
  ii.   *What could be better with the group? (least helpful)*
  iii.  *How can we improve? Do more/less of anything?*
  iv.   *In an open group, because we regularly have new group members, reflect back on     when you first became part of this group. What did the group do/provide that made you feel safe and welcome?*
  v.    *What do you need from the group that you have not gotten?*
  vi.   *Is anything holding you back from achieving your goals?*

c)  The counselor/client relationship.
  i.    *What is working with me/us leading this group?*
  ii.   *What could be better or more helpful in regards to leading the group?*
  iii.  *If no response: "I wonder what it would be like if you needed something else   or if something wasn't going great for you.."*
  iv.   *Do you have any requests as far as activities/topics covered in this group (e.g., in this group, other groups, and in-patient rehabilitation experiences)?*
  v.    *Other comments, questions, or concerns?*

## Processing Questions:

1)  What have you learned about yourself after participating in today's group?
2)  What was it like for you to provide the group facilitators feedback? Did group feel different for you today as we focused on this feedback?
3)  How will you use the information from today's group in your recovery journey?

## Special Considerations:

It is important for the counselor to keep in mind and clearly communicate the purpose of the group check-in along with the option of limited evaluation and disclosure in order to respect members from various cultural backgrounds.  Additionally, in is imperative to keep in mind that feedback will differ depending on the stage of change for each substance abuse group member thus; their evaluation of group dynamics, progress, and evaluation of the counselor will vary greatly (Velasquez, 2001). Additionally, providing feedback is difficult, as is receiving it. Modeling how to accept and use feedback—even when difficult—will be paramount for the clinician. Ultimately, the therapist is the determinant in decision making to apply feedback in future sessions, and would benefit the group to discuss concerns as to why a member's feedback may have not been applied.

## Adaptations:

The activity that has been presented is directed towards an open substance abuse group therapy session. However, because of the way in which this activity approaches the therapeutic relationship, it can be applied in a variety of settings and closed groups. The activity generates a reflective and learning atmosphere to potentially ignite any group's development.

## References:

Ahn, H., & Wampold, B. E. (2001). Where oh where are the specific ingredients? A meta-analysis of component studies in counseling and psychotherapy. *Journal of Counseling Psychology*, 48(3), 251-257. doi:10.1037/0022-0167.48.3.251.

Gazda, G. M. Ginter, E.J., & Horne, A.M. (2001) *Group counseling and group psychotherapy: Theory and application.* Boston: Allyn and Bacon.

Gladding, S. T. (2003) *Group work: A counseling specialty.* (4th ed.) Upper Saddle River, N.J.: Merrill,

Lambert, M. T., & Shimokawa, K. (2011). Collecting client feedback. Psychotherapy, 48(1), 72–79. doi:10.1037/a0022238.

Norcross, J. C., & Hill, C. E. (2004). Empirically supported therapy relationships. *The Clinical Psychologist*, 57(3), 19-24.

Norcross, J. (2012, September). Tailoring the treatment to the individual patient: Evidence based relationships. Lecture conducted at Auburn University, Auburn, AL.

Safran, J. D., Muran, J. C., Samstang, L. W., & Winston, A. (2005). Evaluating alliance-focused intervention for treatment failures: A feasibility and descriptive analysis. *Psychotherapy, Theory, Research, Practice, & Training*, 42, 512-531.

Sorensen, J. L., Midkiff, E. E. (2002). Bridging the gap between research and drug abuse treatment. *Journal of Psychoactive Drugs*, 32, 379–382.

Velasquez, M. M. (2001). *Group treatment for substance abuse: A stages of change therapy manual.* Guilford Press, New York: NY.

## *Author Notes:*

*Melissa M. McConaha* has served as a Graduate Assistant for CSD 5620-Group Counseling during master's work and co-led the experiential portion of the course, led groups in a community mental health setting, led Phase 1 Groups for Troup County's Federal Adult Drug Court, and assisted East Alabama Medical Center in revising group curriculum led by mental health technicians.

*Amanda M. Evans* has experience as a group facilitator specifically for inpatient psychiatric and adolescent female populations, taught a masters-level group class for two years, and served as the 2012-13 secretary for ALASGW.

*Kelly J. Veal* has over 8 years of experience leading substance abuse groups for court-mandated offenders within Georgia's Troup County DUI/Drug Court, Adult Felony Drug Court and Family Drug Court Programs.

*Elliot E. Isom* has led adolescent groups in a community mental health setting, and led Phase 1 Groups for Troup County Georgia's DUI program.

*Serey B. Bright* has facilitated group therapy at an inpatient psychiatric hospital for over two years working with a diverse population of group members with a variety of mental health issues including substance abuse.

*Juliana Groves Radomski* has group counseling experience in community mental health, working with children and adolescents' coping mechanisms.

*Sam Booker* has three years of group work experience as a School Counselor in a K-12 setting followed by two years of experience working as a career counselor at Auburn University.

## *Correspondence:*

Questions and comments related to this activity may be directed to:

Dr. Amanda M. Evans, PhD, LPC, NCC
Auburn University
2068 Haley Center, Auburn, AL, 36840-5222
Email: amt0004@auburn.edu
Phone: 334-844-7695

# Fear in a Hat

*By Heather L. Smith*

## Population:
Adults with normative cognitive and personality functioning

## Stage of Group:
Orientation or Transition

## Type of Group:
Counseling, Therapy

## Rationale:

Fear is a phenomenon that can be helpful or harmful within human relationships. During the orienting and transition stages of group work, individuals can struggle with concerns around what to expect from the group, what to share with the group, and what the norms will become (Erford, 2010). This activity provides members with a structure for sharing fears, which may not be fully conscious. Allowing fears to be brought safely forth into the public arena (LUFT, 1969), provides more material and a success experience with which the group can later use for creating norms (Tuckman, 1965) and addressing other concerns (Cassidy, 2007).

## Goals:

Participants will:
1) experience universality with other members around the human phenomenon of fear.
2) become more secure sharing with other members.
3) become more cohesive as a group.

## Materials:

1) Paper for writing
2) Writing utensil
3) Hat to hold members' slips of paper

## Time Allotment:

The group should be no less than 10 members in order to ensure a degree of anonymity. With 10 members this activity takes approximately 7-8 minutes <u>without</u> the processing. Group leaders can expand or reduce the total time depending upon the intent and extent of processing.

## Directions:

Step:

1) Ask members to consider the following sentence, *"In this group, I am most afraid that..."*

2) Then ask members to finish the sentence by writing on their slips of paper, ensuring them that their responses will remain anonymous.

3) When all members have put their responses in the hat, mix up the papers.

4) Pass the hat around the group, instructing each member to pull out a slip of paper and read the complete sentence aloud with the response on the paper. Ask members to refold the paper after reading it.

5) After each group member has completed the task, collect the papers and dispose of them confidentially.

## Processing Questions:

1) Were there any themes that you heard?
2) What was it like to hear members' fears?
3) How did this activity affect you in terms of sharing with this group?
4) Fears are a normal human phenomenon, and thus, occur in groups like ours as well. A good way to cope with fears is to have them openly acknowledged without being subject to ridicule. How might this group ensure member safety from ridicule?
5) What do you need to look for when selecting individuals outside this group to share your (non-group-related) fears?

## Special Considerations:

Since this activity requires each member to both write and read, it may be difficult to use with individuals with low reading/writing skills, vision or language impairments, or those new to the English language. Also, it may not be appropriate for populations struggling with reality testing or phobias.

## Adaptations:

This activity might be adapted for use with select groups of adolescents. Group leaders might want to provide writing utensils such that all members have the same ink/pencil to decrease the likelihood that a member could figure out who wrote a specific fear. Group leaders need to assess and control for inappropriate/damaging comments after a fear response is read. Additionally, group leaders may need to make adaptations for those with visual or motor difficulties.

# References:

Cassidy, K. (2007). Tuckman revisited: Proposing a new model of group development for practitioners. *Journal of Experiential Education, 29*, 413-417.

Erford, B. T. (2010). *Group work: Processes and applications*. Boston, MA: Pearson.

Luft, J. (1969). *Of human interaction*. Palo Alto, CA: National Press. Specifically Johari's Window.

Tuckman, B. (1965). Developmental sequence in small groups. *Psychological Bulletin, 63*, 384-399.

# Author Notes:

*Heather L. Smith* is an Assistant Professor of the Practice of Human Development Counseling at Vanderbilt University and a Staff Therapist at the Vanderbilt Psychological & Counseling center. She has had twelve years of designing and facilitating group work and nine years teaching group counseling.

# Correspondence:

Questions and comments related to this activity may be directed to:

Heather L. Smith, Ph.D, LPC-MHSP, NCC, LDN, RD
Box 90; 230 Appleton Place
Nashville, TN 37203
h.smith@vanderbilt.edu

# Following Directions

*By Chelsea Latorre, Kenneth Comer, & Paula McWhirter*

## Population:

This activity may be best suited for groups of adults who primarily work together and struggle with effective communication. The group can range from a minimum of 10 to a maximum of 20 individuals; however, the group must contain an even number of individuals for this activity. Refer to the adaptations section for suggestions on conducting this activity with different populations.

## Stage of Group:

Transition

## Type of Group:

Task/work

## Rationale:

Communication plays a major role in how information is passed through different environments and directed towards different populations. Interpersonal therapists emphasize interpersonal communication as fundamental, both for the development of the self and the self in relationship to others (Sullivan, 1953). As such, the development of effective communication is essential for both interpersonal and intrapersonal growth. A subset of leadership development focuses on communication as a key aspect for effectively relaying information and producing more successful outcomes. Learning techniques of effective and leadership communication is critical in many capacities and environments. This activity will enhance individuals' understanding of effective communication and process how to best apply communication in their own environments.

## Goals:

Participants will:
1) identify key factors in effective communication and non-effective communication.
2) develop, demonstrate and discuss components of effective communication.
3) process application of effective communication in leaders and other roles within their environment.

# Materials:

1) Sheets of paper
2) Writing Utensils
3) Poster Board
4) Chairs and tables (if necessary)

# Time Allotment:

This activity can take anywhere from 20 to 45 minutes, including processing questions. With a larger group, the activity may take a longer time to conduct and to process. With younger groups, this activity may take more time to process.

# Directions:

Step:

1) The room should be set up as follows:

   a) Draw a figure on a sheet of poster board. Cover the sheet of paper and place the poster board in the center of the room.

   b) Have enough chairs for half of the individuals completing the activity in a line facing away from the poster board.

2) Have each individual team up with one other individual within the group.

   a) If there are many different age groups within the group, it may be best to pair individuals that are closest to each other in age.

   b) This activity may work best if pairs are individuals who do not typically work with each other.

   c) (Optional) Facilitators can create a short activity to have the pairs decide which individual will be labeled "A" and which one will be labeled "B".

3) The "A" group is told to go inside the room and take a seat in one of the chairs. They are given a sheet of paper and a writing utensil.

4) The "B" group remains outside. The facilitator informs the group that they are going to be giving instructions to their partner on how to draw the figure that is drawn on the poster board behind their partner. The "B" individuals will only have visual access to the picture and will have to direct their partner on how to accurately reflect the picture through communication.

   a) First, group "B" will be informed that they are to demonstrate any type of bad communication (i.e. yelling, showing frustration, unclear directions, etc).

   b) Leaders will tell group "B" that when they are directed to change the activity, they are to demonstrate what they may consider to be "good" communication.

5) Facilitators will lead group "B" members inside to pair up with their partners. Group "B" members will stand in front of their seated partner and facing the poster board.

6) Facilitators will remove the cover over the figure on the poster board and ask for the activity to begin. Group "B" members will direct their partners to accurately draw the image that is presented on the poster board.

7) After approximately 3 minutes of "bad communication", facilitators will make an announcement to change the activity. This will let group "B" individuals know to change to "good communication."

8) Allow approximately 3 minutes to continue and observe reactions.

9) Conclude the activity with debriefing and processing.

## Processing Questions:

   1) As a member of group "A", what differences did you notice throughout the activity? How was your interaction with your partner?
   2) As a member of group "B", what were your thoughts and emotions during this activity? What did you notice and observe from your partner?
   3) What would you describe as successful in this activity? What form of communication would you prefer?
   4) What individuals or group of individuals in your experiences demonstrate the kinds of the communication you experienced during this activity?
   5) How can you apply this activity to your everyday life and experiences?

# Special Considerations:

1) For this activity, understanding power relationships within the group is imperative prior to initiating the activity. The dynamics of the group may change if there is a power differential within the group and within the pairs (i.e. a boss and their subordinate; older member and younger member). Understanding roles and dynamics within the population the facilitator will use is highly important to administer and process this activity.

2) It is important to remain cautious of individuals in the group who have any disability and how that can have an effect on the outcome of this activity.

# Adaptations:

The authors focused on administering this activity to groups that are in the transition stage because they have already created relationships with individuals, and this activity may lead the group towards the working stage. Furthermore, this activity can be adapted to be completed with groups in the working stage; however, the authors encourage facilitators to change processing questions according to their observations throughout the activity and monitor any negative or harsh behavior.

This activity can be adapted to have both groups experience the role of directing their partner to replicate the drawing on the poster board. Additionally, facilitators may want to give no direction to the Group B members to observe what kinds of communication techniques are being used. Using this adaptation, facilitators can observe what techniques individuals commonly use in their interactions with others. Processing questions will reflect what techniques were observed and their strengths or weaknesses.

Furthermore, facilitators should be aware of the developmental level of the group that they are conducting this activity with. For younger task groups, this activity may need more time spent on processing the activity rather than on the activity itself.

# References:

Sullivan, H. (1953) *The interpersonal theory of psychiatry.* New York: Norton.

# Author Notes:

*Chelsea Latorre* is a Graduate Student at the University of Oklahoma. She has experience working as a group facilitator at the Calm Waters Center for Children and Families.. Additionally, Chelsea has had experience developing, organizing, and leading curriculum for group psychoeducational sessions with teenagers in her experience with the Sooner Upward Bound program offered through the University of Oklahoma Community Counseling program. Chelsea currently is interning at the A Better Chance clinic and has interest in working with adolescent children and teenagers.

*Kenneth Comer* is a Graduate Student at the University of Oklahoma. He has conducted couple, family, and individual therapy through both his practicum at the University of Oklahoma as well as through his work with Catholic Charities, St. Joseph's Counseling Center. Through practical and experiential evidence attained, Kenneth works to develop group activities to aid individuals in understanding how differing personality styles may be at the core of some challenges found in certain relationships.

*Paula McWhirter* is a Professor of Counseling at the University of Oklahoma, specializing in positive psychology and group therapy interventions for individuals, children and families. She has been a group therapist and professional member of the *Association for Specialists in Group Work* for over 20 years.

# Correspondence:

Questions and comments related to this activity may be directed to:

Chelsea Latorre
University of Oklahoma
19800 Slaughterville Road
Lexington, OK 73072
chelseaann@ou.edu

# Giving ~ Thanks

*By Allison K. Arnekrans*

## Population:

Both male and females would benefit from this activity. This group would be appropriate for participants ranging from early adult (18-25) through older adult (25-55). This activity can be conducted in outpatient settings, including: community agencies, schools, hospitals, and private practice. This activity would work well in groups that have goals centered on personal growth, rebuilding trust, improving self-esteem/worth etc. Participants with issues such as abuse, depression, eating disorders, terminal illness, injury, anxiety, and relational issues may benefit from this activity. Participants must be able to demonstrate insight into their situation and behavior.

## Stage of Group:

Working

## Type of Group:

Counseling/Therapy

## Rationale:

While we often receive feedback on our negative or self-sabotaging characteristics from ourselves and others, it is imperative that we are also provided with compliments and encouraging feedback that helps us to know our strengths and positive qualities. In an effort to improve self-esteem, rebuild trust, and receive constructive feedback about our experiences, this group activity focuses on reflection of feedback through letter writing. Letter writing has been documented in the professional literature as important for personal growth and has been used with multiple populations (Hagedorn, 2011; Hoffman, Hinkle, & Kress, 2010) in a variety of settings (Tubman, Montgomery, & Wagner, 2001). Using Person-Centered and Cognitive-Behavioral techniques that focus on the unique thoughts and feelings of the individual, writing letters and receiving feedback should symbolize growth, unity as a group, and insight from the group process into a place of forgiveness and thankfulness.

## Goals:

**Participants will:**
1) be able to identify a time within the group structure when they were upset or felt regret about something they said or did. Upon identification, participants will forgive themselves and provide positive feedback through letter writing.
2) be able to identify a person within the group that affected them physically, emotionally, or mentally. Participants will write this other person a second letter to provide positive feedback and encouragement.

3) spend time in reflection and insight into the group process, as well as improve their self-esteem.

## Materials:

Each participant will each need:
1) Formal letterhead paper
2) Envelopes
3) Writing Utensil
4) An empty show box with a hole in the top
5) Markers
6) Colored paper
7) Stickers to decorate the letters/boxes

## Time Allotment:

For most groups, this activity should take between 20-30 minutes. Large groups and/or participants with lower cognitive functioning may require more time. Additional time may be required for participants who need assistance with writing the letters and/or decorating.

## Directions:

Step:
1) Provide each participant with two sheets of heavy letterhead paper and two envelopes.

2) Provide each participant with a shoe box for them to decorate and/or put their name on. Arrange the boxes on a separate table away from the group circle.

3) Describe that the first letter should be addressed to them and the second letter to another person in the group with whom they appreciate.

4) Encourage each participant to think about something they have done or said throughout the group process that they possibly regret or would have done differently. NOTE: Should the participant not be able to identify anything, encourage the participant to write a letter of self-gratitude and thankfulness for their presence within the group.

5) Challenge the participants to write a letter to themselves explaining what happened, what they would have done differently, and finally to provide an apology to themselves. Within the apology, there should be signs of forgiveness (e.g. acceptance, taking responsibility, identifying solutions for the future, etc.).

6) To conclude the letter, allow the participants to compliment themselves through positive language and encouragement. Give them space and time to decorate their card.

7) Go through a visualization exercise in which the group member visually releases themselves from the guilt, resentment, or embarrassment, of what they said/did during the group that caused a problem. Ask the participants to seal the letter and reopen it when they are feeling overwhelmed and/or upset at another point in their lives. Remind participants that no one is perfect and to remember the value of forgiving ourselves and others.

8) The second letter should be addressed to someone within the group whom demonstrated a feeling, action, interaction, or moment in which the participant felt thankful or helped. This letter should be a sentiment of thanks to the person for what they did or said that the participant found impactful and worthy of thanks. Remind the participant that this letter should also include positive encouragement and appropriate compliments.

9) Organize each participant's box on a separate table, clearly marked with each name. As the participants finish their letters, have them step up to drop the letters in the boxes. Let the participants know that that may sign the other letter or leave it anonymous.

10) Provide a quiet time period in which participants can grab their box and read their letters.

11) Upon conclusion of the activity, have the participants reflect on and discuss the following questions.

## Processing Questions:
1) How did it feel for you to reflect on the group sessions and think about your words and actions?
2) Was it easy to find something to forgive yourself for?
3) How can you take this activity and use to in your everyday life? Is it appropriate to forgive yourself?
4) What was it like for you to take the time and acknowledge someone else in the group with kind words and encouragement?
5) How did it feel to receive kind words and positive communication from others?
6) Did you remember doing or saying the things indicated in the letter you received?

## Special Considerations/Cautions:
1) Some participants, depending on their level of participation and involvement in the group, may have difficulty coming up with something to forgive themselves for as well as something positive about another person. If this happens, encourage the participant to think about their role in the group and have them write a letter acknowledging positive behaviors for which they are proud. Remind the participants that the first letter is about honoring our own personal contributions to the group and letter two is acknowledging others' contributions.

2) If the participant is unable to think of something that another person has done or said in the group worth acknowledgement, encourage the participant to discuss the group process and how it has helped them. Some participants may be able to create a whole list of positives for others and only errors for themselves, while others find it difficult to praise others altogether. Encourage both groups to identify at least 1-2 things to talk about in each letter, regardless of the significance or intensity of the compliment or error.

## Adaptations:

This activity can be adapted for younger audiences (i.e. children & adolescents) by allowing participants to color or draw rather than to write. Less insightful responses may result. This activity could also be used with incarcerated individuals or offenders in a locked facility. Crafty materials, scissors, or sharp objects could be omitted from the original design.

## References:

Hagedorn, B. (2011). Using therapeutic letters to navigate resistance and ambivalence. *Journal of Addictions & Offender Counseling, 31*(2), 108-126.

Hoffman, R., Hinkle, M., & Kress, V. (2010). Letter writing as an intervention in family therapy with adolescents who engage in nonsuicidal self-injury. *The Family Journal, 18*(1), 24-30.

Tubman, J., Montgomery, M., & Wagner, E. (2001). Letter writing as a tool to increase client motivation to change: Application to an inpatient crisis unit. *Journal of Mental Health Counseling, 23*(4), 295-311.

## Author Section:

*Allison K. Arnekrans* is a Doctoral Candidate and practicing Professional Clinical Counselor-Supervisor. She has led both adult and child portions of multiple groups in a community mental health agency, as well in the classroom. Previous group topic include: social skills, ADHD, parenting, family management, divorce, anxiety, anger management etc. Allison has served as Past President, Vice President, and Secretary of the **Ohio Association for Specialists in Group Work** in (2010-2013) and currently is an Ad-Hoc Reviewer for the *Journal of Specialists in Group Work.*

## Correspondence:

Questions and comments related to this activity may be directed to:

Allison K. Arnekrans, MA, PCC-S
Doctoral Candidate at the University of Toledo, Toledo, Ohio
Youth & Family Clinical Therapist at Harbor, Toledo, Ohio
The University of Toledo
2801 W. Bancroft Street, Toledo, Ohio 43606
asandro@rockets.utoledo.edu

# Group Work with African American Women: Using Vision Boards for Self-Reflection and Goal-Setting

*By: Angela Coker, Karen Banks, Brianne Overton,*
*Carol Robinson & Jennifer Culver*

## Population:

African American College Students (see explanation below)

Visions boards may be useful with many diverse populations across the lifespan. In a therapeutic setting, vision board activities would fit under the topic of creative arts therapy. Creative arts therapy includes a variety of human expressions such as dance, drama, singing, drawing, and other expressive arts. Molina, Monteiro-Leitner, Garrett, and Gladding (2005) have discussed the usefulness of integrating creative arts therapy in multicultural group settings as a means of helping members explore, make meaning, and express their thoughts and feelings. We have had the most experience using vision boards with African American college women. Many African American women have family histories of sharing their ideas, hopes, and dreams through creative arts (Walker, 1983). Further, the use of culturally-informed rituals has also been identified as an effective intervention in working with African American groups (Parham, 2005). Integrating vision boards into group work may be viewed as a ritual activity or group intervention with African American female group participants. Vision boards allow for the manifestation and creation of cultural rituals of collectivism and personal affirmation. If implemented correctly, vision boards can be an important ritual/activity where group members are invited to revisit their goals and affirmations during subsequent group meetings. Vision boards have become very popular since the advent of the book *The Secret* (Bryne, 2006) that stresses the Law of Attraction. The Law of Attraction states that individuals draw into their lives the things to which they give the most attention. Vision boards can be a therapeutic and simple way to help group members conceptualize life goals and create a visualization of their aspirations.

## Stage of Group:

Working Stage

This activity could work during any stage of the group process, however we have found that it is most effective during the working stage when group members have had an opportunity to get to know each other and identify possible personal goals.

## Type of Group:

Psychoeducational

We have used vision board group activities largely with African American female college students. The primary focus of the groups have generally been psychoeducational in nature.

## Rationale:

While group work has been recognized as an important tool in assisting individuals with growth and change (Corey, 2012), research remains sparse regarding creative usages of group work techniques with African American women (Pack-Brown, Whittington-Clark, & Parker, 2002). The vision board activity is one technique we have found useful in providing group members with an opportunity to explore their values, interests, and goals for the future in an artistic and creative fashion. A vision board is a compilation of assorted images, words, or important items that represent an individual's hopes and dreams for the future. Typically, these images taken from magazines and are mounted on a large poster board, but some individuals may opt to develop a vision board electronically. Vision boards can also be useful for some introverted group members who may exhibit less verbal expression, but who want to fully participate in the group process. We have also found that using vision boards as a therapeutic technique has the power to assist African American women in exploring and dismantling internalized racialized gender stereotypes (Collins, 1990; hooks; 2000) and/or beliefs about the intersections of race, gender, and sexual orientation (Lorde, 1984). Incorporating culturally-affirming vision board activities into group work with African American women can also allow for group cohesion and communal sharing. Group participants can offer each other positive feedback, encouragement, and introduce themselves to life possibilities they may have not previously considered. This activity is a departure from the traditional group setting where group members may be sitting in chairs in a circle. It allows for creativity and entertainment in a therapeutic setting.

## Goals:

Participants will:
1) explore and clarify life goals in a communal, creative, and therapeutic environment .
2) engage in self-reflection and personal affirmation.
3) express themselves using artistic and creative methods.

## Materials:

1) Large paper (11x14) or poster board (one per person)
2) Markers
3) Scissors
4) Glue
5) Tape
6) Culturally-affirming magazines that highlight African American women in a wide variety of positive professional activities and life circumstances

## Time Allotment:

This is an activity that can be done in one group setting, or over several group settings. If done in one group session, we recommend group facilitators plan for about 90 minutes to complete this activity.

## Directions:

Step:

1) Introduce the concept of a vision board to the group and explain the rationale for the activity. The group leader can use the following sample script to introduce the activity: *"Today we will be learning about vision boards. A vision board is a collage of visual images that individuals create to signify their goals and dreams. These images can be material things such as money, a dream home, or a fancy car. Vision boards can also highlight our desire for non-material things such as inner peace, positive relationships with significant others, or even physical fitness. Vision boards can be a fun and creative way for individuals to clarify and affirm life goals. I am going to invite each of you to work independently within our group today to create your own vision boards. At the same time feel free to interact with each other."*

2) Each group member should have a poster board and access to magazines and art supplies along with sufficient physical space to work.

3) Invite group members to cut and paste the pictures and words onto their boards.

4) Group members can color, decorate, or add encouraging words onto their boards as freely as they choose.

5) Once group members' vision boards are complete, invite each member to share their vision board with the group and process the activity.

6) Encourage group members to take their vision boards home and hang it in a space where they will see it daily.

## Processing Questions:

1) How was this activity/experience for you?
2) What did you learn about yourself through creating your individual vision board?
3) What did you learn about other group members as a result of seeing their vision boards?
4) Did the process of creating a vision board help you think about your goals for the future?
5) In what ways has this activity caused you to think, feel, or behave differently?

## Special Considerations:

1) Encourage group members to think beyond the context of the film/book *The Secret*. This activity is not about thinking something materialistic into existence; it is about visualizing goals, the law of attraction, and focusing on positive energy and thoughts.

2) Consider bringing in examples of vision boards from peers or other group leaders to show the group. However, it is important that group members are encouraged to create a piece unique to their own lives and goals - not a copy of someone else's work.

3) This activity should not be a forum for making a "pop culture" poster. Be aware that some younger group members may gravitate towards images of celebrities or elaborate lifestyles that may appear unrealistic to some. It is important for group facilitators to be supportive and encouraging, and not judgmental about a group member's aspirations.

4) While this is a creative activity, it does not require a high level of artistic ability. Remind group members that this activity is not about how artistic they are, but more focused on encouraging them to visualize their values and ambitions.

5) Group members with difficulties participating generally are able to enjoy this activity as the majority is personalized. Group facilitators are encouraged to practice techniques of linking and universalizing (Yalom, 1995) in order to encourage group members to share ideas and images with each other.

## Adaptations:

1) This activity can be done in a shorter amount of time, depending on how much time group facilitator may want to devote to collective group processing.

2) If large poster board is unavailable, a standard size piece of paper will work.

3) This group activity could also be done electronically if each group member has a laptop device.

4) This activity works well for many types of groups and age ranges. Modify magazine selection to fit group characteristics (e.g., age, sex). For example, when using this group activity with adolescents or teenagers, it is important to use positive age-appropriate magazines that fit the group's developmental stage and interests. Some magazine selections may include, but are not limited to publications such as *Right On!*, *Seventeen*, *Teen Vogue*, and *J-14*. What is important is that the images found in these magazines are affirming, offer hope and validation.

## References:

Byrne, R. (2006). *The secret*. Atria Books/Beyond Words.

Corey, G. (2012). *Theory and practice of group counseling* (8th ed.). Pacific Grove, CA: Brooks/Cole.

Collins, P. H. (1990). *Black feminist thought: Knowledge, consciousness, and the politics of empowerment*. New York: Routledge.

Hooks, b. (2000). *Feminist theory: From margin to center* (2nd ed). Cambridge, MA: South End.

Lorde, A. (1984). *Sister outsider*. Freedom, CA: The Crossing Press.

Molina, B., Monteiro-Leitner, J., Garrett, M. T., & Gladding, S.T. (2005). Making connection: Interweaving multicultural creative arts through the power of group interventions. *Journal of Creativity in Mental Health, 1*(2), 5-15. doi: 10.1300/J456v01n02_02.

Pack-Brown, S. P., Whittington-Clark, L. E., & Parker, W.M. (2002). *Images of me: A guide to group work with African-American women.* Farmington, MA: Microtraining Associates.

Parham, T. A. (2005). *Working with African American clients* [DVD]. American Psychological Association. Available from http://www.apa.org/pubs/videos/4310618.aspx

Walker, A. (1983). *In search of our mothers' gardens*. New York, NY: Harcourt Brace Jovanovich.

Yalom, I. D. (1995). *The theory and practice of group psychotherapy* (4th ed.). New York, NY: Basic Books.

## Author Notes:

*Angela D. Coker* is an Associate Professor of Counseling and Family Therapy at the University of Missouri - St. Louis. Her areas of scholarship include women's issues, group work, and the internationalization of counseling. She is the author of numerous articles, book chapters, and co-editor of the book *Experiential Activities for Teaching Multicultural Competence in Counseling* (Pope, Pangelinan, & Coker, 2011). She is a 2011 Fulbright-Hays scholar who has examined cultural diversity in Brazil. In 2013 she served as a sabbaticant in the Department of Educational Foundations at the University of Botswana where she conducted research on how culture impacts the practice of counseling in Botswana. She has also provided professional development training for UNICEF, in addition to community outreach in Namibia. She has over 10 years' experience leading groups both nationally and internationally. Her primary area of group work has been in leading groups designed for women.

*Karen D. Banks* earned her Bachelor's degree in Communication from Millikin University in Decatur, IL. She completed her Master's of Education – Community Counseling at the University of Missouri St. Louis and is currently seeking licensure as a Professional Counselor. Karen works with children, families, and young adults on issues such as behavior struggles, dealing with divorce, coping with grief and loss, depression, academic success, and other mental and social concerns. She also enjoys public speaking and gives presentations and training on mental health and social well-being to both school age children and adults. She has several years of experience leading groups for women across the lifespan.

*Brianne L. Overton* is an Adjunct Instructor at the University of Missouri – St. Louis. Ms. Overton received a Masters of Arts in Thanatology in 2008. She is currently a grief counselor in the St. Louis, MO metropolitan area. She supports grieving children and teenagers that have experienced a significant loss. Ms. Overton is the Founder of Bereavement, Life, & U, which offers comprehensive death education services and community outreach and support to grieving families affected by a significant loss. While studying at the University of Missouri – St. Louis, *Ms. Overton* co-facilitated a support group for African-American women called *SisterScholars* for over two years, in addition to experience conducting group work for children and young adults who experience grief and loss.

*Carol Robinson* is currently pursuing a Ph. D. in Counseling/Counselor Supervision and Education at the University of Missouri – Saint Louis. She is concurrently completing training in Psychodynamic Psychotherapy at the Saint Louis Psychoanalytic Institute where she maintains a private practice. Her long term research interests include examining the effects of microagressions on women of color and lesbians. Carol Robinson has experience leading groups for African American women in community and higher educational settings. She also conducts outreach groups to the LGBT community in the St. Louis metropolitan area.

*Jennifer Culver* is a Counselor Education Doctoral Student at the University of Missouri St. Louis. Culver earned a Master of Arts in Clinical Mental Health Counseling and a Certificate in Addictions Counseling from Indiana Wesleyan University. Culver holds a Bachelors of Arts degree in Communication Studies and Black Studies from the College of Wooster. She is committed to research addressing the mental health needs of Black women as her research interest include body image, help-seeking behaviors, stress, and intimate partner violence. She is particularly interested in addressing these issues as they pertain to minority women and women of the African Diaspora in particular.

## Correspondence:

Questions and comments related to this activity may be directed to:

Angela D. Coker, Ph.D., LPC, NCC
Department of Counseling and Family Therapy,
University of Missouri – St. Louis,
456 Marillac Hall, One University Blvd.,
St Louis, MO 63121-4400.
cokera@umsl.edu

# High, Low, A-Ha!

*By Lindsey Fields & Delini Fernando*

## Population:

This activity has been successful with groups of Undergraduate First-Year students; please see the adaptation section for additional suggestions.

## Stage of Group:

Orientation (and can be repeated throughout the life of a group)

## Type of Group:

Task, Psychoeducational, or Counseling

## Rationale:

Few first-year college students have the opportunity of processing their experience of college. These students face many challenges including leaving home, making new friends, managing their classes and study schedule, balancing different activities related to the college experience. As a result of their experiences, some students thrive while others struggle (Astin, 1997). A shared college context allows a safe place for these first-year students to engage in self exploration and shared experience, and find the support they need (Light, 2004). This particular activity works well as an opening activity that can be repeated throughout the group process on a regular basis. This activity also works well in a classroom setting as students can often find more than just academic support in their classrooms by making connections with each other.

## Goals of the activity:

Participants will:
1) get to know their fellow group members.
2) identify commonalities among their experiences in college, but positive and negative.
3) experience support from fellow group members for a current or ongoing struggle.
4) identify sources of support in college.

## Materials needed to conduct the activity:

1) Note cards
2) Pens or pencils

## Time Allotment: This activity can take 20 minutes for small group (8 members or less) and

more time for a larger group. This activity has been successful with groups as large as a college class of 20-45 students and the time ranges from 45 minutes to an entire class time of an hour and 20 minutes.

## Directions:

Step:

1) Ask members to take a notecard and write down:

   a) Something positive that happened in their lives within the past week (the "high")

   b) Something negative that happened in their lives within the past week (the "low")

   c) Something they learned this past week in school or about themselves (the "A-Ha!")

2) Give them a few additional minutes to write down anything else they wish to share with the group leader (or course instructor) that they might not want to share with the group.

3) Ask participants to also write down any questions they have about potential resources on campus or support services they may need.

4) When everyone has finished, ask each person to introduce themselves by name and share whatever they would like from their notecard. How much each participant shares may vary.

5) Ask members to make observations about the kinds of struggles group members are sharing and provide support or ideas to promote success to the person sharing.

6) Identify commonalities by linking members' common experiences, and thank each member for sharing.

7) Gather the cards at the end of the activity so you are able to read through each statement and provide written feedback, campus resource suggestions, or sources of support if the group member chose not to share that particular event out-loud during the discussion.

## Processing Questions:

1) Would anyone like to share what this experience was like? OR What were your initial reactions to the activity?
2) What was it like to talk about your positive experiences?
3) What was it like to talk about your negative experiences or struggles?
4) What did you learn about yourself from this activity?
5) What did you learn about others, or from others, in this activity?
6) How does it feel to know that you share some experiences with others in this group?
7) What have you learned from this activity that you might apply in your life during the coming week?

## Special Considerations:

More time may be needed the first time this activity is utilized in the group, as group members become more familiar with the activity, the time needed will shorten.

## Adaptations:

This activity can be adapted for use with high school students, and additional topics such as grief groups and adolescent's coping with the divorce of their parents. Using this activity with adjustment issues is also well received. The processing questions may need to be adapted to suit the particular target group.

## References:

Astin, A. (1997). *What matters in college: Four critical years revisited.* San Francisco, CA: Jossey-Bass, Inc.

Light, R. (2004). *Making the most of college: students speak their minds.* Cambridge, MA: Harvard University Press.

## Author Notes:

*Lindsey Fields* is an Academic Counselor at the University of North Texas. She has had six years of experience in teaching First-Year Seminar and Career Exploration coursework with undergraduate students. Her group work experience additionally includes training First-Year Seminar instructors and Peer Mentors on activities around group dynamics, personality and interest assessments, and college adjustment issues in social, academic, and emotional contexts; leads college student groups in residence halls.

*Delini Fernando* is an Associate Faculty member at the University of North Texas. She has group work experience with numerous populations, supervises group facilitators, teaches masters and doctoral level group counseling courses at University of North Texas; has specialized training and experience in group work and family counseling.

## Correspondence:

Comments and questions about this activity may be directed to:

Lindsey Fields, M.S. and M.Ed., LPC
Academic Counselor, University of North Texas
1155 Union Circle #311277
Denton, TX, 76203-5017
Lindsey.Fields@unt.edu

# Improving Your Sexual Communication

*By Rachel Hardin & Paula McWirther*

## Population:

All consenting adults age 18+ in a relationship/partnership/union.

## Stage of Group:

Orientation

## Type of Group:

Psychoeducation/Counseling

## Rationale:

Communication has proved itself time and time again to be a large part of a relationship. According to Rehman, self-disclosure can enhance relationship closeness and intimacy thus increasing sexual satisfaction and ultimately relationship satisfaction as well. Research also shows that being transparent in the sexual realm requires intimacy and risk taking that can improve the relationship as a whole (Montesi, 2011). So in the matters of sexual satisfaction, it is necessary to have healthy communication with your partner. It's important to be open and honest with your partner so expectations are clear, spoken, and reasonable. This way needs and wants are being met, while both partners are being satisfied.

## Goals:

Participants will:
1) gain a clear understanding of what the other person likes/dislikes sexually.
2) be more comfortable with talking about sex and related issues with one another.
3) increase in sexual satisfaction, and in turn relational satisfaction.

## Materials:

1) Research material about communication in couples may be useful for the facilitator to act as a reference point.
2) Journals may also be provided for couples to use when reflecting on homework. This group is mostly discussion focused and driven, therefore few materials are needed.

# Time Allotment:

The course will be conducted in 2-hour sessions for 4 sessions, exploring the topics of sexual communication and sexual satisfaction. If additional counseling is needed, couples will be referred to a more long-term individual counseling setting. Note that we describe the facilitation for two sessions in full detail. This comprises the basic format and should be replicated for facilitation of the final two sessions.

# Directions:

Step:

Session 1: Sexual Communication

1) It's important that each couple introduce themselves and a little bit about why they are in the group.

2) After each couple has shared, the facilitator reminds group members that the first two group sessions focus on sexual communication, with the final two sessions focusing on sexual satisfaction. The facilitator will seek to process these separately throughout.

3) The facilitator asks each couple to consider their current level of sexual communication *as a couple*; each individual participate will be asked to rate themselves as a couple in terms of their sexual communication on a scale (from 1-10) ranging from very poor (1) to highly effective (10). Each individual is asked to generate a number on the scale; therefore, couples may vary considerably in their rating of themselves as a couple.

4) Based off their responses, the instructor will probe each couple to elaborate further on what their sexual communication looks like. The instructor will then present some research on how sexual communication effects sexual and relational satisfaction.

5) Break: If needed, a short break could be taken at this time.

6) The facilitator will then go around the group asking each member's reactions to their partner's response to the previous question. Each couple will speak individually to the group to allow full participation and attention from each member. Afterwards, short explanations or elaborations can be given from the couples, if needed.

7) Next, all will be asked to reflect on the number that they provided about their sexual communication as a couple (see #2 above). Couple by couple, each individual of each dyad is asked what would need to happen in order to move their number higher on their current sexual communication scale (#2 above). Specific actions (by either partner) or examples are encouraged regarding something they would like to improve in regards to their current sexual communication. Couples take turns sharing with the larger group individually once again to allow for full participation

and attention from each member. As participants imagine what specific action(s) they would need to take or that their partner would need to take in order to improve their current sexual communication, this is processed with their partner. Partners are asked about their reactions and willingness to consider the actions discussed.

8) As each couple shares, the facilitator explores the specific actions discussed. Couples are asked if they would be willing to engage in a specific action as homework, in order to improve their communication. Only actions that are considered respectful and desirable to *both* members of the couple are considered. If agreement is reached, the facilitator notates the actions agreed to my each member of each couple.

9) The facilitator closes by validating members' willingness to discuss the issues, reiteration about the importance of acceptance in communication, and with a reminder that the homework will be discussed at the next session.

Session 2: Sexual Communication

1) This session is dedicated to processing the assigned homework. Couples are asked about the action agreed on to facilitate increased sexual communication. Couples are asked to share their attempts made, including reactions of self and partner. Any positive steps are validated and barriers are explored.

2) Begin and end this session with more information about sexual communication. Validate couples for healthy changes in thoughts, or in actions. Elaborate on the importance of open, honest, positive, non-blaming/judgmental communication in the relationship.

Note that content within each step below is to be shared among all group members, with couples taking turns sharing with the larger group. Sessions 1 and 2: Sexual Communication

For the final two sessions, this two-session pattern is repeated, but the topic of sexual satisfaction is explored.

## Processing Questions:
1) How effective do you think your level of current sexual communication is in your relationship?
2) What area of your sexual relationship would you like to see improvement in?
3) What was it like hearing your partner say they weren't satisfied with something in your sexual relationship?

## Special Considerations:

It would be important to make sure each member is okay with possibly having couples of the same sex or different religions in the group. It would also be important to assess the groups' needs by age. Due to the sensitive nature of the group, all participants must be 18 years or older and in a committed relationship, with both members of the couple present.

## Adaptations:

It may be necessary to split the groups up by sexual orientation or religious/spiritual affiliation. When considering age of the participants, activities and homework must be appropriate for the capabilities of the age. For example, special adaptations made be necessary for older couples who are not capable of doing certain activities that a younger couple may be willing or able to do.

## References:

Montesi, J. L., Conner, B. T., Gordon, E. A., Fauber, R. L., Kim, K. H., & Heimberg, R. G. (2013). On the relationship among social anxiety, intimacy, sexual communication, and sexual satisfaction in young couples. *Archives of Sexual Behavior, 42*(1), 81-91. doi:10.1007/s10508-012-9929-3

Montesi, J. L., Fauber, R. L., Gordon, E. A., & Heimberg, R. G. (2011). The specific importance of communicating about sex to couples' sexual and overall relationship satisfaction. *Journal of Social & Personal Relationships, 28*(5), 591-609. doi:10.1177/0265407510386833

Rehman, U., Rellini, A., & Fallis, E. (n.d). The Importance of Sexual Self-Disclosure to Sexual Satisfaction and Functioning in Committed Relationships. *Journal of Sexual Medicine,8*(11), 3108-3115.

Smith, A., Lyons, A., Ferris, J., Richters, J., Pitts, M., Shelley, J., & Simpson, J. M. (2011). Sexual and Relationship Satisfaction Among Heterosexual Men and Women: The Importance of Desired Frequency of Sex. *Journal Of Sex & Marital Therapy, 37*(2), 104-115. doi:10.1080/0092623X.2011.560531

Willoughby, B., & Vitas, J. (n.d). Sexual Desire Discrepancy: The Effect of Individual Differences in Desired and Actual Sexual Frequency on Dating Couples. *Archives of Sexual Behavior, 41*(2), 477-486.

## *Author Notes:*

*Rachel Hardin* is an employee at Griffin Memorial Hospital where she conducts Recreational Therapy group counseling/psychoeducational classes. In addition to teaching from pre-existing core curricula, Rachel creates group therapy curricula about a variety of issues. She also provides counseling at Crossroads Youth and Family Services working with first time offenders through the Teens and Parents in Partnership (TAPP) psychoeducational program, which teaches teens and parents about multiple aspects of healthy parent/child relationships, with a focus on communication.

*Paula McWhirter* is a Professor of Counseling at the University of Oklahoma, specializing in positive psychology and group therapy interventions for individuals, children and families. She has been a group therapist and professional member of the Association for Specialists in Group Work for over 20 years.

## *Correspondence:*

Questions and comments related to this activity may be directed to:

Rachel S. Hardin, B.A., M.Ed. Candidate
University of Oklahoma Community Counseling
3001 Pheasant Run Rd. Apt. 260
Norman, OK. 73072
RachelHardin@ou.edu

# Keep It Simple: Feeling Awareness to Promote Mindfulness

*By Jane Warren*

## Population:

This activity can be very effective for inpatient and outpatient adults with addictions problems.

## Stage of Group:

Orientation

## Type of Group:

Counseling, therapy

## Rationale:

This group experience allows the participants to experience mindfulness. Mindfulness can be defined as intentionally paying attention to the present moment experience (Kabat-Zinn, 1994). *Right* mindfulness is identified as focusing the mind, not allowing distraction to overtake the focus (Dali Lama, 2002). Hanh (1991) acknowledged how the mind wanders, but practicing right mindfulness allows recognition of when the mind wanders, noting what it focuses on, and then returns to focus. Mindfulness enables awareness and acceptance of thoughts, feelings, and physical sensations, and promotes acceptance in a nonjudgmental way (Marcus & Zgierska, 2009). Mindfulness skills can support coping strategies in many challenging situations (Warren, 2012). Mindfulness develops and deepens over time and is not about getting anywhere or fixing anything; instead, it is an invitation to be where one already is and to know the inner and outer landscape of each moment. Through mindfulness techniques, habits can be recognized and changed (Dali Lama, 2002). Being aware of thoughts and emotions as they arise, without trying to medicate, judge, or control them, increases self-awareness. This self-awareness supports self-efficacy, change, choice, and wisdom (Dali Lama, 2002).

## Goals:

Participants will:
1) Have a time to focus on inner feelings and ground one self.
2) Use a simple artistic creation to identify the current feeling.
3) Non-judgmentally identify and experience a feeling.

## Materials:

1) Drawing paper
2) Crayons, paint, colored pencils, pencils, and/or pens

## Time Allotment:

Five minutes to create the image, ten minutes to share image and experience in dyads, and thirty minutes to process as a whole group (Forty-five minutes).

## Directions:

Step:

1) The group leader will ask all of the group members to relax and take a couple of deep breaths. *"I would like you all to relax, close your eyes, imagine you are in a warm, safe place, and now take some deep breathes. Continue this relaxation for 3-4 minutes."*

2) All participants will be given a white piece of paper and simple drawing/coloring materials (colors, colored pencils, finger paints, pencils, pens).

3) Each participant will be asked to then draw and create on the paper what and how they are feeling at the moment. *"Please now take this blank paper, think of it like your mind, and draw on it, how you are feeling right now. This feeling experience is you own creation. I could be an animal, a color, and or an image of any form, shape, and color that expresses your body feeling right now. A feeling is an experience in your body, not a thought in your mind."*

4) After about five minutes to create the image, they will then be asked to pair up with a person sitting by them and share their picture, what it represents, what it meant to them, and what they learned. They are asked to do this for five minutes each. *"Now that you are finished with your drawing, for about 5-10 minutes, please share with someone next to you: What you discovered, felt or recognized. Remember please there are no judgments about your experience or your creative tasks. One you have shared, please ask the person with whom you have shared, to now share with you, in the same, nonjudgmental, descriptive way."*

5) Then for about 20 to 30 minutes the whole group is asked to voluntarily share what they learned about themselves, from their dyad, and any insight into drawing a feeling. *"Now we will ask you to share as a whole group, what you learned, felt, recognized or experienced. Please know you can choose to share or not to share."* The following questions could be asked to facilitate this discussion:
   a. *What was this experience like for you?*
   b. *How is it to take 5 minutes and focus on a feeling?*
   c. *How is a feeling different from a thought?*

6) They are each asked to identify what the take away might be from the experience. *"Now we would like you to think about what this experience has meant to you, and what you might take away with you for use in your process of recovery."*

## Processing Questions:

1) What does this feeling experience tell you about where you are today?
2) What is your take away today?
3) How might this exercise be used to help you center or ground yourself during the week?

## Special Considerations:

If someone were to show notable distress from the feeling experience, follow up and support might be needed. Special considerations will include awareness of cultural, gender, and age differences in expression and in management of feelings. If group members were considerably fatigued, the experience may be more difficult. Processing of the feeling is important so the participants do not leave with unfinished feelings.

## Adaptations:

A diverse type of artistic materials could be used such as clay, and/or arts and crafts materials with glue and small artistic supplies. The experience itself can be self-contained itself meaning it could be sufficient without any follow-up group. This experience can be used to center for a group continuation or simply used as a stand-alone activity as a self-regulation skill, a mindfulness template, or a validation that feelings are ok. This can be a starting point for change if the feelings were something not fitting to what the participant wanted to feel and can be a way to "say" what is not said in other situations. This exercise can be used for any and all ages. It can be very useful for many applications such as self-regulation for anger management; for children who are in situations where feelings are not validated; for persons who are new to the United States and are learning to express themselves; and for grief where feelings are often intense.

## References:

Dali Lama, H. H. (2002). *How to practice: The way to a meaningful life.* (J. Hopkins, Trans.). New York: Atria Books.

Hanh, T. N. (1991). *Peace is every step: The path of mindfulness in everyday life.* New York: Bantam Books.

Kabat-Zinn, J. (1994). *Wherever you go there you are.* New York: Hyperion.

Marcus, M. T. & Zgierska, A. (2009). Mindfulness-based therapies for substance use disorders: Part 1. *Substance Abuse, 30*, 263-265. doi:10.1080/08897070903250027

Warren, J. (2012). Applying Buddhist practices to recovery: What I learned from skiing with a little Buddha wisdom. *Journal of Addictions & Offender Counseling, 33*, 34-47.

## Author Notes:

*Jane Warren* received her PhD in Counselor Education in 1987; then worked as a full time clinician with addictions, mental health, and couple and family individual and group work in a community mental health center for 23 years. Presently as a full time Faculty person, she teaches Group Procedures class in a CACREP-accredited Master's counseling program

## Correspondence:

Jane Warren PhD LPC LMFT LAT
Professional Studies Department - Counseling Program
Room 338 Education Building
University of Wyoming
Laramie, Wyoming 82071
Jwarren4@uwyo.edu

# Life Stages and Group Stages: Asking the Existential Questions

*By Susie Thomas*

## Population:

Because the focus is on existential themes and life stages, this activity is most appropriate for adults or older adolescents. It was originally designed for graduate students in a counselor education program, but could easily be adapted for use in other Populations/settings (see "Adaptations" below).

## Stage of Group:

Working, termination

## Type of Group:

Counseling, therapy

## Rationale:

When groups are working well, members progress through various stages (Corey, 2012; Yalom & Lescz, 2005). It can be helpful to promote awareness of the work that has been done, and/or what still needs to be done. In addition, group members are in various stages in their own lives, and may or may not have resolved developmental crises or tasks associated with a current or previous stage. This activity involves blending existential questions of meaning, loss, and transition with Erikson's psychosocial stages or the accompanying crises/tasks (Erikson & Erikson, 1997). Gestalt and creative arts techniques can be integrated into the session as well. The purpose of the activity is to create a space in which group members can process intrapsychic or interpersonal issues from their own lives, or issues that have surfaced in group.

## Goals:

Participants will:
1) reflect about existential themes in their own lives and in the life of the group itself.
2) bring issues of trust, shame, identity, and integrity into the here-and-now in group through movement, art, and verbal expression.
3) become more aware of their own struggles and more conscious of their experience in group.

272

## Materials:

1) Chairs (one for each member, plus several extra for Gestalt applications)
2) Paper (enough to depict each of Erikson's stages/tasks)
3) Tape
4) Markers, Crayons, or colored pencils

## Time Allotment:

90 minutes is ideal for this activity. Because the activity can be modified to include expressive arts and Gestalt applications, the time frame might be expanded to allow sufficient time for more creative expressions of themes that arise in the activity. The group leader should also allow 5-10 minutes for Set-up.

## Directions:

Step:

1) Set-up the space. Paper signs displaying each of Erikson's stages <u>or</u> crises should be spread far enough apart so that one or more members could stand or sit near a sign. The signs can be:
   a) placed in a timeline (i.e., from infancy through late adulthood, on the walls or floor);
   b) posted on opposite sides of the room (e.g., "Trust" on one wall and "Mistrust" on the opposite wall); or
   c) taped to chairs so that members can speak to or from the stage/task in a Gestalt empty chair application.

2) For groups involving participants who have already studied Erikson's model (e.g., graduate counseling students), the group leader can make the signs and verbally review them briefly when introducing the activity to ensure recall.

3) The group leader asks members to engage with the stages or crises. Example: *"today we are going to examine how various themes might exist in group and in your relationships with one another. I would like to invite you to..."* (see sample prompts below).

4) The group leader Encourages members to move around the room and respond out loud regarding their own experiences (*"I worried a lot when I was in elementary school"*), or to other group members (*"I notice that you are standing near the word 'Shame' and I wonder what you need right now"*). Some group leader prompts are suggested below, with variations based on whether the group is focusing on the stages or the crises/tasks:

For applications using Erikson's psychosocial stages:

a) "Stand near the stage where you are currently in your life. What are you most aware of in this stage? Who is here with you? What needs to be said here?" Or, if using chairs, "Sit in a stage you would like to know more about. What is it like to be in this place? What needs to be said *from* here?"

b) Move to a stage you were in during another time in your life. What was true then? What needs to be said from (or 'to') this stage?"

c) "Move to a stage you are afraid of. What are you aware of in this stage? What do you need here?"

For applications using Erikson's crises/tasks:

a) "Move to the place where you feel you are now in group. What is it like to be here? Who is here with you, and who is not? Is there someone you would like to invite to join you in this place?"

b) "Would you like to move to a different place? If so, who could help you to make that move? What would need to be different for you to go to this place?"

c) "Notice the place opposite you in the room. Speak to that place."

5) The group leader should monitor the progress of the activity and be mindful of time, leaving adequate space for processing questions.

## Processing Questions:

1) What did you notice about yourself during the activity?
2) What feelings were you aware of? What feelings, if any, are present now?
3) What did you notice about other group members?
4) Is there anything you would like to say to another group member?
5) How does today's experience influence your process of moving forward?

## Special Considerations:

1) This activity involves examining existential themes and the use of Gestalt and expressive arts techniques. Therefore, members may experience uncomfortable feelings associated with loss, loneliness, transitions, etc.
2) Gestalt techniques have the potential for catharsis, and addressing existential issues may lead to feelings of fear and anxiety.
3) The group leader needs to use great care and good judgment in protecting group members and providing safe containment during the activity, especially in situations where members are encouraged to speak directly to one another, because some topics may provoke feelings of vulnerability.
4) In situations where the mobility of group members is limited, the requirement to move around the room can be omitted and group members can verbally identify stages/tasks.

## Adaptations:

For groups in which members may not be familiar with Erikson's model, the group leader can explain the model more directly prior to engaging in the activity. In this instance, it may be more meaningful to have the group members design the signs with color or visual imagery and talk together about the terms in one group session. The original activity could then occur in a second session.

In addition to adaptations based on population/setting, the activity itself can be modified. One of the benefits of this activity is the potential for multiple creative adaptations, based on the nature of the group. In some groups, members are mostly focused on understanding their own issues; in other groups, the main focus is on the group process itself, and dynamics that need to be surfaced and processed. This activity can be modified to address the needs of either type of group, by using the stages and crises to help members reflect on their own relationships and life issues or on the issues that have arisen within the group.

## References:

Corey, G. (2012). *Theory and practice of group counseling* (8th ed.). Belmont, CA: Brooks/Cole.

Erikson, E. H., & Erikson, J. M. (1997). *The life cycle completed.* New York: Norton & Co.

Yalom, I. D., & Lescz, M. (2005). *The theory and practice of group psychotherapy* (5th ed.). New York: Basic Books.

## Author Notes:

*Suzy Thomas* is an Associate Professor of Counselor Education at Saint Mary's College of California. She has had fifteen years of group work experience, including designing and facilitating groups in K-12 schools and teaching Group Theory and Practice to graduate counseling students.

## Correspondence:

Questions and comments related to this activity may be directed to:

Suzy Thomas, Ph.D.
Saint Mary's College of California
Kalmanovitz School of Education
P.O. Box 4350
Moraga, CA 94556
sthomas@stmarys-ca.edu

# "Light Shadows" Art Activity

*By Quinn M. Pearson*

## Population:

Outpatient adults with substance-related or other mental health disorders; see below for adaptations with groups for adolescents, inpatient adults, and grief

## Stage of Group:

Working

## Type of Group:

Counseling, therapy

## Rationale:

This activity is grounded in Carl Rogers's classic assertion regarding self-acceptance and change, a dialectic that is espoused by the contemporary practice of dialectical behavior therapy (DBT; Neacsiu, Ward-Ciesielski, & Linehan, 2012). Because the focus on behavioral change was seen as invalidating by group members, radical self-acceptance was added to form the fundamental dialectic in DBT which combines validating and accepting group members while helping them change (Dimeff & Linehan, 2001). This stance seems to echo that of C. Rogers (1961), who wrote, "We cannot change, we cannot move away from what we are, until we thoroughly *accept* what we are. Then change seems to come about almost unnoticed" (p. 17). This activity incorporates the power of expressive arts to provide stimulating and challenging experiences that allow for creative self-exploration and healing (N. Rogers, Tudor, Tudor, & Keemar, 2012).

## Goals:

Participants will:
1) Experience feelings associated with difficult experiences or personal attributes.
2) Increase self-acceptance.
3) Access healing properties of internal creative processes.

## Materials:

1) Blank paper—8½ by 11 inches or larger
2) Box of crayons for each participant
3) Song—"That I Would Be Good" by Alanis Morissette
4) MP3 player, computer, etc. with speakers

## *Time Allotment:*

60 minutes is the approximate time needed to complete this activity. For groups containing more than 8-10 group members, allow for 15 additional minutes.

## *Directions:*

Step:

1) Provide each group member with paper and box of crayons.

2) Prepare group members for the experience by informing members that they will be asked to complete an art activity, listen to a song, and complete a second art activity. They will work independently without interacting until all activities are complete. Inform group members that they may elect to share the content of their art or to keep the content private, and they will be asked to process their reactions to, feelings about, and insights from the experience. *"This activity will consist of three parts—an initial art activity followed by a song and a second art activity. You will have the opportunity to discuss your experience at the end of the second art activity. When processing the experience, you will have the option of describing the content of your artwork or keeping it private."*

3) For the first art activity, ask group members to reflect on something that is difficult, painful, shameful, or guilt inducing about themselves, a past experience, or a memory. *"Think about an experience, a memory, or a personal quality that is very difficult, painful, shameful, or guilt inducing."*

4) As they reflect on this experience and/or personal quality, ask them to express the experience in color in the center of the paper. Encourage them to use their non-dominant hand, if they are comfortable doing so. *"As you reflect on the difficult experience or personal quality, in the center of your paper, use your non-dominant hand to express this experience using color. If you're not comfortable using your non-dominant hand, you may use your other hand. Using your non-dominant hand allows you to focus on the emotion rather than creating a work of art."*
   a. (In some groups, the group leader may want to ask group members to first draw a box in the center of the paper and to express the experience within the box.)

5) Without discussing the experience, play the song, "That I Would Be Good," by Alanis Morissette.

6) Ask group members to use color to surround the center with love, acceptance, and, if necessary, forgiveness. Suggest that they use the hand (dominant or non-dominant) with which they are more comfortable. *"Returning to your art work, use color to surround your painful, difficult experience with love and acceptance and, if necessary, forgiveness. Use whichever hand, your dominant or non-dominant one, feels more comfortable."*

7) Process the experience.

## Processing Questions:

1) What was that experience like for you?
2) What feelings surfaced during this activity?
3) What surprised you the most about this experience?
4) What did you learn from this experience?
5) What is the first thing you will notice that will tell you this activity made a difference in your life?

## Special Considerations:

If the group is being conducted in a setting in which confidentiality among members has not been established, group leaders should instruct group members *not* to share the content of their art. Inform group members that they will have an opportunity to discuss their experience of completing the activity.

## Adaptations:

1) If the group is based on a certain theme (e.g., addictions or grief), in the first part of the art activity you may ask them to focus on the most shameful or painful aspect related to that theme.
2) For adolescent groups, a different affirming song might be used to match the music preferences of the group members.
3) If group leaders are concerned that the difficult experience in the first art activity may be overwhelming (e.g., in an inpatient setting or grief group), they can either provide paper with a box drawn in the center of the paper or ask group members to draw a box in the center of the paper. Group members would be asked to complete the first art activity inside the box.

## References:

Dimeff, L., & Linehan, M. M. (2001). Dialectical Behavior Therapy in a nutshell. *California Psychologist, 34,* 10-13.

Morissette, A. (1998). That I would be good. *On Supposed Former Infatuation Junkie.* Beverly Hills, CA: Maverick Records.

Neacsiu, A. D., Ward-Ciesielski, & Linehan, M. M. (2012). Emerging approaches to counseling intervention: Dialectical behavior therapy. *The Counseling Psychologist, 40,* 1003-1032. doi:10.1177/0011000011421023

Rogers, C. R. (1961). *On becoming a person: A therapist's view of psychotherapy.* Boston, MA: Houghton Mifflin.

Rogers, N., Tudor, K., Tudor, L. E., & Keemar, K. (2012). Person-centered expressive arts therapy: A theoretical encounter. *Person-Centered and Experiential Psychotherapies, 11*(1), 31-47. doi:10.1080/14779757.2012.656407

## Author Notes:

*Quinn M. Pearson* is a Professor of Counselor Education at the University of North Alabama. She has taught group counseling courses for the last 18 years and has facilitated counseling, therapy, and psychoeducational groups in various settings, including university, inpatient, outpatient, and intensive outpatient settings.

## Correspondence:

Questions and comments related to this activity may be directed to:

Quinn M. Pearson, Ph.D., LPC
University of North Alabama
UNA Box 5154
Florence, AL 35632
qmpearson@una.edu

# Mindfulness through Yoga: An Empowering Group Format

*By Hailey N. Martinez*

## Populations:

Inpatient or outpatient adult and youth

## Stage of Group:

Any stage

In the *orientation and transition stages* of group work, focus is on mindfulness activities: breathe work, body awareness, emotions, thoughts, open awareness, and becoming centered and grounded in the present moment. The leader is looked upon to create a safe atmosphere and demonstrate acceptance of every member. Through focusing on getting the group members acquainted with becoming present in the here-and-now and aware of their breath, this exercise allows for them to become centered in their own experience.

In the *working and termination stages* of group work, integration of body movements through yoga is built upon the existing foundation created through the mindfulness practice. The yoga sequence can be used along with the grounding, centering, and breathing exercises. In these latter stages, group members are able to experience more of what is happening in their bodies and what thoughts and emotions are connected to their experience in the present moment. The compilation of all the exercises in the later stages of group work allows for individuals to share with one another, after the trust has been established. More so, it allows for further process and accessing creativity in articulating one's experience. Using this exercise to close the group, allows for individuals to participate in a shared experience, and to continue to experience connection within the group as termination occurs.

## Type of Group:

Psycho-educational, Counseling

## Rationale:

Mindfulness is the practice of actively attending to the present moment of what is coming up in the space of the here-and-now, observing nonjudgmentally and compassionately (Brown, Marquis, & Guiffrida, 2013). Various techniques can be incorporated into a mindfulness practice. Yoga provides a combination of postures, breathing exercises, concentration, and meditation to attain balance and increased self-awareness (Rybak & Deuskar, 2010). Utilizing yoga within a group format creates space where destructive patterns of thinking and behaving can be explored, and honored for the process in which is brought forth through the group experience. Implementing a mindfulness-based yoga format into group work can aid in an individual's ability to take skills acquired within the group experience into one's everyday life practice. Thus, mindfulness discipline aids in responding to defensiveness and reactivity in a more compassionate and present manner both with oneself and others (Schure, Christopher, & Christopher, 2008).

## Goals:

Participants will:
1) Increase body awareness.
2) Develop awareness of thoughts and emotions, observing non-judgmentally with focus in the present moment through breath work.
3) Gain an increased sense of connection with one's body through yoga sequences.
4) Gain an increased awareness of emotions and memories stored in the body through yoga sequences.

## Materials:

1) Yoga mats/Chairs
2) Talking stick
3) Drum/meditation bowl/crystal singing bowl (optional)
4) Sweet grass/sage stick (optional)

## Time:

1-1.5 hours, depending on the preference of time spent participating in each activity

## Directions:

Suggestions for creating the atmosphere:

1) Allow for a designated space for each group member to practice the yoga asanas (poses), based on their own ability level, and whether or not there is space for yoga mats or the use of chairs is more applicable.

2) Essential Oils (EO) can be used within the session to help ground and center the group members. This is a practice that has hypothesized benefits and is optional. EO can be placed on the wrist and inhaled for 30 seconds to 1 minute, or EO can be placed in a diffuser in the group room. EO's: *cedar wood-* promotes relaxation, balance, and increased mental focus; *lavender-* used for relaxation, depression; *vetiver-* used for ADHD, hyperactivity, mental focus; *peppermint-* increased alertness, oxygenizing for places of tension; *balsam fir-* used for depressive symptoms.

3) Sweet grass and sage has been used in Native American Indian traditions for centuries, providing purification and spiritual purposes. This is an optional activity for those who have experience with these materials and can take the form of placing it in a metal, glass, clay bowl, or an abalone shell- and burning as incense. Sweet grass is used for the higher realms of consciousness, in particular, the spiritual realm. Sage is used as type of incense for "smudging," clearing the space of negative energy and as a grounding activity to set intention for the group.

**Step:**

1) The following exercises can be implemented while seated in a chair or on a yoga mat. *Grounding:* allows for individuals to becoming present in the moment by tuning in to what is happening in their body. By learning how to ground oneself provides one with the tool to return to a safe space if at any point in the mindfulness exercises, one finds themselves becoming triggered or unable to remain present. Bringing a call to the present moment can include using a drum, a Tibetan meditation bowl, or a crystal-singing bowl. Inviting group members to become present in the moment, letting go of any thoughts or expectations. The group leader might say, *"I invite you to sit tall, stretching through the crown of your head; shrugging your shoulders up towards your ears (inhaling), and on the exhale- rolling your shoulders back. I invite you to close your eyes if you feel comfortable doing so, or simply pick a space on the floor directly in front of you to gaze at. Bring your awareness to the soles of the feet."*

2) *Centering:* building off of the grounding exercise, centering increases awareness for what is happening in the body. Tuning in to one's thoughts, emotions, and what one is experiencing in their body, the ability to become present in the moment with non-judgmental awareness is expanded. The group leader might say, *"Beginning at the soles of the feet, move your awareness up through your feet to your ankles, to the knees, hips, up the spine, to base of the skull, and ending at the crown of your head. "*

3) *Breath Awareness:* provides a vessel for returning to the present moment. When a traumatic event is experienced, breath is absent and thus storing the traumatic event, and holding the memory of the traumatic event in our body. Breathing helps to release tension and create space in areas of our body that are stagnant and holding memory and connected emotion. The group leader might say, *"I invite you to bring your full awareness to your breath, not controlling your breath in any way; simply noticing where your breath falls- does your chest or stomach move more? Not placing any judgment or thought onto your breath, simply noticing."*

4) *Yoga Sequence:* extending beyond the physical aspects of a yoga practice. Yoga can aid in reconnecting with the body, and beginning to come into relationship with one's self in a new light through mind-body connection. The yoga sequence is self-paced and is adapted to meet the individual's needs in the present moment. The yoga sequence begins after the grounding, centering, and breath awareness exercises. It is suggested for the sunflower sequence (in a standing position), seated posture (sitting in a chair), and seated cat and cow (sitting in a chair) - postures to be used first; followed by any variation of the following poses. Other yoga poses are optional as well, leaving room for the facilitator to adapt a sequence that is suitable for the population being served. As the majority of these poses are instructed for individuals seated in chairs, it is also possible to adapt these postures for practice on the mat. The facilitator must be mindful of using inviting language when guiding the group through the yoga sequence; using words such as: invite, encourage, etc.

Moving from breath work to yoga sequence: The group leader might say,

*"Now, I invite you to come to a standing position in Tadasana/Mountain Pose; using your breath, move your awareness to the soles of your feet, and imagine a long line drawing through the center of the sole of your foot and moving up through your legs, up your spine, and out the crown of your head, stretching tall to the sky."*

*Tadasana/Mountain Pose: is the beginning position for all standing poses. Begin by standing hip-width apart. Lift and spread your toes on the floor, finding your balance point from the center of the sole of your feet. Flexing your thigh muscles, lifting your kneecaps. Press your shoulder blades into your back, widening and releasing the shoulders down your back. Relaxing your jaw, placing your tongue to the roof of your mouth (to promote softening in the jaw). Relaxing and softening your forehead, eyebrows, cheeks, eyes.*

Below are a series of yoga positions that the group leader could use and language for facilitation of the positions.

### Sunflower Sequence

1) Begin standing. Start with your feet apart and your toes turned out to the side at 45-degree angles. Inhale, reach the arms high, and keep the shoulders relaxed.
2) Exhaling, lower your arms to a "T" position while bending your knees and hinge forward at the waist. Be mindful to remain neutral in the spinal column.
3) Continue hinging forward and release the arms down so that they cross in a sweep near the ground. Shoulders may round at this part of the sequence.
4) Inhale, begin sweep the arms back up toward the starting position. Bring arms wide hitting the "T" position on the way up. Straighten the legs.
5) Return to the starting position.
6) Exhaling, simultaneously bend your knees and lower your arms to a "T" position with your palms facing up to form Sun pose.

### Proper Seated Posture/S-Spine

1) Sit all the way back in the chair and lift your shoulders up and back like bird wings.
2) Place your feet flat on the floor and parallel.
3) Align your hips, knees, and ankles to make a 90-degree angle.
4) Inhale, lifting your heart and extending the top of your head to the sky.
5) Face your head forward with the chin parallel to the ground. Ears align over shoulders.
6) Your spine should have alternating curves (lumbar, thoracic, and cervical) in the form of an "S." No "rainbow back."
7) With one hand, reach behind your lower back. If seated correctly, you should feel a slight inward curve in your lower (lumbar) spine.

### Seated Cat and Cow

1) Sit sideways on you chair with your feet firmly on the floor and hands on your knees.
2) Begin with a neutral spine in Proper Seated Posture. Draw your shoulders up and back like bird wings.
3) Inhale. Extend your spine by lifting your tailbone and the crown of your head upward. Press your chest forward and up, into Cow position.
4) Exhale. Draw your buttocks down, and curve your back by pulling your navel into your spine. Bring your chin to your chest for Cat position.
5) Move with powerful inhale and exhale breaths, alternating back and forth from Cow to Cat. As you get more comfortable, increase the pace.

### Seated Kite

1) Sit in a chair in Proper Seated Posture, performed by placing both feet planted firmly on the floor, hip-width apart.
2) Inhale and reach your head up to the ceiling, lengthening your spine. Exhale.
3) Inhale and raise your arms up over your head. Press your palms together with straight elbows pressing your arms into your ears.
4) Your hand fly high like a kite. Sway with the breeze, moving your arms and body right and left, front and back, using your inhale and exhale breaths.
5) Hold the position for 3-5 breaths.

### Chair Down Dog

1) Start either seated/standing to use a chair for support. Position the chair in front of you and adjust to your height.
2) Stand in Mountain Pose (Tadasana)/sit in proper-seated posture. Legs are hip-width apart and feet are pressed firmly on the ground.
3) Inhale and lift your arms up to the sky. Hug your upper arms to your ears.
4) Exhale and hinge forward from your hips, reaching out for the back of the chair in front of you.
5) Holding onto the chair, and without letting go, inhale an lift your arms up and away from the floor
6) Exhale and press back with your heart and hips toward your legs, lengthening your torso. Keep your back in an S-spine. Gaze at the floor.
7) Hold the position for 3-5 breaths.

### Standing Chair Lunge

1) Place back of chair firmly against the wall. Stand in front of the chair, about 1 foot away, with feet a few inches apart, toes facing forward.
2) Hinge from your waist and place both hands on the chair seat in front of you, palms down.
3) Step back with your right foot, keeping the right leg straight. Push the ball of your right foot into the floor. Bend your left knee over your center toes. Do not allow your knee to go past your toes.
4) Now, in the lunge position, using the chair for balance and support. Press right heel down to stretch your calf.
5) Breathe 3-5 powerful breaths while holding the pose.
6) Step forward with your right foot and bring both feet together. Repeat for the left leg.

<u>Corpse Pose</u>
1) Sit on the floor with knees bent, feet on the floor, and bring your arms out in front of you. Make a c-curve with your spine and slowly begin to lower onto your spine. Imagine flattening out the spine, from the tailbone to the base of the skull. Pressing firmly into the floor.
2) Now walk out your legs, pressing the calves of your legs firmly into the mat.
3) Allow your body to soften, opening your palms to the sky, and allowing your feet to fall open in either direction.
4) With each breath, giving your body permission to let go and relax.

## Processing Questions:
1) What are you leaving here with today?
2) What will you do differently today, this week, this month?
3) How will participating in this group today impact what you do next?

Homework: Questions for the individual to process prior to the next group session:
1) What was this experience like for you?
2) What were you noticing about your thoughts during this experience?
3) What emotions were you experiencing?
4) What were you noticing in your body?
5) Do you notice anything shift throughout this experience?

## Special Considerations/Cautions:
It is recommended if a group leader has interest in expanding their facilitation of group work using yoga, to seek further training with a registered yoga school. Special consideration needs to be taken with physical abilities or constraints (e.g. previous injuries, pregnancy) of group members that would require modification to particular yoga poses. Group members may need permission from their physician in order to engage in some of these activities. It is necessary for leaders to have knowledge and training in the yoga poses and know variations of the poses for individuals who need adaptations to the poses. Additionally, sensitivity to smells should be considered if using suggested essential oils or scented herbs.

## Adaptations:
The activity serves as a basic guideline, leaving room for flexibility in the way one chooses to structure the group format. The yoga sequence provides a basic layout of yoga asanas that can be adapted to using yoga mats, in place of chairs. More so, the choice can be made to incorporate a completely different yoga sequence than the one provided.

Also, this activity is suitable for group members of all age groups, as well as being able to integrate the basic guidelines into a variety of different settings. More specifically, it has been used with survivors of sexual assault (SA) and domestic violence (DV) (Emerson, Sharma,

Chaudry, & Turner, 2009). Practicing these activities helps to restore the relationship with one's body, while increasing one's awareness of the trauma that becomes stored in the body. Specifically, SA and DV survivors will be able to re-connect with their bodies, and safely explore one's emotions and thoughts. Below are some processing questions that could be used for working with SA and DV survivors.

1) Connected to your situation, what were you noticing about your experience?
2) When experiencing those thoughts or memories, where were you feeling it in your body?
3) What beliefs do you hold for owning these parts of your experience as your truth?
4) How do these beliefs serve you in your everyday life?

In a study conducted on adolescent sex offenders, results showed relaxation being viewed as positively reinforcing, as well as an increase in controlling impulses and unwanted thinking patterns (Derezotes, 2000). This activity can be adapted to use in working with registered sex offenders (SO's), providing increased awareness of the body and mind. Practicing mindfulness invites the individual to become increasingly aware of one's thoughts and identify triggers and thinking errors. For SO's, a specific goal is to create empathy for what one is experiencing in the present moment as their awareness increases, as well as for their fellow group members as they share their own experience. The SO's will also become increasingly more aware of when they are experiencing a trigger, and thinking errors.

Process Questions for SO's group:
1) What thoughts were you noticing come up through this experience?
2) When thinking of those thoughts, where were you noticing them in your body?
3) How do you differentiate between the positive thinking and negative-unhealthy thinking errors?
4) How will the following exercises help for you to identify when you are experiencing those unhealthy patterns of thought or behavior?

# References:

Brown, A. P., Marquis, A., & Guiffrida, D. A. (2013). Mindfulness-based interventions in counseling. *Journal of Counseling & Development*, 91(1), 96-104.doi: 10.1002/j.1556-6676.2013.00077.x

Derezotes, D. (2000). Evaluation of yoga and meditation trainings with adolescent sex offenders. *Child & Adolescent Social Work Journal, 17(2), 97-113.*

Emerson, D., Sharma, R., Chaudhry, S., & Turner, J. (2009). Trauma-sensitive yoga: Principles, practice, and research. *International Journal of Yoga Therapy*, 19, 123-129.

Ristuccia, C., & Geddes, L. (2011). Yoga for small spaces. *Say It Right, 1ˢᵗ Ed.*

Rybak, C., & Deuskar, M. (2010). Enriching group counseling through integrating yoga concepts and practices. *Journal of Creativity in Mental Health*, 5(1), 3-14.

Schure, M. B., Christopher, J., & Christopher, S. (2008). Mind-body medicine and the art of self-care: Teaching mindfulness to counseling students through yoga, meditation, and qigong. *Journal of Counseling & Development, 86*(1), 47-56.

Zinn, J. K. (1990). Full catastrophe living: Using the wisdom of your body and mind to face stress, pain, and illness. *Random House, Inc.*, New York, NY.

## Author Section:

*Hailey Martinez* is a Doctoral Student at Idaho State University in the Counselor Education and Supervision PhD program. She serves as a graduate student and new professional committee member for the **Association for Specialists in Group Work**. She works for a non-for-profit agency specializing in group work with adolescents, sexual assault and domestic violence survivors, as well as facilitating a trauma-focused yoga class for clients and staff. She has facilitated group work with intellectually disabled sex offenders. She also leads adventure-based counseling groups and has facilitated a mindfulness small group for first year master's students in counseling. Her group work interests include: adventure-based and experiential group work; trauma-focused group work; social advocacy and group work; social justice and group work; international group work; and multicultural group work.

## Correspondence:

Questions or comments related to this activity may be directed to:

Hailey N. Martinez, M. Coun, LPC, NCC, Doctoral Student
Idaho State University
921 S. 8th Ave., Stop 8120
Pocatello, ID 83209-8120
marthail@isu.edu

# Modified Polar Sculpture

## Population:

The Modified Polar Sculpture can be utilized with adult groups in inpatient and outpatient clinical settings. (see adaptation section for other populations of interest).

## Stage of Group:

Orientation, working, or termination

This experiential learning activity can be used during a number of group stages depending on the purpose of the activity, the goal of the group, or the current level of group functioning. The Modified Polar Sculpture (MPS) is an activity that enables group members to create visual representations of the internal conceptualization they have regarding their relationships with others. If used in the early stage of group formation, the MPS may enhance group cohesion and trust as group members are making themselves 'known' to one another (Corey, 2004). During the working stage the MPS is utilized to facilitate the connection of emotions and thoughts regarding past, present and future relationships. At this stage, the focus is on creating pathways for change. And finally, when used during the termination stage of a group, the MPS allows group members to identify changes that have occurred and to illuminate the growth experienced.

## Type of Group:

Counseling, psychotherapy

## Rationale:

Research suggests that people conceptualize or map their complex interpersonal relationships internally (Constantine, 1978). Sculptures or spatialization techniques enable people to create a visual, symbolic representation of relationship maps. Early research on families (Kantor, 1975) suggested that distance regulation is a core mechanism for understanding families in terms of both physical and metaphorical space. The MPS facilitates access to participants' metaphorical maps with an emphasis on emotional connection and the meanings associated with distance regulation. Once accessed, the visual representation can be processed and used as an agent of change. This powerful experiential activity can "cut through excessive verbalizations, intellectualization, defensiveness, and projection of blame" (Costa, 1991, p. 123), which people frequently use when discussing intimate relationships.

## Goals:

Participants will:

1) access their internal relationship map and make it external and visual.
2) develop awareness of perceptions and feelings related to one's interpersonal relationships.
3) take ownership and responsibility for feelings and to enhance new opportunities for relationship growth and change (Costa, 1991).

## Materials:

1) Enough furnishings (chairs, lamps, small tables, etc...) to represent each group member's family members.
2) Sufficient space for each group member to place their representations and for the group to process the activity is needed. Access to several rooms is usually needed.

## Time Allotment:

The required time is dependent upon the number of group members. The MPS is appropriate for groups that range in size from 3 to 8 participants. Group members will need 15-25 minutes to arrange his/her sculpture. The whole group works on this at the same time. After group members complete the sculpture, each group members is then given 30-40 minutes to process the experience with the group leader and other members.

## Directions:

The directions for the original polar sculpture focused on a person's primary parental figures (Constantine, 1978). The directions for this activity have been expanded to include family members deemed important by the participant.

Step:

1) The group leader gives the following directions: *"The purpose of this activity is to create a visual representation of your family relationships. You may select any of the available furnishings to represent yourself and your family members. Please arrange the furnishings in relation to one another according to your view of your family and the relationships family members have with one another. The furnishings may be placed in any location and in any configuration within the space available. After completing the arrangement, please put yourself in position among the arrangement and remain silent for several minutes in order to connect with associated feelings and thoughts."*

2) The group leader waits until each group member has finished the sculpture and had time to sit within the arrangement for a few minutes. At that point, the group leader guides each group member to move around their arrangement and make any needed adjustments to the furnishings like moving them closer or further away, angling them in various ways, and so on. As they move through the furnishings, they are instructed

to take a moment and acknowledge the developing feelings and thoughts. They are to do this until the arrangement of the furnishings 'feels right'.

3) No one speaks until each group member has time to finalize his/her sculpture. Once complete, the group leader facilitates processing the sculptures with the group members.

## Processing Questions:

1) How did you get to the arrangement you finally chose?
2) How are you feeling about the sculpture as you observe it?
3) What changes would you like to see?
4) If you could move the furnishings the way you would like your family to be, what would that look like?
5) How will your relationships with family members and others close to you change as a result of your experience here today?

## Special Considerations:

1) Because group members are being asked to experience and share sensitive relationship information, group safety and confidentiality are essential. This experiential activity can have a powerful impact on group members and elicit strong emotional reactions. Group facilitators must be prepared for this and monitor members' responses.
2) This activity may not be appropriate for group members with disabilities that limit mobility unless the group leader can provide appropriate accommodations.

## Adaptations:

The MPS can be used effectively in clinical training programs to assist students in the exploration of family-of origin issues that will likely impact therapeutic relationships. With this adaptation the group leader is a clinical faculty member. The instructions do not require modification for use with this population. The process questions should be modified to include the following additional question: How will todays experience influence your relationships with future group members?

The MPS can also be adapted for use in a wide array of organizational structures. In business settings the purpose of the activity would be to strengthen relationships with co-workers in order to improve inter-office communication leading to improved performance and productivity. This adaptation will require the group leader to modify the instructions by asking participants to create a visual representation of their co-worker relationships rather than their family relationships. For this adaptation process questions 4 and 5 will need to be replaced with the following questions:

1) If you could move the furnishings the way you would like your co-worker relationships to be, what would that look like?

2) How will your relationships with co-workers change as a result of your experience here today?

## *References:*

Corey, G. (2004). *Theory and practice of group counseling.* Belmont, CA: Thomson Brooks/Cole.

Costa, L. (1991). Family sculpting in the training of marriage and family therapists. *Counselor Education and Supervision, 31*(2), 121-132.

Constantine, L. L. (1978). Family sculpture and relationship mapping techniques. *Journal of Marriage and Family Counseling, 4*, 13-23. doi: 10.1111/j.1752-0606.1978.tb00508.x

Hernandez, S. L. (1998). The emotional thermometer: Using family sculpting for emotional assessment. *Family Therapy, 25*, 121-128.

Kane, C. (1996). An experiential approach to family-of-origin work with marital and family therapy trainees. *Journal of Marital and Family Therapy, 22*(4), 481-488. doi: 10.1111/j.1752-0606.1996.tb00222.x

## *Author Notes:*

*Pat Sims* is an Assistant Professor at the University of Southern Mississippi (USM) and W. Jeff Hinton is an Associate Professor at USM. Both authors have served as Program Director for the Marriage and Family Therapy Program at USM with significant experience in training therapists and in group process for over 20 years. In addition to training therapists, both authors have been group facilitators for multiple therapeutic groups including anger management, adults molested as children, grief, and at-risk adolescents.

## *Correspondence:*

Questions and comments related to this activity may be directed to:

Dr. Pat Sims
The University of Southern Mississippi
Department of Child and Family Studies
118 College Drive, Box 5035
Hattiesburg, MS 39406
pat.sims@usm.edu

# My Photograph for Today

*By Heather L. Smith*

## Population:

Adults with normative cognitive and personality functioning

## Stage of Group:

Orientation or Transition

## Type of Group:

Counseling and psychotherapy groups

## Rationale:

Counselors are ethically responsible to work collaboratively with group members to devise integrated counseling plans that are consistent with the group member's abilities and circumstances (ACA Code of Ethics). At times, counselors must provide additional options for communication to reduce disparities in services. Using photography and spoken language honors individuals who might struggle with traditional counseling, such as those who are not accustomed to direct eye contact or direct questioning, those unaccustomed to individualistic language, and those new to the English language.

## Goals:

Participants will:
1) be supported in developing the norm of taking turns when speaking.
2) increase a sense of hope from learning about options for sharing ideas with the group.
3) experience non-judgment and validation of his/her expression.
4) learn new information about other members.

## Materials:

1) Laminated photos of scenes and objects without significant stand-alone meaning (2-3 times the amount of photos as people in group).
2) Space to place the photos for viewing around a room.

## Time Allotment:

This activity takes approximately 20 minutes for 10 members.

## Directions:

Step:

1) Place photographs around the room for easy viewing.

2) Tell members that when you are finished providing instructions, they are to walk around the room making sure to view each photograph briefly.

3) Ask them to practice awareness of their own reaction to each photograph, noting one that is somehow meaningful or symbolic for them in a positive way.

4) Tell them that as the group leader, you will watch to make sure everyone has had an opportunity to view each photograph. Once they have viewed all the photographs and identified one that is specifically meaningful or symbolic to them, they will return to the group and share how the photograph is meaningful to them. The group leader may say something like, *"Who would like to start by showing us your photo and sharing how it's meaningful or symbolic?"* and encourage each member to share.

5) Be sure to state that more than one individual can choose a particular photograph and that they will just take turns holding it while sharing.


## Processing Questions:

1) What do you think about this activity?
2) Were there any themes that emerged?
3) Sometimes verbal expression is limiting. How might you use other methods to share during the group?
4) In what ways are you comfortable sharing information?


## Special Considerations:

This activity might not be appropriate for use with populations struggling with reality-testing such as those who experience hallucinations or delusions. Additionally, leaders may need to make adaptations for those with visual or motor difficulties.


## Adaptations:

This activity might be adapted for use with select groups of adolescents. Group leaders need to assess and control for the likelihood of inappropriate comments.

## References:

American Counseling Association. (2005). *Code of ethics*. Alexandria, VA: American Counseling Association.

## Author Notes:

*Heather L. Smith* is an Assistant Professor of the Practice of Human Development Counseling at Vanderbilt University and a Staff Therapist at the Vanderbilt Psychological & Counseling center. She has had twelve years of designing and facilitating group work and nine years teaching group counseling.

## Correspondence:

Questions and comments related to this activity may be directed to:

Heather L. Smith, PhD, LPC-MHSP, NCC, LDN, RD
Box 90; 230 Appleton Place
Nashville, TN 37203
h.smith@vanderbilt.edu

# Picking Up Your Baggage

*By Paula L Rainer & Michelle R. Ghoston*

## Population:

This group activity is suitable for adults who are enrolled in graduate school. This group activity is utilized for adults in building resiliency through adversity. The adversity for this activity represents balancing your schedule, family, work, and class work as a graduate student. This activity will be conducted for the purpose of overcoming adversity/stressors to achieving life balance during graduate studies.

## Stage of Group:

Transition

## Type of Group:

Psychoeducational

## Rationale:

The objective of this group is to identify and facilitate coping mechanism for stressors. In life we all have stressors (baggage). Although we are all different we all experience life circumstances that threaten our goals and life balance. In order to start to acknowledge and mitigate our life stressors we have to identify them. This group activity provides a venue to identify group participants' life stressors (baggage) and reflect on strategies for balance or nullification of those stressors. The rationale of this activity is to create an in-depth activity which allows the participants to immediately move into the transition phase of a group.

Upon identifying their stressors the group participants start to process the depth of how the stressor can potentially impact their goals. During the processing phase of the group the solution focus exception (Davis & Osborn, 2000; Simon & Berg, 2002) question will be used to explore times of resiliency when the participants have successfully navigated the stressor. The relief that group participants will experience comes from processing the exceptions to conquering stressors and bonding with other participants who are experiencing similar challenges.

## Goals:

Participants will:
1) identify underlying stressors.
2) process previous success with overcoming stressors (baggage).
3) increase self-efficacy (Bandura, Caprara, Barbaranelli, Gerbino, & Pastorelli, 2003) about handling the stressor.

# Materials:

1) Small lunch size brown paper bags (one per participant)
2) Two different colors of paper (10 sheets of one color and 10 sheets of another color)
3) Pens (one per participant) and one pair of scissors
4) Plastic baggies (one per stressor category)

# Time Allotment:

If you have 5-10 group participants this activity can be executed in 1 hour. The more participants the less time they can share. All participants do not have to share their experience during the process. Group participants can also learn through the sharing of others.

# Directions:

Step:
1) Preparation
   a) Prepare the sheets of paper by cutting them in even portions (approximately 1 inch).

   b) Choose one color for all of the stressor categories.

   c) If the group includes 10 group participants you should create 10 slips of paper to denote each stressor category. For example, if you write down a stressor of "school" you should provide 10 slips of paper to denote school, just in case all ten participants consider school as a stressor. The stressors can include some basic stressors like work, significant other, pets, in-laws, relatives, health concerns, children, finances, friends, emotional support, etc.

   d) Preferably, you can also create the slips of paper in a word or excel document and cut them into strips.

   e) Also prepare about twenty blank slips of paper for group members to write in their own personalized stressors that are not provided on the prepared slips of paper.

   f) Place the slips of paper in baggies with a label denoting the stressor.

   g) With the second colored sheet prepare blank slips of paper (approximately 1inch) to be used later for solutions.

   h) Place the slips of paper in plastic baggies with a label denoting solutions.

2) Execution
   a) The group leader facilitates introductions of the group members. The group leader explains to the group that they are participating in a psychoeducational group with an objective to minimize or eliminate the impact of stressors (baggage) during graduate school.

b) Say to the group, *"we all have experienced a great deal of stressors and we need to acknowledge that by picking up our baggage."* Instruct every group member to pick up their baggage (brown bag), saying *"some of our baggage is heavier than others."*

c) Next, say to group members, *Please look through the sealed plastic baggies and select which baggage you are carrying and place it in your brown bag. Also there are blank sheets of paper for you to list baggage which is not listed on the pre-prepared slips of paper."*

d) The group members are then directed to share their baggage with the full group or the person seated next to them.

e) After they share they should pick up the blank second colored slips of paper and write down exceptions when they have been successful in the past navigating the current or a similar life stressor. Invite the group participants to share their exceptions. Say to the participants, "I would like to invite you all to share past stressors where you were able to successfully navigate similar stressors by implementing an exception."

f) Invite group members to share their identified coping strategies and skills. Say to the group, "please share the coping strategies and skills you identified to manage this stressor."

g) After everyone has shared, begin the processing question portion of the activity.

## Processing Questions:
1) What type of emotional or visceral response did you experience as you placed the stressors in your bags?
2) Explain any rational cognitions which have emerged during this group exercise which will assist you in considering new exceptions to decompress your stressors?
3) As a group member describe any physiological responses to identifying exceptions (Davis & Osborn, 2000) and solutions to your stressors (baggage)?
4) What are some themes of stressors or solutions among group participants?
5) How did this group activity validate your ability to identify and conquer stressors?
6) Describe your steps for implementing solutions as a result of this exercise.

## Special Considerations:
Keep in mind that this group activity is best used if the people in the group have a similar life experience (getting through a graduate program, experiencing a health crisis, divorce, etc). A level of safety for sharing vulnerabilities needs to be established for group members. Rules must be developed at the onset of the group to let participants know that they will share private information which might invoke vulnerabilities and emotions.

## Adaptations:

The types of groups which this activity can be used for are numerous. Those groups include support, anger, academic, self-esteem, marriage, growth, substance abuse, health, anxiety, cutting, ADHD, and disability groups for example.

This group can be adapted by allowing a family system/or friendship group to anonymously place slips of paper (denoting stressors) in one large brown bag which impacts the family system or group. The group leader then pulls out the slips of paper and requires the group members to develop solutions/exceptions or past stories of resiliency.

This group can also be adapted to groups for children. The group participants can have assistance in managing the stressors associated with learning disabilities, ADHD, English Language Learners, Gifted Students, and students with Autism.

## References:

Bandura, A., Caprara, G. V., Barbaranelli, C., Gerbino, M., & Pastorelli, C. (2003). Role of affective regulatory efficacy in diverse spheres of psychological functioning. *Child Development, (74)*3. 769-782.

Davis, T. E., & Osborn, C. J. (2000). *The solution focused school counselor: Shaping professional practice.* NY: Brunner-Routeldge.

Simon, J. K., & Berg, I. K. (2002).Solution focus brief therapy with adolescents. In R.F. Massey & S.D Massey (Eds.), *Comprehensive handbook of psychotherapy.* (Vol. 3, p. 133-152).

## Author Notes:

*Paula L Rainer* is a middle school Director of Counseling in Virginia, adjunct professor at George Mason University, and Center for Life Strategies Counselor in Residence. She has over nine years of group counseling experience in public schools, universities, and community settings.

*Michelle R. Ghoston* is an Assistant Professor at Gonzaga University, in Spokane, Washington and Canada. Dr. Ghoston has over 10 years of experience working with groups in clinical and higher education settings.

## Correspondence:

Questions and comments related to this activity may be directed to:

Paula L. Rainer, Ph.D
2508 Congreve Court
Herndon, VA 20171
Paularainer.phd@gmail.com

# Planting Daffodils

*By Carrie VanMeter & Jon M. Coventry*

## Population:

Transgender adults who are in the process of transitioning

## Stage of Group:

Orientation

## Type of Group:

Counseling, Therapy

## Rationale:

Change is hard and this activity is a way to encourage group members to see how small changes can lead to achieving big goals. Bockting & Coleman (2007) described the transition process as stages involving growing and changing which aligns well with the concepts reflected in the Daffodil Theory story (Edwards, 2004). Research indicated that during the transition period individuals can experience loss on multiple levels including social support and financial loss (Budeg, et al. 2012; Park, 2008). Having the ability to developing facilitative coping skills which includes seeking out social support, learning new skills, changing behaviors to positivity adapt, as well as finding alternative means to seeking happiness have shown to decrease anxiety and depression in the transitioning population (Budge, Adelson, & Howard, 2013, p. 546). In this activity, group members nurture something that needs to be taken care of to grow and develop which is a great parallel to their own transitioning process and helps them to begin developing facilitative coping skills. Group members explore how they must take care of themselves to grow and develop and find ways to support their goals. The activity helps group members to start thinking about a small change they could start that day.

## Goals:

Participants will:
1) gain awareness that small changes can lead to achieving greater goals,.
2) learn to set goals.

# Materials:

1) The Daffodil Theory by Jaroldeen Asplund Edwards. As of this printing, the story could be found at:
   http://intentblog.com/daffodil-principle-story-inspire-you/
   OR
   http://ezinearticles.com/?Applying-The-Daffodil-Theory-into-Business-Practice&id=9993
2) daffodil bulbs (variety pack)
3) small planters
4) acrylic paints (variety of colors; may also use any paint that would stay on clay planters)
5) paint brushes
6) planting soil

# Time Allotment:

1- 1.5 hours

# Directions:

Step:

1) Introduction: Say to group members, *"Today I would like to invite you to participate in an activity designed to help with goal setting. First we will read a story together and talk about the meaning we find. The story might resonate differently with each of you and we will want to explore these different interpretations. After that we will do a group activity that you will be able to take home with you. Before we get started I would like you all to take a few moments to write down your answers to the following questions related to your future goals of transitioning: a) Where do you see yourself in 6 months, 1 year, and 5 years? b) How do you motivate yourself to work towards your goals?"* Give the group members enough time to write down their answers and then ask them to set those aside so they can focus on the story.

2) Read the Daffodil Theory story to group members. Stop and process the story with group members before continuing the activity. You may ask the group questions such as: *"What messages are you taking from the story?"*, *"What do you think it was like for the woman to plant the bulbs year after year?"*, *"Can you relate the character Carolyn in the story?"*, *"Why do you think Carolyn was reluctant to go see the daffodils?"*, *"Do you have any people like Carolyn's daughter in your life, pushing you to plant your own daffodils?"*, *"What are you waiting for to start planting daffodils? Until you start taking hormones? Until you have the money for your surgery?"*, and/or *"What would it take for you to plant your own field of daffodils?"*

3) Give each member a daffodil bulb, planter, paint, brushes, and dirt. After the group members have all of their supplies ask them: *"Now I want each of you to pick up the daffodil bulb and take time to really look at it. How would you describe the daffodil bulb, what can you tell about it just by looking at it? What can't you tell by just looking at it?"* At this point Group leaders can relate the process of the growth stages of the flower to the transitioning process. Make the point that it is hard to tell from the beginning how

something will end but you know that you will need supplies along the way. But you have to plant the bulb first to see any change. Direct the group members to start by decorating their planters first and you could say: *"There is no right way to decorate your planter and no one needs to be an artist to make something beautiful. Keep in mind these planters are going home with you."*

4) After the group members have decorated their planters, instruct them to place the dirt inside but before they plant the blub challenge members to think about what their daffodil bulb could represent for them. The group leader could say *"Earlier you all wrote down some ideas of where you want to be in the future, some goals. Now before you plant your blub think about what goal it could represent for you. After you have decided plant your blub."*

5) After all group members have finished planting their blubs say *"I would like to invite each of you to share your planter and goal with the group."* After everyone has shared continue on with the processing questions.

6) After completing the processing questions, encourage the members to care for the bulb over the next few weeks and to work towards the goal they set.

## Processing Questions:
1) How do you plan to nurture your plant?
2) What steps do you plan to take to nurture yourselves?
3) What is one thing you are taking away from completing the activity?

## Special Considerations/Cautions:
Leaders should be aware that the materials for this activity could be costly and could be modified based on what might be available and affordable in their areas. It is important to take into consideration group members with motor disabilities (painting) and allergies (plants) and to adapt the activity as appropriate. If a group member for whatever reason would not want to take the plant home the leader should be prepared to process this with the group member. If possible the group leader can offer to hold onto the plant for a while, but with the intention for the group member to take over care for the plant when ready.

## Adaptations:
This activity has the potential to be used with any group that has a focus on change promotion and goal setting. It could also be used at the termination stage of group as a way to keep members engaged with their goals after group has ended.

## References/Credits:
Bockting, W., & Coleman, E. (2007). Developmental stages of the
    transgender coming out process: Toward an integrated identity. In R. Ettner, S.
    Monstrey, & E. Eyler (Eds.). *Principles of transgender medicine and surgery* (pp. 185–208). New
    York, NY: The Haworth Press.

Budge, S. L., Adelson, J. L., & Howard, K. A. (2013). Anxiety and depression in transgender individuals: the roles of transition status, loss, social support, and coping. *Journal of Consulting and Clinical Psychology, 81* (3), 545–557. DOI: 10.1037/a0031774

Budge, S. L., Katz-Wise, S. L., Tebbe, E. N., Howard, K. A. S., Schneider, C. L., & Rodriguez, A. (2012). Transgender emotional and coping processes: Facilitative and avoidant coping throughout gender transitioning. *The Counseling Psychologist.* Advance online publication. doi:10.1177/0011000011432753

Edwards, J. A. (2004) *The Daffodil Theory.* eBook: Deseret Books.

Matai, D. K. (2009). The daffodil principle-A story to inspire you [Blog post]. Retrieved from http://intentblog.com/daffodil-principle-story-inspire-you/

Park, C. L. (2008). Testing the meaning making model of coping with loss.*Journal of Social and Clinical Psychology, 27,* 970–994.

Schilling, J. (2005). Applying the daffodil theory into business practice. Retrieved from http://ezinearticles.com/?Applying-The-Daffodil-Theory-into-Business-Practice&id=9993

## Author Notes:

*Carrie VanMeter* is an Assistant Professor at Walsh University in Canton, Ohio. She has worked with a variety of populations in a group setting including: batterers, juvenile sex offenders, survivors of domestic violence, anger management, and school based groups. She also teaches group counseling processes to school counselors in training.

*Jon M. Coventry* is a Supervising Clinical Counselor for Community Services of Stark County, Inc. in Canton Ohio. He is also an adjunct faculty member at Walsh University. He has facilitated many different group experiences, including groups in elementary, middle and high schools, as well as grief groups with adults and children, trauma and debriefing groups, LGBTQ groups, and family therapy in community settings.

## Correspondence:

Comments and questions related to this activity should be directed to:

Carrie VanMeter, Ph.D., PC, PSC
Walsh University2020 East Maple Street
North Canton, Oh 44720
cvanmeter@walsh.edu

# Pride & Prejudice

*By Jared S. Rose*

## Population:

This activity is designed for older adolescents/adults infected with HIV. It can also be adapted for other marginalized populations (see adaptation section).

## Stage of Group:

Working

## Type of Group:

Counseling, Therapy

## Rationale:

Even after more than 30 years of the pandemic, human immunodeficiency virus (HIV) infection and acquired immunodeficiency syndrome (AIDS) is still highly stigmatized. People living with HIV (PLHIV) experience this stigma at a very personal level. At some point since their diagnosis, PLHIV will have been discriminated against because of their HIV status, or at a minimum are concerned of such discrimination. Some individuals who have lived with HIV for many years have learned to overcome the fear and/or pain of stigma. Some such individuals have even developed ways to use their diagnosis to help educate or empower others. This activity encourages group members to share their feelings and experiences surrounding stigma and discrimination. Those who experience trepidation regarding discrimination are given a safe space to express their concerns, while those who have "been there, done that" and now feel comfortable or proud of where they have come can serve as role models. For PLHIV, addressing the social stigma of the disease is a key component in addressing overall mental health (Hammer, 2005; Khalsa, 2006).

## Goals:

Participants will:
1) recognize and acknowledge that they face stigma and possible discrimination, which itself is empowering.
2) voice their thoughts and feelings around stigma and discrimination (issues some newly diagnosed may not yet have faced).
3) experience encouragement to serve as role models to others when they no longer are concerned about stigma and discrimination.
4) identify problem solving and coping skills for when they face prejudices of others.

## Materials:

None (can be done vocally)

## Time Allotment:

1-2 hours (depending on number of group members)

## Directions:

Step:
1) Ask group members to take turns telling the group:
   a) Their thoughts and feelings regarding the stigma surrounding HIV and AIDS.
   b) If they have been discriminated against because of their HIV status; if so, by whom, how, when, etc. (If not, are they concerned it may happen? If so, in what setting, by whom, etc.).
   c) If they have ever addressed HIV discrimination head-on; if so, how, what it felt like to stand up for themselves, etc.
   d) Support systems they have who they can turn to when faced with prejudice because of their HIV status.

2) Allow group members to respond to others' narratives, facilitating group discussion as organically as possible. Some prompt/processing questions to interject would be:
   a) Who else felt the same way? How did you overcome it?
   b) Who else had similar situations happen to them?
   c) How might others combat similar experiences?

## Processing Questions:

1) What was it like to participate in this group today?
2) What was the most important thing you learned or that stuck out to you about the group today?
3) Do you view discrimination/stigma differently after today? If so, in what ways?
4) What are you going to do differently in the next day/week/month as a result of participating?

## Special Considerations:

This activity often brings up issues of social justice and advocacy. As such, facilitators should be prepared for group members that may wish to take action in response to an individual or establishment that has discriminated against a fellow group member. Further, some group members may realize they have cause for legal action based on discrimination of their medical condition and therefore knowing legal help in the area that is willing to take on HIV/AIDS cases is helpful to know and be able to share.

## Adaptations:

This activity is could be adapted to work with children and may also be helpful for work with other marginalized populations, such as lesbian/gay/bisexual/transgender/queer (LGBTQ) group members. Information requested of group members to share, and corresponding processing questions, should be adapted to meet the unique needs of the population.

## References:

Hammer, S. M. (2005). Management of newly diagnosed HIV infection. *New England Journal of Medicine, 353,* 1702-1710. doi: 10.1056/NEJMcp051203

Khalsa, A. M. (2006). Preventive counseling, screening, and therapy for the patient with newly diagnosed HIV infection. *American Family Physician, 73*(2), 271-280.

## Author Notes:

*Jared S. Rose* is a licensed Professional Counselor working in both community mental health and private practice settings, as well as pursuing his doctoral degree in Counselor Education and Supervision at The University of Toledo. He has spent over 20 years working with individuals infected, affected, or at risk for HIV. Such work has included many years facilitating a counseling group for HIV-positive men. His work in the field of HIV/AIDS has included providing HIV counseling, testing, and education to thousands of Ohio residents, and training hundreds of helping professionals to provide HIV-counseling, testing, and referral services. Mr. Rose has also co-authored a state-wide, public health HIV/STD prevention education program in conjunction with the Ohio Department of Health, where he has infused the curriculum to include core counseling techniques.

## Correspondence:

Questions and comments related to this activity may be directed to:

Jared S. Rose, MA, LPC/CR, NCC
InnerView Behavioral Care
27475 Holiday Lane, Suite #2
Perrysburg, OH 43551
Jared.Rose.IBC@gmail.com

# Rebuilding a Rock at a Time: A Group Activity for Natural Disaster Survivors

*By Delini M. Fernando*

## Population:
Adult survivors of natural disasters

## Stage of Group:
Working

## Type of Group:
Counseling

## Rationale:

In the aftermath of a natural disaster, survivors often find themselves without a home or with a badly damaged one with a few salvageable personal items. These individuals often find it difficult to start rebuilding their homes or move to a new home in another neighborhood. Finding hope and motivation to rebuild or move can sometimes feel like an arduous task. Most survivors are able to have their immediate needs met: food, water, temporary shelter, clothes and a few personal items (Fernando, 2009). Although these experiences are common for disaster survivors, few have the opportunity to process the trauma of losing their home or seeing it badly damaged and uninhabitable. A group allows a safe place for these survivors to grieve their lost home and belongings and to find a way to look to the future and a new or rebuilt home (Fernando & Hebert, 2011).

## Goals:

Participants will:
1) experience positive coping through instilling hope.
2) experience healing through sharing trauma stories related to losing their home.
3) be aware of other survivors' experiences thereby reducing some of the isolation they may feel regarding their losses.
4) have the opportunity of tap into their inner resources of strength that are necessary to look toward the future.

## Materials:

Four round river rocks (palm size), each marked with a black sharpie pen: Strength, Hope, Healing, Trust

## Time Allotment:

One two-hour session

## Directions:

Step:

1) Review the purpose of the activity. For example, *"this activity will help you to share your thoughts and feelings about your experience of losing your home and/or belongings."*

2) Show participants the rocks and inform them that during the session they will be given the opportunity to share and talk about hope, strength, healing, and trust.

3) Explain to participants that as they hold each rock they can talk about what it means for them in relation to rebuilding or moving to a new home. For example, *"As you hold and look at this rock that says "Hope" what does that mean to you?"* or *"How does it feel to hold this rock that says "Hope?"*

4) Begin with the rock marked "Hope" and continue with "Trust," and "Strength" ending with "Healing."

## Processing Questions:

1) What was it like to do this activity?
2) What feelings were the strongest for you? Why?
3) What is one thing you could do when you feel less hopeful for the future?
4) How can we be hopeful for each other?
5) How does it feel to know that you share these feelings and thoughts with others in this group?
6) What feelings come up for you when you hear someone else's story?
7) What are some of the ways we can reach out to one another?
8) What can you do differently today or this week as a result of what you learned from this activity?"

## Adaptations:

1) One session can be centered on one rock and its descriptor.
2) The processing questions may need to be adapted to suit the particular rock that is used, for example, *"What feelings were the strongest for you when you held the 'healing' rock?"*

## References:

Fernando, D. M. (2009). Group work with survivors of the 2004 Asian Tsunami: Reflections of an American trained counselor. *Journal for Specialists in Group Work, 34,* 4-23, doi: 10.1080/01933920802600816

Fernando, D. M., & Hebert, B. (2011). Resiliency and Recovery: Lessons from the Asian tsunami and Hurricane Katrina, *Journal of Multicultural Counseling and Development, 39(1),* 2-13.

## Author Notes:

*Delini M. Fernando* is an Associate Professor of Counseling at the University of North Texas. She has eighteen years of group work experience including family counseling. She regularly teaches the group counseling course at UNT.

## Correspondence:

Questions and comments related to this activity may be directed to:
Delini M. Fernando, PhD
Associate Professor, University of North Texas
1155 Union Circle #310829
Denton, TX, 76203-5017
Delini.Fernando@unt.edu,

# River of Life

*By Daria Borislavova White*

## Population:

This activity is intended for adults who are survivors of trauma or abuse.

## Stage of Group:

Working

## Type of Group:

Counseling

## Rationale:

Research on trauma suggests impact on the neural connections in the brain, the left-right brain communication, and traumatic events' silencing of the human psyche (Cozolino, 2010). Creating a coherent narrative after trauma is an element of the healing journey, especially with those exposed to prolonged traumatic events (Cozolino, 2010). Traumatized individuals struggle to make meaning of the trauma within the greater narrative of their life-story.

The River of Life is an exercise that incorporates drawing, narrative, and sharing with others to assist group members in creating a holistic view of their own development, life, and identity formation (Morgan, 2002). The river/water metaphor is something that everybody can connect to regardless of age, culture, religion, or socioeconomic background. The flow of a river and the life-giving power of water are archetypes that connect to the human psyche and open up the imagination to look at one's life not as a simple chronological line but as a force of nature that continues its flow through different turns and stages.

## Goals:

Participants will:
1) create an integrated view of one's life that incorporates different influences, events, important people (shapers), and place traumatic events within the context of one's experience and background.
2) gain confidence in sharing with others one's life-story.
3) appreciate differences and similarities of experience when listening to others.

## Materials:
1) paper
2) markers
3) crayons

## Time Allotment:
15 minutes for drawing; up to 45 minutes for sharing. It could take longer depending on the group and how deep facilitators want to explore the themes and issues discussed.

## Directions:
Step:
1) Imagine your life as a river, a river with a beginning and tributaries down its course; pools and shallows; boulders and rapid turns; at times lazy and quiet and then rapid and torrential (Morgan, 2002).

2) Draw your river and represent in it the significant traumatic events you have experienced finishing at the river mouth where you currently are. There are no restrictions as to how the river will look. You could use symbols and key words, poetic phrases, and particular colors in creating this visual image of your life.

3) Share the river with another member of the group or with the entire group.

## Processing Questions:
1) What did your river signify to you? What were surprises and new insights for you? How did you recognize important people/shapers?
2) What were times of courage and growth? How did these inform the difficult experiences you have been through and what you want for the future?
3) What similar themes did you find when sharing with your partner/other members of the group and what did you learn in regards to your own story?
4) How could you apply the new insights to life outside this group?

## Special Considerations:
1) Are group members ready to discuss traumatic events? What if emotions difficult to cope with become apparent in a member of the group? Consider who the members in the group are and how those who are more reflective could serve as anchors for the others during the discussion.
2) Are pairs prepared to deal with intense affect? If there might be a problem with strong affect, consider working through this exercise as a whole group.

3) If using with adolescents – questions need to be situated in the world of the adolescent. Consider beginning with a list of events adolescents in the group have experienced – births, role of parents and siblings, family transitions, illness and death, best friends. As they look at the river of life and the traumatic events they could think about who else was impacted by what happened to them and what they hope for from this point in their journey.

## Adaptations:

This exercise has been used with trauma victims in different cultural settings, but it could also be used in a variety of groups including those dealing with disordered eating and substance abuse. This activity could be also incorporated in discussions of identity, spiritual journey, significant attachments, and developmental stages. When an entire community has shared an experience of trauma, members could draw the river together by creating a public mural.

## References:

Cozolino, L. (2010). *The neuroscience of psychotherapy: Healing the social brain.* New York: W. W. Norton.

Morgan, R. L. (2002). *Remembering your story: Creating your own spiritual autobiography* (2nd ed.) Nashville, TN: Upper Room.

## Author Notes:

*Daria Borislavova White* is a Doctoral Student at James Madison University. She has a graduate degree in conflict transformation with a focus on trauma healing and has worked with marginalized populations and religious leaders in Eastern Europe.

## Correspondence:

Questions and comments related to this activity may be directed to:

Daria Borislavova White, M. A., M. S.
Department of Graduate Psychology
70 Alumnae Dr., MSC 7401
James Madison University
Harrisonburg, VA 22807
whitedb@jmu.edu

# Sharing Our HIV Diagnosis Experiences

*By Jared S. Rose*

## Population:

This activity is designed for older adolescents/adults infected with HIV. It can also be adapted for individuals with other chronic illnesses (see adaptation section).

## Stage of Group:

Orientation

## Type of Group:

Psychoeducational, Counseling/Therapy

## Rationale:

Learning of one's human immunodeficiency virus (HIV) infection is a life altering event. In addition to an overwhelming sense of having to handle a chronic health condition, individuals are met with a wide-range of emotions including guilt, shame, and fear. Depression as a result of facing an illness, anxiety due to lack of self-efficacy for their disease and isolation for fear of disclosing one's status to loved ones are quite common. What's more, when first diagnosed people living with HIV (PLHIV) are sometimes left feeling completely abandoned because some medical professionals do not provide immediate psychoeducation and support. Being able to discuss their diagnosis experience with others who have been in similar situations is incredibly empowering for PLHIV. Through this exercise, individuals bond quickly with their fellow group members; have their thoughts, feelings, and behaviors during a painful period of their life normalized; and discover creative, new avenues of finding comfort and strength in disclosing their status to others. All of which can improve mental and physical health for PLHIV by increasing social support, as well as disease-specific coping strategies and self-efficacy (Hult, Wrubel, Bränström, Acree, & Moskowitz, 2012; Kraaij et al., 2008; Siegel & Schrimshaw, 2007).

## Goals:

Participants will:
1) begin building therapeutic bond with other group members.
2) identify personal, non-group support systems.
3) gain information related to viral load (VL) and CD-4 cell-count fluctuations as means to normalize physical health issues and reduction of intense mood symptomology.

## Materials:

None (can be done vocally)

## Time Allotment:

1-2 hours (depending on number of group members)

## Directions:

Step:
1) Ask group members to take turns telling the group of their diagnosis experience. Request they feel comfortable sharing in their own way but that it includes the following points:

   a) When they were diagnosed.

   b) Where they were tested for HIV and who first told them they were HIV positive (and how they were told).

   c) What they first thought when they were told they were HIV positive, how they felt, and what they did when they left the testing location.

   d) Their VL and CD-4 count at time of initial infection.

   e) If they have told others they are HIV positive, who they have told including the first person they told and why; if they have not told anyone of their HIV status, what concerns they have about disclosure.

2) Allow group members to respond to others' narratives, facilitating group discussion as organically as possible. Some prompt/processing questions to interject would be:
   a) Who else felt the same way?

   b) Who else at their time of initial diagnosis didn't have someone explain to them what VL and CD-4 count meant as it related to their HIV infection?

   c) How many others when they were first diagnosed thought they would never be able to tell their family of their diagnosis? Their friends? Their intimate partner(s)?

d) Who was the first person you told of your diagnosis? Why that person? How did they respond?

e) For those who have been living with HIV for some time, at initial diagnosis did you think your VL and CD-4 count could improve to the healthy levels they are now?

## Processing Questions:

1) What was it like to participate in this activity today?
2) What is the most important thing you learned or that stuck out to you in group today?
3) What sources of support do you have in your life? What supports might you seek out or utilize differently as a result of participating in today's group?

## Special Considerations:

Be prepared for intense emotions as individuals re-connect with their diagnosis experience; it often brings a resurfacing of those initial emotions. Often with sharing one's diagnosis experience thoughts and emotions surrounding the person that infected them also surface. Addressing that issue is best served by a separate exercise. Therefore it is appropriate to acknowledge and validate this for a group member when it comes up, but focus on keeping the members on task for this activity. Also be ready to link individuals to area resources such as infectious disease physicians, mental health services for family or intimate partners, etc. (a pre-constructed referral guide is recommended).

## Adaptations:

This activity is also helpful with open groups when new group members join and they are able to quickly and easily identify with their peers by hearing the narratives of those around them. Additionally, this activity can be adapted for children or for other illnesses or chronic health conditions situations (e.g. cancer, chronic pain). Information requested of group members to share, and corresponding processing questions, should be adapted to meet the unique needs of the illness or condition.

## References:

Hult, J. R., Wrubel, J., Bränström, R., Acree, M., & Moskowitz, J. T. (2012). Disclosure and nondisclosure among people newly diagnosed with HIV: An analysis from a stress and coping perspective. *AIDS Patient Care & STDs, 26*(3), 181-190. doi: 10.1089/apc.2011.0282

Kraaij, V., Garnefski, N., Schroevers, M. J., Van Der Veek, S., Witlox, R., & Maes, S. (2008). Cognitive coping, goal self-efficacy and personal growth in HIV-infected men who have s ex with men. *Patient Education and Counseling, 72*(2), 301-304. doi: 10.1016/j.pec.2008.04.007

Siegel, K., & Schrimshaw, E. W. (2007). The stress moderating role of benefit finding on psychological distress among women living with HIV/AIDS. *AIDS Behavior, 11*(3), 421-433. doi: 10.1007/s10461-006-9186-3

## Author Notes:

*Jared S. Rose* is a licensed Professional Counselor working in both community mental health and private practice settings, as well as pursuing his doctoral degree in Counselor Education and Supervision at The University of Toledo. He has spent over 20 years working with individuals infected, affected, or at risk for HIV. Such work has included many years facilitating a counseling group for HIV-positive men. His work in the field of HIV/AIDS has included providing HIV counseling, testing, and education to thousands of Ohio residents, and training hundreds of helping professionals to provide HIV-counseling, testing, and referral services. Mr. Rose has also co-authored a state-wide, public health HIV/STD prevention education program in conjunction with the Ohio Department of Health, where he has infused the curriculum to include core counseling techniques.

## Correspondence:

Questions and comments related to this activity may be directed to:

Jared S. Rose, MA, LPC/CR, NCC
InnerView Behavioral Care
7475 Holiday Lane, Suite #2
Perrysburg, OH 43551
Jared.Rose.IBC@gmail.com

# Stereotypes and Profiling

*By Lynn L. Brandsma & Gregory K.P. Smith*

## Population:

Young Adults and/or Adults. This exercise may be particularly helpful in a multicultural training or instruction type of setting. It could have potential benefit in a diversity training activity for teachers in school districts struggling with achievement gap issues between various races and/or children of differing socioeconomic status.

## Stage of Group:

Working

## Type of Group:

Psychoeducational, Counseling or Therapy

## Rationale:

The purpose of this activity is to foster an appreciation of the nature and effects of stereotypes and profiling. Through personal stories and discussions it is hoped that individuals can examine the similarities and differences of both stereotyping and profiling and look at the relationship, if any, between the two. In listening and speaking to each other with respect and honesty perhaps this activity can help to broaden the world view of some to include experiences they may not, and most likely, will not ever have. This view is supported by research in Acceptance and Commitment Therapy (ACT) showing promise that how one relates to others' experiences differing from their own is particularly useful in accepting diversity and multiple ways of thinking (Hayes, Pistorello, & Levin, 2012).

## Goals:

Participants will:
1) define stereotypes and profiling.
2) examine the possible relationship between stereotypes and profiling.
3) share personal experiences from their lives of being stereotyped and/or profiled.

## Materials:

1) The hand-out
2) Pen or pencil

## Time Allotment:

90 minutes

## Directions:

Step:

1) The group leader briefly gives a definition of stereotypes and profiling.

2) The group members take a few minutes to individually answer the questions on the hand-out.

3) The group leader asks the members to share their answers one at a time allowing enough time for sufficient discussion for each response if need be.

4) The leader should allow the conversation to go where it needs, however it is important for him/her to be cognizant of people who may be uncomfortable and respond accordingly.

5) Each member is encouraged to be respectful and honest both in answer and in discussion.

6) There should be sufficient time left at the end to discuss the activity as a whole so that the group members can take a step back and examine the value of hearing others' experiences.

## Processing Questions:

1) What was more difficult for you—sharing your own experiences or hearing others' experiences?
2) What do you see as the biggest difference between stereotyping and profiling?
3) What relationship, if any, do you see between stereotyping and profiling?

## Special Considerations:

People will be at different places and it may be a good idea for the leader to explain this before the activity. Some may have knee jerk reactions to some stories and rather than react perhaps a guideline can be set up ahead of time so that such reactions can be announced in a similar fashion (i.e. "that pushes my button because....." or "I have a knee jerk reaction to that statement and I need help from the group in understanding my reaction". These types of guidelines set up ahead of time may keep the discussion moving in a positive direction.

## Adaptations:

It is possible to adapt to a younger population or a population with intellectual challenges by changing the terms to those more developmentally appropriate such as "Differences" and keeping the conversation centered on times they have felt "different".

## References:

Hayes, S. C., Pistorello, J., & Levin, M. E. (2012). Acceptance and commitment therapy as a unified model of behavior change. *The Counseling Psychologist*, 40(7), 976-1002.

## Author Notes:

*Lynn L. Brandsma* is an Associate Professor of Psychology at Chestnut Hill College. Dr. Brandsma has taught Group Process and Leadership at both the undergraduate and graduate levels for 18 years. She has extensive experience facilitating counseling and therapy groups for adolescents and adults with eating and weight related issues. She is also a Board Certified Music Therapist and has led numerous music therapy groups with various populations.

*Gregory K. P. Smith* is a Professor of Recreation, Health and Physical Education in Hospitality and Recreation Management Department at Cheyney University of Pennsylvania. Dr. Smith has extensive experience in facilitating task/work groups in his current role as advisor to the Muslim Student Association, as past advisor to numerous student clubs, and as President of the Faculty Union, APSCUF (Association of Pennsylvania State College & University Faculties) at Cheyney University of Pennsylvania from 2003-2007.

## Correspondence:

Questions and comments related to this activity may be directed to:

Lynn L. Brandsma, Ph.D., LPC, MT-BC
Chestnut Hill College
Department of Psychology
9601 Germantown Avenue
Philadelphia, PA 19118
brandsmal@chc.edu

Stereotyping and Profiling Hand-Out

The stereotypes that have been associated with me include:


I am mostly stereotyped by:


Many people think that:

However:


Most people assume that:

However:


At times I have assumed that:


The stereotype that is the most offensive to me:


If people really knew me they'd know that:


Just because I'm _____ doesn't mean I'm _____


Was there ever a time you felt you were profiled?

If so, how did that differ than being stereotyped?

# Stone Giveaway

*By Ford Brooks*

## Population:

This activity is best utilized with adult group members in treatment for addiction and involved in outpatient or inpatient treatment groups. Appropriate group structures for this activity include intensive outpatient, partial and inpatient groups as well as ongoing recovery groups. The Stone Giveaway is a symbolic process allowing for final comments and appreciation for group members. It can also be used with adolescents in open and/or closed groups.

## Stage of Group Work:

This activity is best suited for the termination stage of open and/or closed alcohol and drug treatment groups.

## Type of Group:

This activity is best used in a counseling group focusing on alcohol and drug addiction issues whereby group member defenses, emotions, and coping mechanisms are addressed.

## Rationale:

Although the termination process is significant for counseling groups in general, a closure process is essential for addiction treatment groups due to the nature of emotional identification, development, and expression in the recovery process (Flores, 1997). Not having appropriate closure with other group members could block the member(s) from experiencing the emotional loss (along with other emotions) associated with group termination (Brooks & McHenry, 2009). For addicted group members there are multiple losses, mainly the loss of the drug followed by the loss of personal relationships. With such significant losses, group members become a part of a new sober life. Proper closure and acknowledgement of the group loss, as well as the significant gains while in group, are important. The Stone Giveaway provides a space for group members to present feedback in a closure activity.

## Goals:

Participants will:
1) experience feedback/wishes for continued growth and change in recovery.
2) have the opportunity to terminate/say goodbye with each other. (Open ended group)
3) experience emotions related to closure and to incorporate the experience into the ongoing recovery process.

320

## Materials:

1) Small polished stones (twice as many stones as group members for a varied selection)
2) Basket for containment

## Time Allotment:

The time allotted depends on how many group members are terminating at the same time and how many members are in the group. If only one member is leaving, the activity may take 10-15 minutes at most. If two members are leaving, it will obviously take more time. The facilitator will want to start this activity in the last portion of group. The group members who are leaving have completed their treatment goals and are prepared to move forward in recovery. Closure with a few members from an open group takes significantly less time than a closed group that is terminating simultaneously. Nonetheless, the process of closure is meaningful to all group members.

## Directions:

Step:

1) The process begins with the counselor placing the basket of stones in the center of the group circle.

2) The counselor describes the following process to the group members:

   a) *"For those of you closing out with the group today, you will select a stone from the basket."*
   b) *"You will then pass the stone to the person on your left or right; your choice."*
   c) *"The person you pass the stone to will share a parting wish for you and any brief comments about your growth."*
   d) *"When that person has finished, the stone is passed to the next person in the circle."*
   e) *"Closing wishes and comments are made to you by each group member as the stone is passed around the group from member to member until the stone comes back to you."*
   f) *"You then make final reflections to the group members and you keep the stone."*

3) This process continues for each person leaving the group.
   NOTE: This process can be quite emotional so facilitators want to prepare for the length of time involved as well as the emotions that come with the final group closure. For example, if it is a ninety minute closed group, the facilitator needs to adjust the group time in order for group members to be able to share and provide feedback.

4) Another option following the activity is to have the departing group member(s) stand in the middle of the group circle while the outside group members stand in a circle around them and place their left hands on their shoulders. The circle on the outside then puts their right hand on the group member in front of them thus creating what looks like a wheel. The counselor can make final comments at this point and the group concludes.

## Processing Questions:

Since this is a closure activity, questions are not utilized but rather, a feedback loop addressing final wishes and thoughts. Although not a direct question, the departing group member(s) are directed to address how it felt to have the well wishes and feedback from each group member.

## Special Considerations

Counselors need to be aware that group members preparing to leave an addiction treatment group may have significant emotional loss related to closure. Moreover, the longer the group has been meeting, the more emotionally laden the termination process.

## Adaptations:

In closed groups, where the entire group is terminating, the individualized thoughts/wishes of each group member are related to each member and takes time. It could take up to two hours for appropriate closure depending on the number of group members. For a closed group, The Stone Giveaway directions for open groups are identical except the entire group is simultaneously closing out.

## References:

Brooks, F., & McHenry, B. (2009). *A contemporary approach to substance abuse and addiction counseling: A counselor's guide to application and understanding.* Alexandria, VA: American Counseling Association.

Flores, P. J. (1997). *Group psychotherapy with addicted populations: An integration of twelve-step and psychodynamic theory* (2nd ed.). New York: Haworth Press.

## Author Notes:

*Ford Brooks* is a Professor of Counselor Education at Shippensburg University in the Department of Counseling and College Student Personnel and is the Coordinator of Internships and Director of the Clinical Mental Health Program. He has 30 years of group experience working primarily with addicted populations in a variety of treatment settings.

## Correspondence:

Questions and comments related to this activity may be direct to:

Dr. Ford Brooks, NCC, LPC, CADC
Shippensburg University,
Department of Counseling and College Student Personnel
1871 Old Main Drive, Shippensburg, PA 17257
cwbroo@ship.edu

# The 4 Ways of Being: A Group Exercise for Members Confronted with Grief and Loss

By Julie Murray, Kaitlin O'Dell, Chris Burkhalter
& Amanda M. Evans

## Population:

This activity would be most appropriate for adults who are experiencing grief and loss. This activity would be appropriate for both inpatient and outpatient populations.

## Stage of Group:

Transition, Working

Ideally this exercise would be introduced by the group leader in the transition or working stage of a group when members are focusing on being vulnerable, attending to their own experiences with grief/loss and have established a relationship with one another in the group.

## Type of Group:

Counseling, Therapy

## Rationale:

Cohesion, understanding, and a sense of belonging that a group counseling format offers can be especially beneficial for individuals who are grieving, as members may be feeling disengaged from the world around them (Corey, 2004). Group work can assist those who are grieving to reengage with life tasks that they previously found meaningful, make connections with others who are struggling with the same issues, and to feel useful as they offer advice and support to other members (Garrow & Walker, 2001). This group exercise introduces the existential philosophy of the 4 Ways of Being coupled with a mindfulness based exercise into therapeutic practice so that group leaders can "complement the grieving process" by exploring feelings associated with grief and loss in a here-and-now humanistic manner (Spillers, 2007). A large body of research supports that mindfulness has both physical and mental health benefits (Carmondy & Baer, 2008; Rausch, Gramling, & Auerbach, 2006). By introducing group members to a mindfulness based exercise, the authors hope to create a supportive environment in the group for members to explore their relationship with each of the 4 Ways of Being and how grief/loss many have negatively impacted the members ability to function successfully in their relationship with the self. This exercise requires trust, vulnerability and openness. Thus, a more intensive type of therapy group may assist in producing the environment conducive to making this exercise successful (Moore & Herlihy, 1993).

# Goals:

Participants will:
1) reflect on how the loss of an individual and or relationship has impacted their ability to function in each of the four ways of being.
2) examine, in the here-and-now, sources of anxiety associated with their loss.

# Materials:

1) 4 Ways of Being Descriptions
2) Mindfulness Script

# Time Allotment:

This entire group exercise will occur over the course of a 90 to 120 minute group. Please reserve approximately thirty minutes for the mindfulness-based exercise. The introduction and Discussion of the 4 Ways of Being can take approximately fifteen minutes. Processing the overall experience may take one hour or an entire group counseling meeting (90-120 minutes) depending on the facilitation style, group member participation, and response to the activity.

# Directions:

Step:
1) Introduce the 4 Ways of Being: according to Van Deurzen (2011), the 4 Ways of Being, also known as the ultimate concerns, can be used in therapy to "remind us of the multidimensionality of existence." Each dimension presents an anxiety-producing dilemma that must be faced in order to move past it.

   a) **Physical Dimension**
   This is how we relate to the natural world around us. It includes our body, our surroundings, our material possessions, our health and our "relationship with our own mortality."
   *Unsolvable dilemma*: Mortality is a fact that we can accept or deny.

   I can relate to this dimension because I: _____.

   b) **Social Dimension**
   This is the way in which we relate to others, our class and race, as well as to classes and races to which we do not belong. We confront the fact that, "no one can know what it's like to be me."
   *Unsolvable dilemma*: The need for individuality combined with the need to be part of a whole.

   I can relate to this dimension because I: _____.

c) **Personal Dimension**
These are our beliefs about our past, our future and ourselves. It involves taking responsibility for our actions.
*Unsolvable dilemma:* We yearn for "unchanging principals to live by" even as we make our own choices.

I can relate to this dimension because I: _____.

d) **Spiritual Dimension**
We use reflection in order to determine our values and gain a sense of an ideal world.
*Unsolvable Dilemma:* Facing "the tension between purpose and absurdity, hope and despair" (pgs. 16-21).

I can relate to this dimension because I: _____.

2) Transition members to the mindfulness-based exercise and employ the Mindfulness Script. The group leader should offer this mindfulness-based exercise in a room large enough so that all group members can be seated comfortably. Group members should be instructed to sit in a relaxed fashion. Members may close their eyes or leave them open depending on personal preference. The group leader should read the following script in a calm manner. Please be mindful of pacing and use of silence while reading the script.

Group leader: *"As you begin to relax, come to a position that is comfortable. Your arms may be beside you or resting in your lap. Close your eyes if you would like, and allow yourself to be still for a moment."*

Pause.

Group leader: *"Begin to become aware of your natural breathing pattern. Notice your thoughts, and become both self-aware and centered in the present moment. You are not trying to eliminate or control your thoughts and feelings, but instead stay with them as they occur."*

Pause.

Group leader: *"Anxious feelings may being to arise and this is natural throughout this exercise as you are faced with difficult thoughts and emotions, but you will notice that as naturally as they occur, they can also be reduced throughout the exercise. Be gentle towards yourself, and allow these thoughts to occur without passing judgment."*

Pause.

Group leader: *"Please take this time to reflect on your loss. Think about the person, relationship, position that has contributed to your feelings of grief."*

Pause.

Group leader: "*Take a moment to notice the way you are using both your body and mind at this time. Be aware of your breathing, and acknowledge the way your body is positioned. You will notice that many of your thoughts are automatic and spontaneous. Allow these thoughts to linger, while accepting any unpleasant feelings that may accompany them. Soon, your thoughts may shift.*"

Pause.

Group leader: "*Take a moment to step back from your thoughts and see them from another perspective. View your thoughts as though they are a movie streaming through your mind. Allow these movies to stream through your mind without trying to figure them out or engage them. Accept the feelings that accompany this stream of thoughts.*"

Pause.

Group leader: "*Continue to sit in a comfortable position with your eyes closed. When your thoughts wander, acknowledge that they have wandered, and then bring your attention and awareness back to the exercise. Once you have brought your attention back to the exercise, pay attention to the here and now.*"

Pause.

Group leader: "*As we had previously discussed, today's group topic is the 4 Ways of Being. Let's introduce these ideas into our mindfulness-based practice. First, we have the Physical Dimension. In this dimension, we consider how we relate to the natural world around us. This might include our body, our environment, and our health. Please imagine yourself existing in the physical dimension.*"

Pause.

Group leader: "*What does the physical dimension look like for you?*" Pause. "*How does it feel to be in the physical dimension?*" Pause. "*Do you feel authentic in the physical dimension?*"

Pause.

Group leader: "*Second, we have the Social Dimension. In this dimension, we consider how we relate to others and acknowledge that we are an individual and that no one can relate to exactly what we are experiencing. Please imagine yourself existing in the social dimension.*"

Pause.

Group leader: "*What does the social dimension look like for you?*" Pause. "*How does it feel to be in the social dimension?*" Pause. "*Do you feel authentic in the social dimension?*"

Pause.

Group leader: *"Third, we have the personal dimension. In this dimension, we consider our beliefs about the past, the future and the self. Please imagine yourself existing in the personal dimension."*

Pause.

Group leader: *"What does the personal dimension look like for you?"* Pause. *"How does it feel to be in the personal dimension?"* Pause. *"Do you feel authentic in the personal dimension?"*

Pause.

Group leader: *"Lastly, we have the spiritual dimension. In this dimension, we can reflect on our values and an ideal world. Please imagine yourself existing in the spiritual dimension."*

Pause.

Group leader: *"What does the spiritual dimension look like for you?"* Pause. *"How does it feel to be in the spiritual dimension?"* Pause. *"Do you feel authentic in the spiritual dimension?"*

Pause.

Group leader: *"Note the thoughts as they arise, while allowing them to be. For the remaining time, allow yourself to sit, relax, and simply be present. Notice your breath going in and out, your chest rising and falling with each breath. When your thoughts begin to wander, bring them back to the present, while accepting them in a non-judgmental way."*

Allow group members to sit in silence for 10 to 15 minutes. The group leader may want to play light, soft music or have members sit in silence.

Group leader: *"As this mindfulness session comes to a close, you may open your eyes. We will begin our process session momentarily."*

It is recommended that the group leader consider providing group members with a break after the mindfulness-based exercise to provide members the opportunity to come out of the mindfulness practice individually and to have some quiet time before returning to the group.

    3) Bring the group back together and process the experiential exercise.

## Processing Questions:

    1) What was the last half hour like for you?
    2) Has your loss/grief affected your ability to live in each of the 4 Ways of Being?
    3) How might you utilize our group to address your feelings related to each of these areas?
    4) What things will you do to continue to process the emotions and thoughts brought up through this exercise?

5) How might you use mindfulness-based stress reduction and/or the 4 Ways of Being to help you cope with your feelings of loss/grief?

# Special Considerations:

It is important for group leaders to be mindful of natural responses to grief and pervasive responses to grief. If a group member appears to be experiencing clinically significant responses to grief, referring that individual to a higher level of care may be recommended. In addition, some individuals who have experienced trauma or abuse may be uncomfortable with closing their eyes in group and it is imperative that this discomfort is normalized and accommodated in the group setting. In addition, individuals who may be experiencing racing thoughts or are in the early stages of grief may not be appropriate for this exercise. Individuals with disabilities that make it difficult or impossible for them to read or write would require the group leader to make further adaptations with portions of this activity.

# Adaptations:

This activity could be adapted to many different populations and presenting issues, but a study done by Lantz & Gregoire (2000) found that existential group therapy may be especially beneficial to couples facing breast cancer. Existential therapy assists these individuals in confronting the anxiety and uncertainty surrounding death. In this same study, secondary reflection, including guided imagery was used to help couples, "notice, discover and recollect the meanings and meaning potentials in life" (p. 320). With further modifications this activity would also be applicable to individuals with bipolar disorder. Goldner-Vukov, Moore, & Cupina (2007) found that examining existential issues such as mortality, isolation and responsibility, along with the use of cognitive interventions, significantly decreased the relapse and hospitalization rates of the participants of their study (p. 32).

# References:

Carmody, J., & Baer, R. A. (2008). Relationships between mindfulness practice and levels of mindfulness, medical and psychological symptoms and well-being in a mindfulness-based stress reduction program. *Journal of Behavioral Medicine, 31,* 23-33. doi: 10.1007/s10865-007-9130-7

Carmody, J., & Baer, R. A. (2009). How long does a mindfulness-based stress reduction program need to be? A review of class contact hours and effect sizes for psychological distress. *Journal of Clinical Psychology, 65*(6), 627-638. doi: 10.1002/jclp.20555

Corey, G. (2004). *Theory & practice of group counseling.* Belmont, CA: Brooks/Cole-Thompson Learning.

Garrow, S., & Walker, J. A. (2001). Existential group therapy and death anxiety. *Adultspan Journal, 3*(2), 77.

Moore, J., & Herlihy, B. (1993). Grief groups for students who have had a parent die. *School Counselor*, 41(1). 54-59.

Rausch, S. M., Gramling, S. E., & Auerbach, S. M. (2006). Effects of a single session of large-group meditation and progressive muscle relaxation training on stress reduction, reactivity, and recovery. *International Journal of Stress Management*, 13(3), 273-290. doi: 10.1037/1072-5245.13.3.273

Singh, N. N., Lancioni, G. E., Wahler, R. G., Winton, A. S. W., & Singh, J. (2008). Mindfulness approaches in cognitive behavior therapy. *Behavioural and Cognitive Psychotherapy*, 36, 359-666. doi: 10.1017/S1352465808004827

Spillers, C. S. (2007). An existential framework for understanding the counseling needs of clients. *American Journal of Speech-Language Pathology*, 16(3), 191-197. doi:10.1044/1058-0360(2007/024)

Van Deurzen, E., & Adams, M. (2011). *Skills in existential counselling & psychotherapy*. Thousand Oaks, CA: Sage Publications.

## Author Notes:

*Julie Murray* is a Graduate Student in Clinical Mental Health Counseling at Auburn University. Julie has experience as a group leader for severely mentally ill populations in a community mental health setting.

*Kaitlin O'Dell* is a Clinical Mental Health Counseling Graduate Student at Auburn University. Kaitlin has experience as a group leader for adjudicated adolescent females.

*Chris Burkhalter* is a Clinical Mental Health Counseling Graduate Student at Auburn University. Chris has experience as a group leader for college students in a career counseling center.

*Amanda M. Evans* is an Assistant Professor and Coordinator for the Clinical Mental Health Counseling Program at Auburn University. Amanda has experience as a group leader specifically for inpatient psychiatric and adolescent female populations, taught a masters-level group class for two years, and served as the 2012-13 secretary for Alabama Association for Specialists in Group Work

## Correspondence:

Questions and comments related to this activity may be directed to:
Dr. Amanda Evans PhD, LPC, NCC
Auburn University
2068 Haley Center
Auburn AL, 36840-5222
amt0004@auburn.edu

# The Mentor Map

*By Amy Ghaemmaghami*

## Population:

Underrepresented college students, LGBTQIA students, international students

## Stage of Group:

Working

## Type of Group:

Counseling

## Rationale:

Mentors are the people who provide helpful guidance, education, protection and support at crucial junctures in our lives. Some anthropologists describe these individuals as "fictive kin," in other words, people unrelated to us by either birth or marriage that have emotionally significant relationships with us that take on the characteristics of family relationships (Schneider, 1997). In this activity, we map the people and places that encouraged our healing, growth, and freedom. The Mentor Map will not only acknowledge and celebrate our mentors, but also express our developing identities, and redefine our family to include people we love by choice. The memories evoked by this activity will remind us not only our vulnerabilities, but also of our resilience as we seek to claim our unique personal history. Furthermore, by mapping our relationships to our mentors, we can share our stories with others in the activity group and empower ourselves to validate our own affiliations and create new relationships within the group (Etherington, 2009; Yalom, 1995).

## Goals:

Participants will:
1) learn the concept of mentors as "fictive kin," who validate their experiences with mentors through storytelling.
2) embrace non-traditional relationships that have shaped the goals, identity and emotional intelligence of the group participants.
3) create a sense of community among the group through sharing of important past relationships, and imparting a sense of hope for nurturing and empowering relationships to emerge within the group.

## Materials:

1) Variety of paper, pens, pencils, colored pencils, markers
2) Processing questions sheet for each group member

## Time Allotment:

90 minutes total time. 5 minutes for meditation. 40 minutes to create the map, 45 minutes for sharing maps with members of the group.

## Directions:

Step:

1) The group will be seated at a conference table or in classroom desks that are pulled into a circle.

2) Since the group is at the working stage you will not need to learn names or have them introduce themselves.

3) Explain that the group will engage in an expressive activity called the Mentor Map.

4) Explain the rationale for the activity. Explain the notion of "fictive kin" and that making a creative map which shows the mentors who have guided the participants on their journeys will affirm the participants' identities and claim those who love them and whom they love by choice.

5) Explain that the group may use paper and pencils, pens and markers provided to create their maps.

6) Explain that their maps are their own creative projects and do not need to look like a standard map, but are a rendering of their bonds with their mentors. Suggest: "You may want to draw lines, arrows, pictures, colors, create a portrait, or use words to describe your mentor and how you feel about that person. Then think of another mentor and repeat the process. At the end of the activity, you may have one mentor on your map or many mentors and we'll process your maps as group."

7) Invite them to prepare for the Mentor Map Activity with a short meditation.

8) Invite the group to reflect: "Close your eyes and think of a person whom you would consider a mentor. Imagine the time, place and culture where that person helped you. Now remember how you felt when you realized that this person cared deeply for you and your wellbeing, your hopes, and your dreams. Now open your eyes and begin to create your map."

9) Suggest to the participants that they may want to start by jotting down a list of their mentors.

10) After 40 minutes, ask the group to put the final touches on their maps. Allow 5 minutes more.

11) Allow 30 minutes for group reflection. Ask the group to go around the table or the circle of chairs and describe their maps. Ask the speaker how she felt when she was making it.

12) Encourage the other members of the group to ask questions or make a positive comment about what they liked in the other group member's map.

## Processing Questions:

1) How did you feel as you created the Mentor Map? What feelings did you experience in your body? Did you notice your body becoming hot or cold? Did you heart rate change, or your breath become easier or more labored? Why do you think your body may have reacted in that way?
2) What was it like when you shared your map with other members of the group? Did you feel happy, sad, proud, or grateful? Put your feelings about the process into words.
3) Describe how you felt about the process of creating the map and becoming a storyteller.
4) What did you like about hearing about others' mentors?
5) Have you ever thought of yourself as a mentor?
6) Did you like the Mentor Map activity? Why or why not?

## Special Considerations:

When conducting this activity with any of the populations, there may be unanticipated emotional responses, so be advised to prepare the members beforehand that this exercise could bring up some negative as well as positive emotions. Prior to beginning the activity, take care to remind the group to be kind and gentle to themselves and one another, participating and sharing their maps only as much as they are able. Also, remind the group that they can be as creative as they like and that this map is not a formal map, nor a formal work of art, but rather a creative representation of their relationships to their mentors.

## Adaptations:

If the Mentor Map activity is conducted with a group that includes a disabled individual who does not have use of a means by which to draw her map, but she is able to talk, the leader may draw the map from the verbal instructions of the individual or change that person's participation to rely on oral processing.

Give the group members 10-15 minutes to do a one paragraph reflective writing on another sheet of paper. Give group members a list of processing questions that they may want to tackle in the reflective writing.

## References:

Etherington, K. (2009). Life story research: A relevant methodology for counsellors and psychotherapists. *Counselling and Psychotherapy Research, 9*(4), 225-233.

Foster, C. (1993). *The family patterns workbook: Breaking free from your past and creating a life of your own.* New York: Perigree Books/Putnam Group.

Keen, S., & and Valley-Fox, A. (1989). *Your mythic journey: Finding meaning in your life through writing and storytelling.* New York: Penguin.

Schneider, D. (1997). The power of culture: Notes on some aspects of gay and lesbian kinship in America today. *Cultural Anthropology, 12*(2), 270-74.

Yalom, I. (1995). *The theory and practice of group psychotherapy* (4th ed.). New York: Basic Books.

## Author Note:

*Amy Ghaemmaghami* is a College Counselor at Bridgewater College (Virginia). She has over five years of group work experience with underrepresented college students, including minority, international, and LGBTQIA students, as well as sexual trauma survivors.

## Correspondence:

Questions and comments related to this activity may be directed to:

Amy Ghaemmaghami, M.A., LPC
Bridgewater College
Counseling Center, 218 Rebecca Hall
Bridgewater VA 22812
aghaemma@bridgewater.edu

# Time is on My Side

*By Leigha Huston & Paula McWirther*

## Population:

Single Parents and/or Divorced Parents

## Stage of Group:

Transition

## Type of Group:

Counseling

## Rationale:

The activity involves visual and tactile representation of participants' time and responsibility stressors. From a Narrative Therapy perspective, the activity enables participants to externalize their considerable time stressors (White, 2007). In doing so, distance is created, as participants are able to separate themselves from their time management stress. This enables them to focus on their relationship with time management; the focus is on the effect of the stressors within their lives, making it easier to evaluate the negative influence of the problem. Participants are then encouraged to engage in the construction of their preferred use of time, to find the alternative best solution for the problem, and to take steps toward actively shaping their identity authentically as a single or newly divorced parent (White, 2007).

## Goals:

Participants will:
1) normalize experience between group members to create a stronger and more trusting bond.
2) allow for cathartic discussion of responsibilities and expectations.
3) set the stage for development of problem solving techniques and better coping mechanisms.

# Materials:

1) One handout per group member (see description)
2) Thirty small items:
   a. fifteen items of one kind and fifteen items of another kind. These items may be similar or different in nature but must be distinct from one another. The first and second sets of items should be the same for all group members. Suggested items: 2 different colors of beans, 2 different colors of beads, pennies. Alternatively, two different items (i.e. 15 beans and 15 pennies) may be used. It is also suggested, but not required, that these be in divided in containers before group for the leader's convenience. For example, small paper Dixie cups: each group member would receive one small paper cup of white beans, and one small paper cup of black beans.

# Time Allotment:

Allow approximately 90-120 minutes for this activity as follows: Each round will require 5-10 minutes for the initial steps (placing of items on handout), followed by 40-60 minutes for processing.

# Directions:

Step:

This activity involves two rounds.

Round One: Explore members' actual/current time schedule.

1) To begin the first round, the group leader gives out the first set of 15 items (i.e. white beans). Group members are instructed that these items represent the amount of time and energy they currently put into activities.

2) Group leaders instruct members to place their 15 items on the portions of the handout that best match how their week usually goes. The 15 items should be divided by the amount of time that the individual currently spends doing each category per week. Sections of activities on their paper may be left blank. Again, these should be representations of what is actually happening in their schedule. If asked for clarification of what each section means, please see 'Handout Notes' - however, do not provide this information without being prompted.

3) Process by allowing members to share their item placement, along with their feelings associated with how items are distributed, reflecting the ways in which they currently devote the majority of their time.

<u>Round Two</u>: Explore members' ideal time schedule.

1) The second round involves members' ideal time spent. For the second round, group members should be instructed to leave the first set of items on the sheet.

2) The facilitator then hands out the second set of 15 items (i.e. black beans)

3) Group members are instructed to place the second set of 15 items representing how they wish things would occur in their week. Again, this should represent their ideal time spent on each activity for the week. If they had no responsibilities - how would they spend their time?

4) Process by allowing members to share their item placement, along with their feelings associated with contrasts between their actual versus ideal time allocation.

## Processing Questions:

1) How has the stress of limited time managed to influence your life?
2) Which area (i.e., work, household responsibilities, etc.) receives the most time during your average schedule? In other words, which area *eats up* most of your time? If we could give voice to that area and allow it to speak, what tone of voice would it use? To whom would it talk? Likewise, to whom would it simply not bother talking? What would it say?
3) Were there any areas that you did not put items on during the first round? These areas seem silent, or unexpressed in your life. What would need to happen for those areas to become stronger in your life?
4) What was the biggest difference for you in round 1 and round 2?
5) What parts of your 'ideal' schedule would you like to see in your 'normal' schedule? Have there been times in your life during which you felt that your ideal schedule was closer to your normal schedule? Share with us, were there any specific situations or individuals in your life which influenced you in a positive way, allowing that ideal schedule to be closer to your normal schedule?

## Special Considerations:

Although this activity is intended to attend to surface level emotions and cognitions, acknowledgement of these stressors may invoke strong emotions. Visualizing time constraints may lead some members to feelings of hurt or anger towards former spouses or lack of social support. Although that is not the original intent of the activity, it may be a useful avenue to explore with group members.

## Adaptations:

If it is necessary to describe the meanings of the different circles on the handout, it may be appropriate to include activities that have been discussed in previous sessions. For example, under 'Self Care' leaving out yoga but stating hunting/fishing. The activities listed are general ideas.

## References:

White, M. (2007). *Maps of narrative practice*. New York: W.W. Norton.

## Author Notes:

*Leigha Huston* is a Graduate Student in Professional and Community Counseling at The University of Oklahoma. Leigha has group work experience through facilitating pre-existing psychoeducational curriculum groups for Sooner Upward Bound and the Second Step program at Educare of Oklahoma City. In addition to teaching from these programs, she also provides counseling services for couples and individuals through her internship with Sunbeam Family Services, Inc. Leigha looks forward to her continued work with clients, with heightened interest in work with client concerns surrounding relational strain, marriage, and divorce.

*Paula McWhirter* is a Professor of Counseling at the University of Oklahoma, specializing in positive psychology and group therapy interventions for individuals, children and families. She has been a group therapist and professional member of the Association for Specialists in Group Work for over 20 years.

## Correspondence:

Questions and comments related to this activity may be directed to:

Leigha Huston, B.S.
220 E. 29th Street
Edmond, OK 73013
Leigha.Huston@ou.edu

# Using Music in a Small Group Setting

By Shawn P. Parmanand & Erin E. Binkley

## Population:

This activity is used primarily with adults, although it can be altered and used with a variety of other populations. Please see the adaptations for ideas on appropriate populations.

## Stage of Group:

This activity is most effective when used for the duration of a short-term group, and is therefore used during every phase of a group. It helps to facilitate the transitions that occur between group stages, as well as facilitating the shifts between content and process.

## Type of Group:

This activity can be used with any type of group. The authors originally implemented the activity with a six-member counseling group that met for eight weeks (Binkley & Parmanand, 2009). However, because of the universal nature of music, the authors believe that this activity could be used with any type of group aimed at promoting connection among its members.

## Rationale:

The authors recommend using this music activity in a small group setting because of its many benefits. Firstly, its use may promote an alternate, non-verbal means of communication for group members. Based on the results of a prior research study that was conducted using this activity, group members may find that this activity facilitates communication, self-expression, connection, and the creation of shared meaning among group members. This activity may also be used as a catalyst to facilitate shifts between content and process within group discussions. Lastly, this activity may promote the development of self-awareness for group members and aid them in creating lasting change in their lives outside of group (Binkley & Parmanand, 2009).

## Goals:

Participants will:
1) Offer group members an alternate, creative means of communicating in group and with other group members;
2) Promote connection among group members and growth within a small group;
3) Promote individual development and lasting change.

## Materials:

1) Music playing device (CD Player, I-Pod docking station, cassette player, laptop computer). The authors recommend group leaders inquire from group participants what medium of music playing works best for the group members during the first session, and adjust music playing devices accordingly.

## Time Allotment:

The intent of this particular intervention is for each member to share a song that reflects who they are, and the meaning they are making out of the group process. Each member takes turns sharing their song at the beginning of each new group meeting. Group leaders should designate the first ten minutes of a group counseling session in order for the group member to play their song, and to explain why they chose that specific song to share with his or her fellow group members.

## Directions:

Step:

1) During the first group session, explain to group members that they will be asked during the course of the group to bring one song that captures who they are, how they hope to benefit from the group process, and/or the meaning they have made from the group process. It is recommended that group leaders delineate a schedule of who will be bringing a song each week to avoid confusion and help ensure every group member brings a song at least once during the course of the group.

2) Review the procedural aspects of the music sharing activity:
   a) The group member sharing a song will open group by playing the song for the group while the other group members remain silent, listening.

   b) The group member who shared the song will explain the reasons for choosing the song. Questions can be asked such as:
      i. *Help me understand what prompted you to bring that song to share with us today?*
      ii. *What was it like to share that song with each of us?*

   c) The group leader will encourage group members to respond by reflecting on their experience of the song, as well as their experience of the song presenter's explanation and reasons for sharing the song. This could include questions such as:
      i. *For those of you who heard the song, what stood out to you?*
      ii. *How does what was shared in that song reflect what's happening here in group?*
      iii. *How does listening to that song help you to connect with one another in the here and now?*

   d) The group leader should consider this opening group activity to be the springboard for transitioning the group into further sharing and group processing, and should facilitate the process accordingly.

3) After reviewing the procedures, the group leader should model the activity by sharing a song to open the first group meeting. This may lower the anxiety level for group members and model the expectations of the activity.

4) The sharing process should be repeated at the beginning of each group meeting, according to the schedule decided upon in the first meeting.

## Processing Questions:

1) What was this experience like for you?
2) What surprised you the most about this experience?
3) How will listening to and discussing this song in group impact you when you leave here today?

## Special Considerations:

Group leaders need to keep in mind that music varies in content and lyrics. Perhaps setting limits on lyrical content might be worthwhile. Also, a level of flexibility is required on the part of group members as group members may choose to sing or play their chosen song rather than a more traditional avenue for sharing music. In addition, due to the potentially sensitive nature of the song content and discussion, group leaders should consider this an activity to be used within a closed group setting.

## Adaptations:

This activity was originally developed and implemented with a group of adults. Additionally, the activity could be effective with children and adolescents as well, given they are old enough to make meaningful song choices. When working with children and adolescents, it may be beneficial to set ground rules in the first meeting regarding appropriate song choice; consider setting boundaries regarding language and lyrical content.

Another adaptation would be to encourage group members to bring in songs that reflect the stage the group is in. For example, group members presenting near the beginning of the group may bring in songs regarding their expectations of the group. During the working stage, members may bring in songs representing self-awareness they are developing. Near the end of the group, members may bring in songs which are reflective of closure.

## References:

Binkley, E. E. & Parmanand, S. P. (2010). Members' experience of using music in a small group setting: A phenomenological study. *American Counseling Association Vistas.*

## Author Notes:

*Shawn P. Parmanand* is a core Faculty Member of the Marriage, Couple, and Family counseling program at Walden University. He has had seven years of group work experience, leading process groups for college-aged students, groups for incarcerated youth, and most recently as a group facilitator for children who are the victims of sexual abuse.

*Erin E. Binkley* is an Assistant Professor at Oakland University. She has seven years of group work experience, facilitating groups in both public schools and mental health agency settings, including process groups for adolescent and adult victims of domestic violence, relationship-building groups for youth and adolescents, and education and team-building groups for both adolescents and adults.

## Correspondence:

Questions and comments related to this activity may be directed to:
Dr. Shawn P. Parmanand, Ph.D., LPC, NCC
Walden University
100 Washington Avenue South
Suite 900
Minneapolis, MN 55401
Shawn.Parmanand@waldenu.edu

# Values Clarification

*By Lynn L. Brandsma & Gregory K. P. Smith*

## Population:

Adults in any group setting assigned a task (e.g., ad-hoc committee)

## Stage of Group:

Orientation

## Type of Group:

Task/Work

## Rationale:

The purpose of this group exercise is for group members to identify values which are important to them both in decision making and in completing a task. Each group member shares their individual values. The group as a whole then looks for common themes and begins to identify those so that the decisions made for the assigned task can be guided by those identified values. There has been a recent trend within the broad field of cognitive behavior therapy (CBT) on helping individuals pursue individualized goals (Herbert & Forman, 2011; 2014). A key part of this process is values clarification. Once an individual is clear about the key themes that are important in his or her life and how these are prioritized with respect to one another, he or she can begin developing goals linked to these values, and then behavior can in turn be directed toward those goals. Among the novel CBT models that most emphasize this process of values clarification are Acceptance and Commitment Therapy (Hayes, Strosahl, Wilson, 2011) and Dialectical Behavior Therapy (Linehan & Dimeff, 2011).

## Goals:

Participants will
1) explore and examine individual values important to the decision making and task completion process.
2) understand others' values important in the decision making and task completion process.
3) identify common values and begin the assigned task from this common ground.

## Materials:

1) Paper and pencil
2) White board
3) Dry erase marker

## Time Allotment:

60-120 minutes (approximately)

## Directions:

Step:

1) Before beginning the activity, the leader may want to briefly summarize the values clarification research stated above and explain its significance as it relates to the group decision making process.

2) Each group member writes down a minimum of 5 values important to them in decision making.

3) Each group member writes down a minimum of 5 values important to them in completing a task.

4) Each group member shares with the entire group their chosen values.

5) The group leader looks for common themes for both decision making and completing a task and writes these on a white board.

6) The leader asks the group to keep these values in mind as they work to complete the task assigned to them.

## Processing Questions:

1) How will the group decide which values to use if there are few common themes?
2) What is the best way to let the identified values guide the process?
3) Will a task group's assignment go more smoothly if group identified values guide the process?

## Special Considerations:

It is important for the group leader to encourage each individual to articulate his/her individual values because the goal is not to convince the group members that certain values are necessarily better, but to foster an understanding of why members value what they do and how these values contribute (or not) to group decision making

## Adaptations:

It is possible to do a similar type of exercise with employees or group members who do not get along well or where morale tends to be low. For these adaptations more time should be given for processing the importance of a group identified value filled workplace or situation. It would also be important for regular follow up meetings in addition to the orientation stage of group.

# References:

Hayes, S. C., Strosahl, K. D., & Wilson, K. G. (2011). *Acceptance and commitment therapy: The process and practice of mindful change* (2nd ed.). New York: Guilford.

Herbert, J. D., & Forman, E. M. (2011). The evolution of cognitive behavior therapy: The rise of psychological acceptance and mindfulness. In J. D. Herbert & E. M. Forman (Eds.), *Acceptance and mindfulness in cognitive behavior therapy: Understanding and applying the new therapies* (pp. 3–25). Hoboken, NJ: Wiley.

Herbert, J. D., & Forman, E. M. (2014). Mindfulness and acceptance techniques. In Stefan G. Hofmann & D. J. A. Dozois (Eds.), *The Wiley-Blackwell handbook of cognitive behavioral therapy* (pp. 131-156). Hoboken, NJ: Wiley-Blackwell.

Linehan, M. M., & Dimeff, L. (2001). Dialectical behavior therapy in a nutshell. *California Psychologist, 34,* 10-13.

# Author Notes:

*Lynn L. Brandsma* is an Associate Professor of Psychology at Chestnut Hill College. Dr. Brandsma has taught Group Process and Leadership at both the undergraduate and graduate levels for 18 years. She has extensive experience facilitating counseling and therapy groups for adolescents and adults with eating and weight related issues. She is also a Board Certified Music Therapist and has led numerous music therapy groups with various populations.

*Gregory K.P. Smith* is a Professor of Recreation, Health and Physical Education in Hospitality and Recreation Management Department at Cheyney University of Pennsylvania. Dr. Smith has extensive experience in facilitating task/work groups in his current role as advisor to the Muslim Student Association, as past advisor to numerous student clubs, and as President of the Faculty Union, APSCUF (Association of Pennsylvania State College & University Faculties) at Cheyney University of Pennsylvania from 2003-2007.

# Correspondence:

Questions and comments related to this activity may be directed to:

Lynn L. Brandsma, Ph.D., LPC, MT-BC
Chestnut Hill College
Department of Psychology
9601 Germantown Avenue
Philadelphia, PA 19118
brandsmal@chc.edu

# Who Am I?

*By Kenneth Comer, Chelsea Latorre, & Paula McWirther*

## Population:

This project is geared toward 10-15 individuals who frequently work together in groups. It can be conducted in most workplace and/or graduate student classroom settings.

## Stage of Group:

Transition

## Type of Group:

Task/Work

## Rationale:

Career choice, according to John Holland (1997), is thought to be an expression of personality within the world of work. Individuals seek out work environments in which they can fully utilize their talents and abilities, and meaningfully express attitudes and values central to the self (Holland, 1997). Holland assumes that a description of an individual's vocational interests is, in fact, the description of their personality. Each person is defined by one of six group of traits (Realistic, Investigative, Artistic, Social, Enterprising, Conventional), which ultimately defines how each individual works with others to complete tasks. Based on Holland's assumptions, our personality influences our group interactions

Many individuals struggle to understand why they find some individuals, or groups of individuals, are more difficult to interact with than others. This group technique is designed to help individuals identify how their personalities may explain interactions in high performance and high task demand settings, common in many work settings.

## Goals:

Participants will:
1) identify individual personality type.
2) develop understanding of different personality types and the effects on group work.
3) process differences among individual personality types and how they influence how group work is completed.

# Materials:

1) Access to the Strong Interest Inventory (Strong, Donnay, Morris, Schaubhut, & Thompson, 2004)
2) Colored paper that coordinates with Primary results indicated by Strong Assessment
3) Six laminated cards with the individual RAISEC traits written
4) An area big enough to have 6 designated spaces

# Time Allotment:

40-50 minutes

# Directions:

Step:

1) Prior to the initial group meeting, each group member will complete the Strong Interest Inventory and arrive to the group meeting with their results. Members will send their individual results to the facilitator, who will color coordinate the results according to the Holland Codes: RIASEC, as follows. First, select a different color to represent each letter code. Next, based on inventory results, identify each member's primary letter code. Finally, assign the corresponding code color to each group member. For example, group members with a primary code of Realistic would be assigned Red, group members with a primary code of Investigative would be assigned Indigo; group members with a primary code of Artistic would be assigned Purple, and so forth.

2) As group begins, provide group members with a colored card representing their primary Holland Code. Refrain from disclosing any meaning behind the colored cards provided. Ask members to break into small groups with those who share their same color. Be sure each small group is comprised of members with the same color cards.

3) Introduce a short, 10-mintue, pre-planned group task and request that members complete the task within their small groups. This group task can involve any activity that would typically encourage participation of all group members working together to complete. For example, group members could be asked to accurately replicate a drawing together, after allowing only one or two group members the ability to see the drawing.

4) Next, ask members to break into different small groups, this time comprised only of individuals with different color cards. If possible, the facilitator should aim to group together individuals of polar opposite, per Holland typology. For example, this would involve placing together: Conventional with Artistic, Realistic with Social, and Investigative with Enterprising. The facilitator should use color cards to group members into small groups, again refraining from disclosing the meaning of the color cards to the group.

5) Introduce another short, 10-minute task and rests that members complete the task within their new small groups. These small groups reflect personalities that are complete opposites.

6) After this activity, the group members and leader will engage in a discussion focused on difficulties within each group activity. The leader will also describe each trait type and discuss with group members the differences in personality traits in order to show the dynamics encountered with in-group members.

## Processing Questions:

1) How was working with the first group?
2) Did you notice a difference in working with the first group compared to the second?
3) Which group did your prefer to work with?
4) In what ways do you feel your overall work was affected by different personalities?
5) How can you apply this activity to your work environment?

## Special Considerations:

All groups will differ in makeup. Even though individuals may have some similar personality traits, it is important to remember that each individual is unique. Members may become defensive or reluctant to participate in the group work, or members may appear to be quiet due to fears and anxieties. Also, struggles of control, confrontation, and conflict may be encountered. The counselor needs to be well versed in dealing with these situations if/when they arise in therapy. Also, special considerations and cautions should be taken when looking at individual's experiences and backgrounds.

## Adaptations:

This activity may be adapted based on the resources of the group. For example, if the group does not have access to the Strong Interest Inventory, leaders can make cards based on characteristics that symbolize the type of each trait on the inventory. Each individual will be given a set of cards with mixed descriptors of traits, and will be asked to narrow the cards down to two cards that best describe themselves. It is important to ask them to consider how they identify themselves and not to focus on what others may have described them to be. Have each group divide into groups based on the color pattern of their two remaining cards and continue the activity as directed above. The authors focused on groups moving from the Transition to the Working stage primarily because of the processing questions that can be applied; however, this activity may be beneficial across different stages of groups. Leaders can adapt the processing questions to the desired stage.

# References:

Holland, J. L. (1997). *Making vocational choices: A theory of vocational personalities and work environments* (3rd ed.). Odessa, FL: Psychological Assessment Resources.

Strong, E. K., Jr., Donnay, D. A. C., Morris, M. L., Schaubhut, N. A., & Thompson, R. C. (2004). Strong Interest Inventory®, (Rev. ed.). Mountain View, CA: Consulting Psychologists Press, Inc.

# Author Notes:

*Kenneth Comer* is a Graduate Student at the University of Oklahoma. He has conducted couple, family, and individual therapy through both his practicum at the University of Oklahoma as well as through his work with Catholic Charities, St. Joseph's Counseling Center. Through practical and experiential evidence attained, Kenneth works to develop group activities to aid individuals in understanding how differing personality styles may be at the core of some challenges found in certain relationships.

*Chelsea Latorre* is a Graduate Student at the University of Oklahoma. She has experience working as a group facilitator at the Calm Waters Center for Children and Families. Additionally, Chelsea has had experience developing, organizing, and leading curriculum for group psychoeducational sessions with teenagers in her experience with the Sooner Upward Bound program offered through the University of Oklahoma Community Counseling program. Chelsea currently is interning at the A Better Chance clinic and has interest in working with adolescent children and teenagers.

*Paula McWhirter* is a Professor of Counseling at the University of Oklahoma, specializing in positive psychology and group therapy interventions for individuals, children and families. She has been a group therapist and professional member of the **Association for Specialists in Group Work** for over 20 years.

# Correspondence:

Questions and comments related to this activity may be directed to:

Kenneth Comer
University of Oklahoma
2041 NW 47th St,
Oklahoma City, OK 73118
kennycomer@ou.edu

# Why Does My Child Want a New Culture? A Group for Immigrant Parents

*By Delini M. Fernando & Natalya A. Lindo*

## Population:
Immigrant parents of adolescents

## Stage of Group:
Orientation

## Type of Group:
Counseling

## Rationale:

Immigrant parents often find it difficult when their adolescent children adopt aspects of the American culture: independent behavior, communication style, language, dress, culinary interests, and worldviews (Nesteruk & Marks, 2011). Few of these parents have the opportunity to process the experience of their children's American ways of being, and their limited understanding of the culture to which their children seem to easily adapt. These parents share a common experience as a result of leaving their home country. A shared cultural context allows a safe place for these parents to engage in self-exploration and shared experience without the added pressure of having to explain their culture, traditions, values, beliefs, and ambitions for their children.

## Goals:

Participants will:
1) increase their understanding of their children's acculturation to the American culture.
2) discuss common experiences related to leaving their home country and learning to acclimate to the host country.
3) increase their awareness of other immigrant parents' experiences thereby reducing some of the isolation participants may feel regarding their children's American behaviors, worldviews, and beliefs.
4) form a support system.

## Materials:
1) Blank 4" by 6" index cards
2) Markers or pens

## Time Allotment:
One and half-hour session

## Directions:
Step:
1) Review the purpose of the activity. For example, *"the purpose of this activity is for us to discuss and share our children's behaviors, values and anything else that might seem strange and new to us. By sharing with others in the group it will help us better understand our children's newly adopted ways."*

2) Using one 4" by 6" card, ask participants to write a short list (up to five) of their teenager's behaviors, worldviews, and/or beliefs that each parent would like to better understand.

3) Have participants rate each item on the list from most important (1) to least important (5).

4) Invite participants to take turns and share the most important concern on their list, why it is a concern, and how the particular concern is different from their culture of origin.

5) Invite other participants to give feedback or share similar concerns.

6) Discuss why adolescents feel they need to adapt to the ways of the dominant culture, and why it is important for their parents to understand their adolescents' need to fit in.

## Processing Questions:
1) What was it like to do this activity?
2) What is it like to discover that others in this group have similar reactions to their teenager's behaviors, worldviews, and beliefs?
3) What is one thing you could do to better understand your son/daughter's American-like behaviors, worldviews, and/or beliefs?
4) How do you think your son/daughter would feel if they knew you were trying to understand their behaviors, worldviews, and/or beliefs that seem new and foreign to you?
5) How does it feel to know that you share these experiences with others in this group?
6) Process with participants that most immigrant parents (who are not in the group) may have similar experiences and feelings.

## Special Considerations/Cautions:

No special considerations were identified by the authors.

## Adaptations:

1)  This activity can be adapted for use with immigrant parents from specific parts of the world. For example, parents belonging to the Far Eastern Asian cultures may have specific concerns that are different to other cultural groups such as parents of Latino groups. Immigrant Muslim parents' religious beliefs and cultural customs differ significantly from other immigrant groups. Therefore processing questions may need to be adapted to suit the particular target group.

2)  Group members can create their lists but then share them with the group without identifying them as their own. For example, all the index cards including participants' individual concerns are placed in a bucket, and then concerns are drawn out of the bucket and discussed as a group.

## References:

Nesteruk, O., & Marks, L. D. (2011). Parenting in immigration: Experiences of mothers and fathers from Eastern Europe raising children in the United States. *Journal of Comparative Family Studies, 42*, 809-825.

## Author Notes:

*Delini M. Fernando* is an Associate Professor of Counseling at the University of North Texas. She has eighteen years of group work experience including family counseling. She regularly teaches the group counseling course at UNT.

*Natalya A. Lindo* is an Assistant Professor of Counseling at the University of North Texas. She has ten years of group work experience including training counselors to work with parents, children and families in a group setting.

## Correspondence:

Questions and comments regarding this activity may be directed to:

Delini M. Fernando, PhD
Associate Professor, University of North Texas
1155 Union Circle #310829
Denton, TX, 76203-5017
Delini.Fernando@unt.edu,

# Your Superhero

*By Stefi Threadgill & Brandy Schumann*

## Population:
Adults dealing with low self-esteem and adjustment issues

## Stage of Group:
Working

## Type of Group:
Counseling

## Rationale:

A strong, integrated sense of self generates positive self-esteem and self-regulation (Oaklander, 2007). A poor perception of self creates disintegration and polarity, which negatively shapes an individual's self-concept and how one experiences him or herself and his or her world. Projective techniques help to provide a safe, non-threatening way to re-experience, reconnect, and increase awareness of challenging feelings and behaviors (Oaklander, 2007). Parts of self that are denied result in unexpressed emotions that create an incomplete gestalt, or fragmented sense of self. Increased self-awareness promotes authenticity and accuracy, which creates an opportunity for change. This activity can increase awareness that personhood is holistic and is not defined only by his or her problem. Additionally, the activity provides the opportunity for social support, normalization of concerns, and increased opportunity to understand that perception is subjective (Berg, Landreth, & Fall, 2013).

## Goals:

Participants will:
1) develop increased self-awareness and an authentic sense of self.
2) develop an awareness that personhood is holistic and not solely defined by their problem or situation.
3) experience increased self-esteem and a sense of empowerment.
4) experience social support and a normalization of their concerns.

## Materials:

1) Materials (cape, wand, armor, cloak, mask, sword, clock, map, money)
2) Art supplies (comic books, magazine photos, markers, play dough)

## Time Allotment:

90-minute group session.

## Directions:

Step:

1) Invite group members to create a superhero. Leaders may say *"Create a superhero of your own personal world using the materials provided. You may use any of the materials provided or use your imagination."*

2) Ask members to name their super heroes and identify the super power they possess.

3) Invite members to share their superheroes with the group using the following prompts:
   a. Describe your superhero.
   b. How are you like your superhero? How are you different?
   c. When do you need the super powers your superhero possesses?

## Processing Questions:

1) What did you experience while doing this activity?
2) What did you learn about yourself from this activity?
3) What did you learn by listening to the superheroes of others?
4) What super powers have you relied on in the past?
5) What super powers can you employ when you are stuck?
6) What superhero in the group could help you on your journey? How?

## Special Considerations:

1) More prompts may be necessary for child and adolescent populations.
2) While working with children with oppositional defiant disorder, the counselor will include the materials in the play therapy room.

## Adaptations:

1) Create your own superhero using art supplies (expressive arts).
2) Describe your own superhero (talk therapy).
3) Other populations for which this activity can be utilized include children and adolescents with externalizing behavioral disorders, such as Oppositional Defiant Disorder. Those developing appropriate personal power, such as individuals suffering from Post-traumatic Stress Disorder, may also benefit from this empowering activity.

## References:

Berg, R.C., & Landreth, G. L,. & Fall, K. A. (2013). *Group counseling: Concepts and procedures.* (5th ed.). New York: Routledge.

Oaklander, V. (2007). *Hidden treasure: A map to the child's inner self.* London, UK: Karnac.

## Author Notes:

*Stefi Threadgill* has received training specialized in group therapy through Southern Methodist University and currently provides group therapy to pre-adolescents to improve social skills and increase self-esteem.

*Brandy Schumann* has a decade's worth of experience delivering group therapy services to children, preadolescents, adolescents, adults and parents. In addition to teaching about group therapy as a Clinical Assistant Professor at Southern Methodist University, she also services the public from her private practice, Therapy on the Square in McKinney, TX, providing groups to address self-esteem, divorce support, social skills and parenting needs.

## Correspondence:

Questions and comments related to this activity may be directed to:

Stefi Threadgill, Student
SMU Counseling Program
Southern Methodist University in Plano
5228 Tennyson Parkway, Bldg 3
Plano, TX 75024-3547
sthreadgill@smu.edu

# Career Narratives in Retirement Groups

*David A. Hermon & Louisa Foss-Kelly*

## Population:
Older Adults

## Stage of Group:
Orientation

## Type of Group:
Counseling

## Rationale:

In 2010 the United States began an 18-year period that will witness seventy-seven million individuals known as the "baby boomers" (those born between 1946-1964) reach the age where they may leave the workforce (U.S. Census Bureau, 2010). While retirement is often viewed as a desirable goal, individuals often struggle with the transition to a greater degree than anticipated (Peila-Shuster, 2011). Narrative therapy has been successfully used in groups with members who are in a variety of transitions (Lane, 2013). The purpose of this narrative-based group activity is to encourage members reflect on aspects of their paid employment that provided identity, purpose, and meaning, as well as grapple with the idea of creating roles (volunteering, encore careers, mentoring, etc.) that will continue to provide the beneficial aspects received from their work.

## Goals:

Participants will:
1) increase introspective nature of how members view one's paid employment and future retirement.
2) identify aspects of their work life that provided opportunities to implement and test their self-concept to find what gave them meaning.
3) identify skills and strengths that they were not able to develop or engage due to confines inherent in their work that may have provided greater meaning.
4) make a plan to engage in activities beyond their traditional paid employment to use their strengths affording members the opportunity to continue to implement and test their self-concept that is satisfying to self and society (Super, 1988).

## Materials:

1) A writing utensil and paper for writing the career narrative.
2) A handout made from the processing questions.
3) A dry erase board for summarizing group responses.

# Time:

Approximately 30 minutes of writing time for group members and 40 minutes for processing questions. Alternatively, writing the career narrative could be given as a homework assignment for members to complete between the first and second group meeting to allow more time to focus on the processing questions.

# Directions:

**Step:** Introduce members to the primary goal of writing a career narrative – to deconstruct (unpack) one's career story, reflect, and construct (re-author) to highlight what was realized and aspects of self yet fulfilled.

1) Reinforce that the career narrative is not fiction and that through the writing process members reflect on their strengths, talents, abilities, and identity bundled in their story (McIlveen and Patton, 2007).
2) Ask members to write in a fairly informal first person narrative.
3) Suggest that members write in blocks and use developmental sections in their writing. Encourage members to begin with a section as far back as childhood to examine dreams of what they believed they would do when they grew up. Below are suggested questions to prompt the members:

   a) What core strengths and abilities did I use in my career?
   b) What strengths went unfulfilled in my work life due to my specific position or industry?
   c) In what ways do current career (or retirement) activities allow me to maintain the life quality I desire?
   d) What competencies and passions would I like to develop? What role would best meet those areas (returning to school, an encore career, volunteering, consulting in my industry, etc.)?
   e) What are my options? Do I want to do nothing and maintain the status quo?
   f) What economic, family, industry trends, or barrier impact my future? Who can help me stay accountable to the goals I set?

**Processing Questions:**
1) What core strengths and abilities did I use in my career?
2) What strengths went unfulfilled in my work life due to my specific position or industry?
3) In what ways do current career (or retirement) activities allow me to maintain the life quality I desire?
4) What competencies and passions would I like to develop? What role would best meet those areas (returning to school, an encore career, volunteering, consulting in my industry, etc.)?
5) What are my options? Do I want to do nothing and maintain the status quo?
6) What economic, family, industry trends, or barrier impact my future? Who can help me stay accountable to the goals I set?

## Special Considerations/Cautions:

1) Many members gain insight from writing their story to a greater degree than talking about their lives. The processing questions set the stage for understanding the impact of writing a career narrative and may lead into additional group meetings. While this activity is an early, orientation stage, group activity it may become the primary topic in group. Group leaders may choose to take this activity and create a group whose purpose is to process the questions listed above and have members create a plan for their future.

2) In situations where reading or writing is difficult for group members, group members may verbally describe their career history.

## Adaptations:

Group leaders working with adults unsatisfied in their current careers, may modify the processing questions listed above to address the needs of members seeking greater satisfaction in their current careers. Some modifications are as basic as changing past tense to present (e.g., "did" to "do") in the processing questions, allowing for reflection and insight of the members' current career stories. Leaders interested in this adaptation are encouraged to consider incorporating the concept of *job crafting* to help members redefine current work to increase meaning and career satisfaction (Berg, Dutton, and Wrzesniewski, 2013; Wrzesniewski and Dutton, 2001).

## References:

Berg, J. M., Dutton, J. E., Wrzesniewski, A. (2013). Job crafting and meaningful work. In B. J. Dik, Z. S. Byrne, & M. F. Steger (Eds.), *Purpose and meaning in the workplace*. Washington, DC: American Psychological Association.

Lane, J. A. (2013). Group counseling for students transitioning out of postsecondary education: A narrative approach. *Groupwork, 23*(1), 34-55. doi: 10.1921/1501230103

McIlveen, P., & Patton, W. (2007). Narrative career counseling: Theory and exemplars of practice. *Australian Psychologist, 42*(3), 226-235.

Peila-Shuster, J. J. (2011). *Retirement self-efficacy: The effects of a pre-retirement strengths-based intervention on retirement self-efficacy and an exploration of relationships between positive affect and retirement self-efficacy*. Ann Arbor, MI: UMI Dissertation Publishing, 3468973.

Super, D. E. (1988). Vocational adjustment: Developing a self-concept. *The Career Development Quarterly, 36*, 351-357.

U. S. Census Bureau (2010). *The older population in the United States: 2010*. Retrieved from www.census.gov/population/age/data/2010.html

Wrzesniewski, A., & Dutton, J. E. (2001). Crafting a job: Revisioning employees as active crafters of their work. *Academy of Management Review, 26*(2), 179-201.

## Author Notes:

*David A. Hermon* is a Professor in the Counseling Department at Marshall University. He received his Ph.D. in Counselor Education from the School of Behavioral Sciences at Ohio University in 1995. Prior to his teaching career, he worked as a Research Assistant on the Life Education Planning Program (LEPP) at The University of Michigan.

*Louisa Foss-Kelly* is an Associate Professor and Clinical Mental Health Counseling Program Coordinator in the Counseling and School Psychology Department at Southern Connecticut State University. She received her Ph.D. in Counseling and Human Development from Kent State University in 2005. She is a Licensed Professional Counselor and National Certified Counselor.

## Correspondence:

Questions and comments related to this activity may be directed to:

Dr. David A. Hermon Ph.D., LPC
Marshall University
1 John Marshall Drive
Huntington, WV 25755
hermon@marshall.edu

# Nourishing the Body and Soul

*By Drew Krafcik*

## Population:

We focused on older adults grieving the loss of their partners. Please see the adaptation section for other applications.

## Stage of Group:

Orientation is the best fit. This activity can be modified for use in various stages of group work. In practice, we implemented the meal throughout the entire group process.

## Type of Group:

Counseling or Therapy

## Rationale:

For older adults, the loss of a partner is extremely stressful and creates significant distress for the surviving spouse (Carr & Utz, 2002; Heinmann & Evans, 1990; M. Stroebe, Hanson, W. Stroebe, & Schut, 2001). The widowed spouse loses one of his or her primary sources of emotional support and must now rely on other relationships for emotional and instrumental support (Ha & Ingersoll-Dayton, 2011). Researchers have found that widowed older adults show increased positive affect and enhanced support satisfaction when they received social support interventions such as being matched with peers who shared similar bereavement experiences or participating in self-help/support groups (Silverman, 2004; Stewart, Craig, MacPherson, & Alexander, 2001). Researchers have also found that the *context* of relationships is more important than the amount of social contact in fulfilling emotional needs of widowed older adults (Cartensen, 1991). Improving the quality of support and focusing interventions on specific aspects of social relationships are thought to influence psychological well-being for surviving partners (Ha & Ingersoll-Dayton, 2011).

In this activity, a co-group leader and I made home cooked meals that we served to our group members, older persons who were grieving the loss of their partners. Many of the group members had not prepared or eaten a home cooked meal since their partner died, and felt comforted by others who understood what that truly means (A. Solomon, personal communication, February 4, 2004). Eating together as part of our group resonated with a natural social ritual that helped members connect and continue eating and being together long after our group formally ended. Members also volunteered to bring in their own favorite foods to share with the group, and this spontaneous evolution energized creativity and a sense of communal contribution and belonging. Part of the potency of eating together was that it was not just practiced, but actually lived. In that sense, we all took away something new, and something we have also always known.

## Goals:

Participants will:
1) feel genuinely welcomed and cared for by the group leaders.
2) improve their physical wellbeing by eating a healthy meal.
3) share community and foster connections with peers in similar life/bereavement situations.

## Materials:

1) Folding tables (round or square)
2) Folding chairs
3) Plates
4) Utensils
5) Napkins
6) Glasses/Cups
7) Vases and flowers (for each table)
8) Tablecloths (for each table)
9) Tea candles (for each table)
10) Meal the group leaders decide to cook/prepare and the necessary materials to accommodate.

## Time Allotment:

An ideal amount of time for sitting and eating together is about 30-45 minutes in the Orientation stage. After the first week, there is a familiarity and acclimation that arises that might result in expanding or reducing the length of allotted time. Make sure to budget extra group leader time for meal preparation, set-up, and clean up. The extra group leader is dependent on group size, meal choice, site accommodations, and whether or not members contribute to the set-up, meal preparation, and clean up (after week one).

## *Directions:*

Step:

1) Choose and prepare the meal.

2) Set up the room before group members arrive. Three round tables with chairs (or however many are needed) are dressed with pressed tablecloths, place settings for 4-6 (e.g., utensils, plates, bowls, mugs, glassware, folded cloth napkins), vases of fresh cut flowers, and lit tea candles.

3) Welcome the group members and invite them to have a seat where they feel most comfortable. For example, the group leader may say something like, "*Hi Mrs. Briscoe, we are so glad you are here. Please feel free to have a seat wherever you might feel most comfortable. We'll be having dinner soon. Can I get you something to drink?*"

4) Co-group leaders serve the meal that has been prepared. (We brought out and served homemade soups, baskets of warm breads, steamed vegetables, fruits, and desserts).

5) Join group members at the tables for dinner once all participants have received their food. (Our presence during dinner was not formal, but warm and engaging).

6) Remain attentive to the needs of group members during dinner (e.g., refresh water, offer seconds, pour tea and coffee). For example, a group leader may say something like, "*John, can I get you some more tea, or another bowl of soup?*"

7) During dinner, invite reflections and ask discussion questions. Discussion questions can include categories such as "casual every day," "health and wellness check-in," and "depth oriented." This continuum allows for exploration, normalization, and assessment. Questions can also be adjusted to fit group stage and frequency of meals together. For example, "*Mrs. Hart, last week you mentioned that you and Mr. Hart had your most important conversations when you were eating dinner together. Do you find that to be true in your dinners now with others?*" Or, "*Abe, I was thinking about you... what was your experience of the Rose Bowl game this weekend? I would imagine it brings up memories of you and Mrs. Hanson together.*" Other examples of discussion questions during the meal include: "*What happens to our (appetites, routines, energy levels, seeing friends, feeling cared about) when we lose our profound loved ones?*" "*With whom do you spend time with in your life now?*" "*What are your dinner experiences like these days?*" "*What special memories do you have of meals with your partner?*" We also asked about everyday life events (like we might over a casual dinner). Inquiries included news, sports, community events, movies, activities, etc. (Small moments of sharing the everyday are lost when we do not have our partners with whom to listen).

8) Clear plates and tables when the meal is winding down. Members may continue to socialize together while you prepare for cleaning. (Prepare means set up for later cleaning. We had a sink to soak dishes and plates but did not actively wash them during group time.) When the group concludes, cleaning usually took about 20-25 minutes.

9) Processing after the activity. We moved the group from the meal location to another on-site space for reflection and processing. See questions below for examples.

10) At the conclusion of the group time, break down the tables, fold tablecloths, put away chairs, pack up supplies, load up left over food, etc. (Consider offering members the chance to take home left-overs.)


# Processing Questions:

1) What are you leaving here with today?
2) How will participating in this group today impact what you do next?
3) How can we use this experience together to help ourselves (and each other) with our losses?


# Special Considerations:

Group leaders should be aware of various dietary restrictions and preferences of the group participants. If including this activity, leaders may choose to ask about dietary needs during the screening process. Group leaders should consider how the food will be prepared; considerations regarding catering or acquiring a meeting space that has a kitchen would be important. Due to the nature of the activity, some costs to group leaders may be significant. Purchasing food and supplies could be costly. Leaders may seek out grants or other funding opportunities to assist with this expense. Group leaders may consider utilizing a co-leader or helper due to the labor-intensive nature of food preparation, site preparation, serving, clean up, and facilitation during the meal. Group leaders should be aware of the intense emotional experiences that come with processing the grief and loss of a partner.


# Adaptations:

This activity could be adapted for use with all groups that may involve loss, like working with parents/children of deployed military members, children who have lost siblings, or teenagers who have lost a peer to suicide, etc. This activity could be made more formal or casual depending on the group needs and circumstances. Adaptable items include food choices, preparation, table-setting materials, group stage implementation, and group member participation.

# References:

Carr, D., & Utz, R. (2002). Late-life widowhood in the United States. New directions in research and theory. *Ageing International, 27*, 65-88.

Carstensen, L. (1991). Selectivity theory: Social activity in the life-span context. *Annual Review of Gerontology and Geriatrics, 11*, 195-217.

Ha, J., & Ingersoll-Dayton, B. (2011). Moderators in the relationship between social contact and psychological distress among widowed adults. *Aging and Mental Health, 15*(3), 354-363.

Heinemann, G., & Evans, P. (1990). Widowhood, loss change and adaption. In T.H. Brubaker (Ed.), *Family relationships in later life* (2nd ed., pp. 142-168). Newbury Park, CA: Sage.

Silverman, P. (2004). *Widow-to-widow* (2nd ed.). New York: Brunner-Routledge.

Stewart, M., Craig D., MacPherson, K., & Alexander, S. (2001). Promoting positive affect and diminishing loneliness of widowed seniors through support intervention. *Public Health Nursing, 18*, 54-63.

Stroebe, M., Hansson, R., Stroebe, W., & Schut, H. (2001). *Handbook of bereavement research: Consequences, coping, and care.* Washington, DC: American Psychological Association.

# Author Notes:

*Drew Krafcik* is an Assistant Professor of the Graduate Counseling Program at Saint Mary's College of California. He has had 6 years of group work experience, including designing and facilitating bereavement, wellness, and forgiveness groups.

# Correspondence:

Questions and comments related to this activity may be directed to:

Drew Krafcik Ph.D., AAPC
Saint Mary's College of California
Kalmanovitz School of Education
FAH 281
P.O. BOX 4350
Moraga, CA 94556
aek3@stmarys-ca.edu

# INDEX

The index is organized utilizing two different structures. First, the group activities are sorted by Topic, then by Activity Type. Only the activity title and page number on which the activity begins are listed.

## TOPIC

## Career

## College Students/Grad Students

## Communication

## Crisis/Trauma

## Culture/Diversity

## Expressive Arts/Creativity

## Family

# Type

## Creative Props

## Arts and Crafts Exercises